"An honest candid, enquirer after the truth I revere"
Robert Burns

This work is dedicated to my 2yrs old twin daughters,
Roberta Burns Hogg and Laken Jeanette Hogg.

The author would like to acknowledge grant assistance towards research from the Dumfries & Galloway Robert Burns Bi-centenary Committee.

ISBN: 1 873586 85 X

Designed, typeset and printed by Clydeside Press
37 High Street, Glasgow G1 1LX

Contents

Preface

This book began in September 1994 as a search for possible "prose essays" which Robert Burns indicated he may write for *The Morning Chronicle*, a radical London newspaper. In a letter of mid-March 1794, the poet offered "prose essays" and radical poetry to the newspaper. The bard went as far as asking for a special "safe" channel and address to carry essays or poems to London, which "spies and informers" could not intercept. It is this promise of the poet's which forms the basis of this work. Until now, there has never been research to find out if the poet composed additional, unrecorded work for the *Chronicle* or to investigate possible "lost" poems, despite the fact that Burns was a regular anonymous and pseudonymous contributor to newspapers of his day. Two of the new poems were found by accident during December 1994. The bulk of the new material was discovered during late 1995 and early in 1996.

Many people have helped, assisted or encouraged this work on its path to print. Foremost was Shirley Bell, Project Manager with Dumfries and Galloway Council's Robert Burns Bi-centenary Committee. Councilors on the Bi-centenary Committee kindly funded the research for three months in early 1996.

I am grateful for the advice of many academic scholars who gave their views on one or two poems or simply encouraged me to continue the research. Not all, in the beginning, agreed with the provenance of the poems, but not all were privy to the full argument presented here. They include a few of the most eminent literary scholars in Scotland - Professor David Daiches, Professor Roderick Watson, and Thomas Crawford. Dr Andrew Noble, senior lecturer in Literature at the University of Strathclyde was the first academic to look over all the new poems. His support has been of great encouragement.

I am grateful to many other Burnsians for their advice or encouragement. They include - in chronological order of who I spoke to or wrote to - Wilson Ogilvie, Alistair Campsie, Jack Hunter, Hamish Henderson, James MacKay, Norrie Paton, Alistair Geddes, Andrew O'Hagan, Michael Donelly, Lou Houson & A.M. Mitchell, Professor Edward Cowen and Gavin Wallace and Alan Jamieson of the *Edinburgh Review*. Roderick Richmond and Robert Pate, my former teachers, kindled an enthusiasm for Scottish literature which is still, profoundly, *in the blood*.

In addition, BBC Scotland's *Omnibus* staff - in particular, producer, Louise Wardle and researcher, Mark Downie - kindly assisted my research efforts. Also from the media world, Brian Morton, himself an expert Burnsian and leading art critic, visited the wilds of Drummore in late January 1996 to make his own, favourable judgments of the poems - "surely Burns". Brian remarked on Radio Scotland, 24th January 1996, that the discovery of the new poems was "of potentially, astronomical proportions". I am also indebted to Martin Treacher, former senior reporter of *The Galloway Gazette*, who first broke the controversy in 1995.

Helpful and instructive comments were made by fellow Burnsians of the Stranraer and District Burns Club. The impeccable chairmanship of Jack Hunter, Galloway's renowned lecturer in Scottish literature, and the eloquent recital of two new poems by President Harry Monteith made for a night of friendly, serious, open-minded discussion. A few points of interest, now incorporated in this work, were made by members of the far-famed Burns Howff Club in Dumfries, whose President, Peter Karmylo, invited me to speak in September 1996. It was a superb night among fellow Burnsians.

I loaned books from Willie Hannah, Jim Hutchison, and Joanne Mullen, guid Drummore neibors. David Wilson, a former colleague at Dumfries & Galloway College, assisted with a computer problem. To my brothers, James and Harry Hogg, I am indebted for their moral and intellectual support. Both brothers gave up a days salary to sit in the Mitchell Library and collate additional notes, facts and poetry now contained in this volume. To Jim, I am deeply grateful for years of stimulating conversation on a myriad of subjects - a pleasure money can never measure. My brother Robert, now of Glasgow, resuscitated and revived my enthusiasm on many occasions when I felt a despairing futility in what I was doing, especially after the media maelstrom of January 1996.

The patience and helpfulness of professional library staff at The Mitchell Library, Glasgow, cannot go unacknowledged. Various members of staff from the Arts Department, the Glasgow Room, and the Science & Technology Department, delivered the most obscure newspapers, journals and books to a bleary-eyed researcher. The fact that one librarian had to dust the mouldy fragments off copies of James

Anderson's *The Bee* and stick labels to them before they were issued, indicates that the books had not been issued for many a decade. I am also grateful to staff at the Ewart Library, Dumfries, and Dumfries Museum for help during my stealth raids to scan old books.

My partner Helen's encouragement was invaluable. She kept me going when serious thrombo-phlebitis put me in hospital and almost made me a martyr to the poems. For tolerating my dogged, almost manic determination to keep going against very difficult odds, I am embarrassingly apologetic. Her only consolation is knowing she too shared my euphoria and tears in finding the poems.

It is my personal decision to provisionally attribute the new poems to Burns. There are, however, many respected Burnsians who now agree with their provenance.

Patrick Scott Hogg, Drummore, Galloway, September 1996.

The Building Blocks –
Contextual Evidence

There is no doubt that poetry by our national bard has been "lost". *The Poet's Rambles on the Banks of Ayr*, a long satirical poem on the aristocratic families who lived by the river, is a perfect example. A verse, or stanza, from *The Dumfries Volunteers* is also "lost"; the poet deleted it after Mrs Dunlop informed him that it mocked a relative of a close friend. Recent research has discovered that an eight verse edition of *Ye True Loyal Natives* was sold in 1862 but was never printed. It will also be shown that manuscripts by Burns were *lost, stolen, destroyed and burned*. Scholars have all been aware that a large cache of letters were withheld, suppressed or destroyed. So, the notion that we have everything penned by Burns, is gazing dumb in dreamland.

This work focuses on radical poems written during the years 1793-96. It is believed by at least one expert that the poet fell cravenly silent during these last years and ceased to write radical poetry. According to the biographer MacKay, Burns became a loyalist Hanoverian bard in his last years. This impression will be shown to be wrong. The Hanoverian government of Prime Minister, William Pitt, was fiercely opposed to the pro-democracy movement in Britain between 1791 and 1796. Burns, it will be shown, was an unstinting supporter of the democratic cause. The divide between the pro-democracy movement and the loyalist Hanoverians, was like oil and water: they did not mix. It is a central plank to *The Lost Poems* that Burns did continue to write radical poetry after early January 1793. It does not seem realistic that Scotland's most famous and most prolific poet wrote a meagre handful of poems during his last three and a half years.

Modern biographers never explain that the poet's so-called "complete" works, or canon, have been an unstable body of poems since his early death in 1796. The bard wrote over 600 works, yet, during his lifetime he was only famed for 74 poems and a few dozen songs. The majority of his material was published posthumously. The evolution of the canon is looked at in detail to show that eruptions of "new" poetry from Burns was commonplace during the 19th century. It was not until the work of Professor Kinsley, as recently as 1968, that the canon was looked at seriously. Kinsley himself asserted that the canon would probably never be resolved and accepted that new finds might yet occur. The so-called Complete Works of Burns have only ever been *literally* the "collected works". So, the notion of the "lost" poems is fixed firmly on empirical evidence, not cranky assumption.

After establishing the contextual framework which shows that democratic poems by Burns were indeed "lost", the new poems, gleaned from newspapers of the 1790's, have been subject to rigorous stylistic analyses to establish their provenance. They are given in two groups. Those which show substantial evidence of the poet's authorship are *provisionally* attributed to Burns, awaiting further analyses from literary experts. The second category *may be* by Burns. It should be noted that even when manuscript evidence has existed in the past, radical poetry by Burns has been rejected by one or two "experts" on highly suspect grounds. Certain anti-radical elements within the Scottish cultural personality have always lived uneasily with a national bard who was primarily a radical, satirical poet. So, it would seem that even manuscript evidence is not the *sine qua non* of canonical acceptance. The strongest circumstantial evidence to support the case for *The Lost Poems* does not come from a crystal ball; it is found in the letters of the bard himself.

Chapter 1

The Canon: Cut Away, Destroyed or Lost

"It is far from likely that the whole democratic effusions of Burns have come down to us."

Dr. Robert Chambers, 1851.

The first block of contextual evidence which point to "lost" poems by Robert Burns is the story of how the bard's poems came down to us. The so-called "complete" works, described as the *canon* by scholars, have been a volatile, unstable body of writings for two centuries. It is widely accepted that Kinsley firmly set the canon "in stone" in 1968. However, Kinsley was more cautious than write with absolute certainty: "The canon of Burns's work will probably never be fully established", he wrote, admitting "some of my judgements, through chance discoveries" may "turn out to be wrong".[1] The canonical door was, therefore, left open by Kinsley because of the possibility that "lost" poems might yet be found. This means, in short, that the canon of Burns is still unfixed.

The Kilmarnock edition in 1786 printed 36 poems - 44, if we count epigrams. Between the first Edinburgh edition of 1787 until the edition of 1793, the canon grew by only 20 poems. From 1793 onwards, it was presumed by the poet's Edinburgh publisher William Creech, that Burns composed no further poetry. Creech was obviously in the dark. Today, it is still accepted that the bard wrote only a handful of poems during his last three and a half years. In 1797 Creech cashed in on the bard's death and fame by republishing the 1793 Edinburgh edition. The 1797 publication contained 74 poems and 8 songs. It is astonishing that Burns' fame during his lifetime, rested upon only 74 poems. The majority of his poems, which total over 200, remained unpublished during his lifetime.

Burns saw many songs published in James Johnson's *Scots Musical Museum* (S.M.M.) before 1796. However, most of the songs - over seventy - sent by Burns to Johnson between 1787 and 1792 were published anonymously. They include a cluster of radical lyrics such as *A Vision, The Song of Death* and *Parcel o Rogues*. The total number of anonymous or pseudonymous works published by Burns from 1786-1796, including *Here's A Health Tae them That's Awa, A Man's A Man, Scots Wha Hae, The Rights of Woman* and so on, is greater than the number of works he acknowledged. Thus, the majority of Burns' published works during his own lifetime were either anonymous or pseudonymous.

The majority of the bard's writings in late July 1796 either lay in his desk-drawer, were scattered among friends, or waited to be published by the song collectors George Thomson or James Johnson. The poet was not publicly known as the author of *Parcel of Rogues, Here's A Health tae Them That's Awa, The Ode for The Departed Regency Bill, Holy Willie's Prayer, Stanzas on Psalmody, Extempore Stanzas on Thomson, Election Ballad to Graham of Fintry, The Rights of Woman, The Slaves Lament, The Tree Of Liberty, The Jolly Beggars, The Address of Beelzebub, Strathallan's Lament, Scots Wha Hae* or *A Man's A Man*. So, works which are now celebrated all over the world, were, during the 1790's, composed by an unknown mystery poet X, whose disguise was either anonymity or a series of pen-names such as A. Briton, John Barleycorn-Praeses, Thomas A Rhymer, Tim Nettle, Agricola, or Duncan M'Leerie. The publicly perceived "Robert Burns" of the late 18th century was not the complex, radical poet we know now.

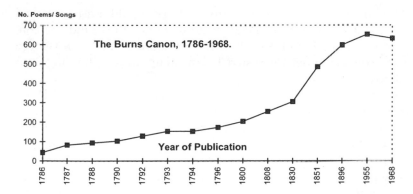

The Burns Canon, 1786-1968.

Anonymity or pen-names were very much a fashion during the 18th century. Burns, however, signed the Oath of Allegiance to the crown when he joined the Excise and was professionally barred from engaging in political or religious controversy. He, therefore, had a strong personal reason for not placing his name to controversial poems or letters sent to newspapers. The dual role of being at the same time the celebrated Scottish national bard and an Exciseman, created many problems for Burns. At one level he had earned the right to speak on national affairs, while on the other, he was supposedly an obedient peasant gauger - the most detested job in Scotland. The poet knew that if he was to continue writing radical poetry such as *A Dream*, it would have to be anonymous or pseudonymous. He observed to Mrs. Dunlop "Politics is dangerous ground for me to tred on".(CL 326) So, anonymous or pen-name poetry may have been fashionable for other writers - for Burns, it was necessity.

It is quite clear that Burns would have instructed George Thomson to publish *Scots Wha Hae* and *A Man's a Man* anonymously or under a pen-name had he lived to see Thomson's publication. He would have been furious if he had known Thomson printed *Scots Wha Hae* with an explanation of how to turn the song into an English anti-French song: Thomson suggested

> By changing *wha* into who, *hae* into have, *wham* into whom, *aften* into often, and *sae* into so, the following song will be English; and by substituting Gallia for *Edward*, and Britain for *Scotland*, it will be adapted to the present time.[2]

While the sedition laws were in force, Burns could not have risked being publicly known as the author. Of course, Burns did not conceal his authorship of *Scots Wha Hae* or *A Man's a Man* to George Thomson. He implicitly trusted Thomson not to pass the songs into the wrong hands.

After the poet's death John Syme headed a Committee in Dumfries to determine what to do with the poet's unpublished writings. Their immediate concern was a subscription volume to raise funds for Jean Burns and her family. Dr Currie, the "entire stranger", stepped forward as a reluctant volunteer biographer and took the "sweepings of his (the poet's) drawer" to Liverpool to prepare his biography of Burns.[3] He complained about the "chaos of the manuscripts". He did not take sole responsibility in deciding what unpublished poems and letters should be suppressed and what to print. He records that "Mr. Syme and Mr. Gilbert Burns made a journey to

Liverpool, where they explained and arranged the manuscripts, and selected such as seemed worthy of the press".[4] Fear of prosecution prompted Currie to edit out radical and bawdy writings. He admitted having to "mutilate many of the individual letters" [5] and boldly announced "all topics are omitted in the writings, and avoided in the life of Burns, that have a tendency to awake the animosity of party".[6] It therefore appears that Currie was forced to censor, cut sections from, or destroy manuscripts. Whether Currie destroyed manuscripts of the new poems presented here will never be known.

It became a fashion to edit out the radical or bawdy content of Burns's writings during the early part of the 19th century. Cromek, in his 1808 edition *The Reliques of Robert Burns*, comments "some of his compositions must be discarded, as inconsistent with that decorum which is due to the public at large".[7] He claims to have left out many works but justifies his decision with the vague explanation "some compositions of his yet remain.. which might render the Editor obnoxious to the letter, though not the spirit of the law".[8] To possess or pass on, written material that was potentially "seditious" was still a criminal act well after 1800. In his *Select Scottish Songs*, Cromek also commented "But blasphemy and ribaldry will not be published by the Editor of these volumes, though written in an unhallowed moment by Robert Burns".[9] The word "ribaldry" could be taken to mean bawdy songs or fierce radical works such as *A Revolutionary Lyric*. So, it is clear, that Burns's writings were passed from editor to editor, who were compelled to censor writings which might damage their own reputation. In the fiercely anti-radical climate of the early 19th century, this meant controversial poetry would have been deliberately destroyed or concealed.

Even as late as 1815, Chambers affirms that the culture of anti-radical oppression had only declined marginally. He records the story of how the Lord Advocate in Edinburgh ordered an "emissary" to trace all the subscribers of a newly launched liberal newspaper, the first in Edinburgh since the *Edinburgh Gazetteer* of the 1790's.[10] Moreover, the fact that early radical poems from Coleridge and even Shelley did not surface until the 1830's or later, indicates that the claustrophobic culture of oppression from 1792 to around 1832 was endemic to Britain. In such a climate of political fear it seems almost certain that radical letters and poems would have been either destroyed or withheld.

During the first decade of the 19th century a plethora of new editions appeared, each adding "new" poems, some authentic, others spurious. By 1810 there had been many editions containing new poetry. Sir Walter Scott, a high Tory unsympathetic to the radicalism of Burns, criticized an 1801 volume, which, he says ".. contains, among a good deal of rubbish, some of his most brilliant poetry".[11] Referring to the appearance of *Holy Willie's Prayer* and *The Jolly Beggars*, Scott went on, "Knowing that these, and hoping that other compositions of similar spirit and tenor might yet be recovered." So, the appearance of "new" poetry by Burns was almost a commonplace event during the early 19th century.

Many works were "recovered" and published. *On the Death of Lord President Dundas* and *The Address of Beelzebub* appeared in 1818. In the 1830's, Hogg and Motherwell's edition added many new works. Thereafter, various radical poems surfaced, including *The Tree Of Liberty* in 1838, *On Some Commemorations of Thomson* in 1856, *A New Psalm for The Chapel of Kilmarnock* in 1867, the first three stanzas of the *Irregular Ode for General Washington's Birthday* in 1872 and *On Glenriddell's Fox Breaking its Chain* in 1874. These works were all radical or satirical compositions. It is probably down to luck and chance that many of these radical works came to light during the 19th century. So, it is clear that radical poetry of Burns was "lost" and did surface by chance during the latter half of the 19th century. It is therefore highly probable that there were other works which did not survive the anti-radical oppression of the period.

It is a known fact that manuscripts are lost. Collector Mitchell, the poet's Excise colleague, owned a "sheaf of first copies of poems and songs by Burns" which were found in Mitchell's desk by his family when he died. Chambers comments that "The bundle was lost by the family, and has never since been heard of".[12] What songs and poems were included is not known. It may simply be that they were a "bundle" of Mitchell's favourite songs or bawdy songs. It is unfortunate that Mitchell's family were so negligent as to lose original manuscripts of Burns. However, it cannot be certain that the lost poems did not include any of the newly discovered works.

The manuscript for *The Tree Of Liberty* appeared in 1838 and thereafter it mysteriously vanished or was deliberately destroyed. In headnotes to *The Tree Of Liberty* Dr. Chambers argues that it was very likely there were other poems which might never be found –

It is far from likely that the whole democratic effusions of Burns have come down to us. For many years, that kind of authorship was attended with so much reproach, that men of humanity studied to conceal rather than to expose the evidence by which it could be proved against him (Burns). And even after the poor bard's death, the interests of his young family demanded...that nothing should be brought forward which was calculated to excite a political jealousy regarding him. Hence, for many years there was a mystery observed on this subject. During that time, of course, many manuscripts might perish.[13]

Chambers' statement is revealing. It refers to the continued culture of oppression and fear which echoed through until the Reform Act of 1832. With such an intensely xenophobic fear of radical ideas, it is understandable that many radical poems only slowly appeared from sources who guarded them with caution. There is little doubt that the appearance of a corpus of overtly radical works after the bard's death would have seriously jeopardized the attempt to raise a sub-scription for the poet's family. So, Dr. Chambers, the most respected Burns editor of the 19th century, believed "many manuscripts" of pro-democratic works by Burns, were lost or perished, during the decades after the poet's death.

Dr Chambers' view is supported by an eye witness account from a Mr John Pattison. Pattison visited Dumfries in late 1795 with his father, also John Pattison, brother to the bard's "worthy, wise, friend", Alexander Pattison of Paisley. John junior recalled that at dinner with Burns and Dr Maxwell during late 1795, "Burns repeated many verses that have never seen the light, chiefly political".[14] Pattison wrote of the visit in 1848 and did so anonymously in the *Glasgow Citizen* newspaper. MacKay includes the story of the visit but skips over this important remark without comment. He states erroneously in a foot-note that Pattison's letter was in *The Glasgow Courier* (not *Citizen* as in Chambers) of January 1848.[15] The anonymous letter by Pattison is not in the *Courier* of January 1848. Moreover, the only source where it is known the letter was by Pattison is in Chambers' biography. By 1848 *The Tree of Liberty* and the fragment of an *Ode to Liberty* (the final stanzas of the *Washington Ode)* had been in print. His comments, therefore, point to other unknown, unrecorded poems. The only problem with Pattison's evidence is that it is vague. He does not include names of poems, pen-names or specific subjects. His eye-witness account, though, is historical evidence which points to lost radical works. So, even by the mid-19th century, it was known that works of the bard had been lost.

The fact of missing or lost letters is not in dispute. It is widely known letters were either lost, withheld or destroyed. MacKay undermines the title of his *The Complete Letters of Robert Burns* by suggesting there is evidence to alert us to "the possible existence of many other letters of Burns hitherto unrecorded".[16] He makes this comment because the list of those who wrote to Burns does not match the list of people he replied to. For instance, it is known there were seven letters written by the Earl of Buchan to Burns, yet there are only three extant letter to the Earl from Burns. Buchan was a leading supporter of the reform movement. It does not seem tenable that Burns would not have replied to every letter from the Earl, whom he greatly admired. Further examples are letters to Burns from Sir W. Cunningham and J. Gregory who thank Burns in their letters for receiving poetry directly from him. The letters from Burns to them have not survived.[17] So, it is an indisputable fact that letters of the bard have been lost.

A letter which has been in print and is not included with MacKay's edition is to Dr Hughes of Hereford, 8th August 1795 where Burns wrote of Bruce slaying the Black Comyn in Dumfries.[18] In addition, a series of original letters from Burns to Robert Aitken were stolen from Robert Aitken's offices and never recovered - "the bundle was stolen by an unfaithful clerk, and, it is feared, destroyed, to prevent detection".[19] The existing letters to Aiken stop abruptly in 1793. Robert Aitken was a close associate of Burns from 1783. It seems remarkable that they corresponded up until 1789, then stopped writing for four years for the bard to continue writing to him as though he had been speaking to him only a month or so ago "I understand that our friend, Mr Muir......" (CL 570) The stolen letters are, therefore, from the period 1793 to 1796. Due to the poet's habit of including poetry in his letters, it is not known whether the stolen Aitken letters contained seditious radical poetry.

The entire correspondence between Burns and a few radical friends has never seen the light. For instance, it is known that Burns wrote to his "friend" Dr Walcot, alias the poet/songwriter, Peter Pindar. Another "friend" of the poet's was Dr. Currie's close associate in Liverpool, the poet William Roscoe. Roscoe held the honour of being the only living poet in 1795 to be quoted by Burns. Roscoe remarked after the bard's death that it was a great honour to know that Burns had planned to visit him in Liverpool in September of 1796. No letters from Burns to Roscoe have been preserved. It is reasonable to suspect the withheld correspondence of Burns to Pindar and Roscoe was of a radical nature. Both writers were radical pro-democracy supporters who published seditious poetry in *The Morning Chronicle*. It is certain, therefore, that the Burns-Pindar and Burns-Roscoe letters were of a radical nature and would have included radical poetry from the bard. Missing letters from Burns to radicals such as Pindar, Roscoe and even Mary Wollstonecraft, author of *Vindications on The Rights of Woman*, almost certainly contained radical poetry.[20] Almost every letter Burns wrote either quotes or mentions poetry. So, lost radical letters equals lost radical poems.

It is known the London office of James Perry, editor of *The Morning Chronicle*, was used as a collection point for manuscripts after July 1796 which may have been sent to friends in or near London. If any manuscripts were handed to Perry and passed to Currie, they have never been recorded.

Manuscripts of Burns regularly appeared in auction rooms in London during the 19th century and early 20th century. A remarkable example of material surfacing out of the blue occurred in 1862. Manuscript letters were sold at auction in London. The story features in the *Glasgow Herald*, in December 1862:

> Some highly curious letters of Burns, the poet, have just been disposed of in a sale by auction at Mssrs Puttick and Simpson, Leicester Square. They consisted of upwards of 20 autograph letters, with some poetry and a commonplace book. The letters have all, more or less, been used by Dr. Currie in his edition of Burns' correspondence; but the originals, just sold, contained many unpublished passages highly illustrative of the genius, peculiarities and eccentricities of the writer, as well as numerous particulars of the personal history of the poet and his family... Divided into 26 lots, they produced over £100.[21]

The "many unpublished passages" are recorded in the auction brochure - advertised in a previous issue of the *Herald* - as lengthy extracts from letters by Burns to Robert Cleghorn, an active member of the pro-democratic group, the Friends of the People. In 1996 we only have access to brief letters from the bard to Cleghorn which match those published by Currie. Letter number 302 to Cleghorn is annotated "remainder missing" as though part of the letter was edited away by Currie or destroyed. Letter 302 reads like a Christmas card note as though the body of the letter was lost. Letter 527 is merely two sentences long. There are 11 letters from Burns to Cleghorn extant - at least one for every year from 1787 onwards. None were collated from the year 1794. So, it seems clear that the letters sold in 1862 contained passages which have never been in print.

The fact that at least one letter from Burns to Cleghorn is missing can be inferred from a letter written by Cleghorn to Burns, where Cleghorn mentions receiving a copy of *The Soldier's Return*, which was composed in 1793.[22] Cleghorn's letter is dated 9th October 1793 and is a reply from a letter by Burns which contained the song. The only letters by Burns to Cleghorn which have survived from around this time were composed by Burns on 12th December 1792 - before *The Soldier's Return* was written - and 25th October 1793, after Cleghorn received the song. In the letter of 25th October, the bard sent him another ballad. (CL 592) So, here is another gap missing in the complex historical picture of what happened to the poet's writings after his death.

More important, this find, unearthed by Glasgow historian Micheal Donnelly in early 1996, reveals that an eight stanza holograph copy of *The Loyal Natives* was also sold, although only 2 relevant stanzas have come down to us. Assuming this material was genuine (the spate of forgeries occurred later in the 19th century and centered around one Edinburgh individual), there is now striking evidence to prove poetry by Burns did surface in 1862 but was suppressed by the buyer. If this happened in 1862, then it certainly occurred in the anti-radical hot-house culture of the 1796-1832 period.

A regrettable example of wanton destruction of original manuscripts occurred on 9th June 1871. Scott Douglas records that he received transcripts of previously unpublished material from a Mr. Greenshields of Lesmahago which helped the "completeness" of his edition. He then goes on, surprisingly, to applaud Mr. Greenshields for burning unknown manuscripts of the bard. Greenshields informed Scott Douglas, "How much it is to be regretted that Burns prostituted his genius! On broad moral ground, I have just finished a bonfire of them: - so here ends the matter".[23] While it may be right to assume that Mr. Greenshields burned only bawdy songs composed by Burns, it is very likely that he would have been aware of the clandestine edition of *The Merry Muses* which contained all the bawdy material of Burns. So, burning original copies of known bawdy songs served no purpose. The material was in print. If Greenshields was prejudiced against radical poetry, it is highly probable that what he destroyed were manuscripts containing pro-democratic poetry. No definitive answer can be drawn as to what was burned, but it is certain the manuscripts were either bawdy or overtly radical.

The notion of anti-radical prejudice ranged against the bard is founded on empirical evidence. A few editors and commentators on Burns's writings during the mid-to-late 19th century were openly hostile to his radical pro-democratic compositions. Scott Douglas, for instance, remarked on *The Tree of Liberty* that its

sentiments.. are so crude and unreasonable, that we would *rejoice* to be informed, some of these days, that the *Mosesfield manuscript*, on being more closely examined, turns out to be not Burns' penmanship after all! [24]

Henderson and Henley, who were also ardent Tory Unionists, followed swiftly with their assessment that the same work was "trash" which Burns did not write.[25] In fact, their view of the poet's radical views was one of detestation; that he was, on balance a "bad man" who refused to "dissemble" his support of the French Revolution and whose early death came at the right time.[26] So, if Mr. Greenshields was an anti-radical Tory who thought like Scott Douglas or Henderson and Henley, he would have had the motive to destroy a group of unpublished radical poems. Indeed, there is every chance that if any additional democratic poems like *The Tree of Liberty* were passed to leading "experts" in the ilk of Scott Douglas or Henderson and Henley, they would have immediately disagreed with their authenticity and might even have burned them. The word "trash" is a very emotive term. It seems a grotesque paradox that a "Burnsian", Mr. Greenshields, could destroy genuine works of the bard.

Moreover, Scott Douglas and Henderson and Henley rejected the song *A Revolutionary Lyric*, which was found in Burns's manuscript. The former concluded that "this production and also *The Tree of Liberty*, if really taken from Burns' M.S., have been merely *transcribed* by him from the pages of some wild *Magazine* of the period."[27] Both are aggressively political works, but display the same humanitarian vision of *A Man's A Man*. Scott Douglas's and Henderson and Henley's views display an open revulsion at the political sentiment of the two works. The remarks of these editors are unscholarly and deplorable, despite MacKay's applause for Scott Douglas as a "scientific" scholar. *A Revolutionary Lyric* has never been proven not to be by Burns. Yet, it has been quietly lobotomized from the canon.

What is most revealing about this episode is that the manuscript of *A Revolutionary Lyric* was not sufficient for it to be accepted to the canon. No scholarly evidence has ever been presented to justify its rejection. Why the jaundiced hysteria of Scott Douglas and Henderson and Henley has been allowed to stand, when it is obvious their personal views crossed over into the realm of their professional task as editors, is bewildering. Nowadays, the bias of 19th century editors has been corrected in the case of *The Tree of Liberty* which is generally accepted, but the case of *A Revolutionary Lyric* is still unresolved. How different is the story of the homeless orphan, the cute, uncontroversial little *Selkirk Grace*, which Burns certainly *did not write* and which *was never found in his manuscript*. It sits snugly next to *Tam O' Shanter* as the second most famous work of the bard, without a shred of evidence to suggest its authenticity. It is astonishing that Kinsley did not mention *A Revolutionary Lyric* in his 1968 volumes and did not list it as a work once accepted as genuine. MacKay follows suit but at least includes it as a historical reject in Appendix B of the *Complete Wordfinder*. Hughes, in *The Real Robert Burns*, published in 1922, has no doubts that it was the genuine article from the bard. It seems that proof of authorship in the form of the poet's own manuscript is not the *sine qua non* for entry to the canon. In fact, there are no established formal guidelines to follow.

A further lost manuscript surfaced in 1872. A large fragment of the poem had been in print for over almost fifty years. The first three stanzas of *Ode for General Washington's Birthday* had been either defaced or deliberately suppressed by Currie. Fortunately, a holograph manuscript was sold in London and was permitted publication. Robert Louis Stevenson comments in 1876:

> A point of curiosity is the rest of Burns's *Ode* about *Washington*, some lines of which appear already in his Correspondence. It is a very poor performance, but interesting as another testimony to the profound sympathy of Burns for all democratic movements.[28]

Stevenson was not impressed by the poem and his judgement "a very poor performance" disguises his obvious dislike of the poem. The *Ode* is, by any standard, a stunning performance in abstract Miltonic style. Dr Chambers' remark about lost "democratic effusions" was vindicated by the chance appearance of the *Washington Ode*.

By 1900, around 500 editions of Burns's collected works had been published worldwide. Around 100 songs were added to the canon during the latter part of the 19th century. Just as everything seemed to settle down with the canon after the turn of the 20th century, James Barke rocked the boat when he published his 1955 edition which allegedly added another 60 works to the canon. After so many unstable eruptions of "new" poetry, James Kinsley stepped in and contracted the canon in 1968, arguing there were 632 works which were "incontrovertibly" the work of Burns. The very fact that debate over the final number of poems and songs written by Burns did not settle down until Kinsley's classic 1968, 3-volume edition, should alert us to the reality that from the period 1796-1968, the canon was an expanding, volatile corpus of poems. This means that as the oppression of the 1790's slowly declined, the appearance of suppressed manuscripts was a matter of chance and luck. Inevitably, as Chambers commented, manuscripts would have decayed and perished.

In the process of Burns's writings being taken to Liverpool and whence to the four corners of the globe, the various editors of his works acted within the cultural constraints of their own period and published only what they could. The bards works were, therefore, siphoned through the anti-radical culture of the 1796-1832 period and then through the genteel culture of both Victorian and Edwardian society. Radical and bawdy works were bound to be casualties in this convoluted process. Chambers, Pinnington[29] and Pattison all point to lost radical works. MacKay points to lost letters. The poet's letters, more often than not, contained poetry. We now know that a "bonfire" of manuscripts did occur and that manuscripts were stolen and lost. This all adds up to lost poetry.

Two hundred years after the bard's death, there is little chance that lost poems would surface in manuscript form. However, the emergence of professionally organised archives in the 20th century inadvertently provided the opportunity to uncover the "lost" poems in the place the bard was likely to have placed them - in the newspapers of his own time. After all, he did promise to write material for *The Morning Chronicle* during mid-March 1794, a topic we will look at in detail later. As Freud comments, the repressed or *suppressed* will always return.

Footnotes

[1] James Kinsley, *The Poems and Songs of Robert Burns*, Vol. 1, p.vi., Oxford 1968.

[2] George Thomson, *Select Collection of Scottish Airs for the Voice*, 1794-1818, p.133, Vol. 3, 1815 edition, London.

[3] Dr James Currie, *The Works of Robert Burns*, Cadell & Davies, 1800.

[4] Op cit., p.vii.

[5] Quoted in Cunningham, p.587, 1834.

[6] Currie, op cit., p.viii.

[7] R. H. Cromek, *Reliques of Robert Burns*, p.vii, Cadell & Davies, 1808.

[8] Cromek, op cit., p.viii.

[9] Cromek, *Select Scottish Songs*, p.225.

[10] Dr Chambers, *The Life & Works of Robert Burns*, Vol II, p.264, Edinburgh, 1851.

[11] In Cromek, *Select Scottish Songs*, op cit., p.229.

[12] Chambers, op cit., Vol. IV, p.144.

[13] Chambers, op cit., Vol. IV, p.78.

[14] Op cit., p.173. Pattison's letter in *The Glasgow Citizen* of January 1848 was anonymous.

[15] Footnote 28 in MacKay, op cit., p.719, erroneously cites the letter by Pattison as in *The Glasgow Courier*.

[16] MacKay, *The Complete Letters of Robert* Burns, p.727, Alloway Publishing, 1987.

[17] See CL, op cit., Appendix C, numbers 97 & 137

[18] Letter to Dr. Hughes of Hereford, 8th August 1795, quoted in H. & H. Vol. IV, p.477, Centenary Edition, 1896. Facsimile copy of original on display in The Burns Room, The Murray Arms Hotel, Gatehouse of Fleet.

[19] Chambers, op cit., Vol. IV, p.226.

[20] Correspondence with Wollstonecraft was first highlighted in Carswell, op cit. 1930 & cited in N. Paton's essay, *Robert Burns and the English Radicals*, 1995, Sea-Green Publications.

[21] *The Glasgow Herald*, 26th December 1862 - unearthed by historian Michael Donnelly.

[22] CL, op cit., p.758, number 271.

[23] William Scott Douglas, *Poetical Works of Robert Burns*, The Kilmarnock Edition, Vol. II, p.417, Thirteenth Edition, Glasgow, 1938.
[24] W Scott Douglas, op cit., p.404.
[25] T. F. Henderson & W. E. Henley, Vol. IV, p.107
[26] Op cit., Vol. IV, p.337
[27] W Scott Douglas, op cit., p.392.
[28] Robert Louis Stevenson, in *The Academy* journal, 12th February 1876.
[29] Edward Pinnington, *The Burns Chronicle*, 1912.

Chapter 2

The Letters and Poems, 1793-6

"If I must write, let it be sedition". Burns, June 1796. (CL 679)

The second block of contextual evidence is a consideration of the poet's political sentiments within his letters and poems between January 1793 and 1796. In this period the poet is supposed to have abandoned radical composition and, according to at least one expert, changed his radical views to become a loyalist Hanoverian bard. So, this section of the argument is pivotal to the new poems. If the poet threw his democratic principles to the wind from 1793, then he could not be the author of any of the "lost" poems, which are all radical effusions. However, if it can be shown that Burns continued to hold radical views during his last years *and* composed controversial radical poetry *and* was still sending such poetry to newspapers and journals, then the keystone of *The Lost Poems* is firmly in place. With pieces missing from the canonical jig-saw, confirmation of the poet's radical creativity in the post-1793 period establishes the likelihood that the poet wrote other works which went unrecorded after his death.

In his recent biography, MacKay comments that the poet's letters are "remarkably apolitical" from "mid-1793 onwards".[1] Is this true? We know that letters from this period were withheld and many went unrecorded. Given the oppressive culture of the 1796-1820 period, the remarkable feature is that so many letters from this period were collected at all. It seems clear that many of the "unrecorded" letters were of a radical nature and date from the last three and a half years of the poet's life. So, even if the poet's letters which have come down to us, are "remarkably apolitical", it is obvious that an amount of political flavouring was suppressed: the unrecorded correspondence to Roscoe, Cleghorn, Ainslie, Wollstonecraft, Masterton, and so on. So, the notion of "apolitical" is suspect from the outset. When looking back to an era when it was effectively a criminal act to speak in support of the reformist case outwith parliament, we should not confuse the cautious, relative silence of the poet *in public*, with an acceptance of the status quo.

If we are to accept MacKay's view at face value, it seems that Burns wrote only one "side-swipe at the contemporary situation", meaning one political remark, during the 1793-1796 period.[2] The bard's "side-swipe", also described as an "oblique" remark, is his explanation to Thomson of the inspiration behind *Scots Wha Hae*. Burns informed the song collector that the patriotic Ode was imaginatively conceived with one foot in the 14th century, thinking on Bruce and Wallace, while the other was fixed in the context of late August 1793, "with the glowing ideas of some other struggles of the same nature, *not quite so ancient*". (CL 582) The "*not quite so ancient*" is the "oblique" hint, or "side-swipe". In *The Complete Letters* a footnote states that this is a reference to "the trial of Muir and Palmer for sedition, then taking place at Edinburgh".[3] This is partly correct. The Reverend Fysche Palmer was not tried at Edinburgh, but at Perth on 12th September 1793, well after Thomson received the song. By implication, the poet is relating the battle waged against foreign oppression by Wallace and Bruce with the contemporary struggles of the reform movement against oppressive sedition laws. So, amid the political and cultural context of 1793, the theme of *Scots Wha Hae* was, in the words of the bard "Liberty & Independence". (CL 582). The old Scottish national anthem, therefore, viewed in proper context, is a song laden with political overtones which relate to the ideological debates of 1792-3.

Crawford has shown that the line "Let us do - or die!", from *Scots Wha Hae*, is adapted from a French revolutionary oath.[4] More or less the same words were the final triumphant chant of the Convention of the Friends of the People, who met in Edinburgh in late 1792. So, there is more than a mere "oblique" reference to the contemporary situation. It is due to the political overtones of the song that Burns was cautious about it being published under his own name and asked that Mr James Perry, editor of *The Morning Chronicle*, print the song anonymously. The song is proof of the poet's continued radical composition. The notion that *Scots Wha Hae* is only a 14th century hymn to Wallace and Bruce is romantic, unhistorical, and ignores the bard's own remarks.

So, are there really no comments by Burns during this latter period on the issue of radical politics? On 6th April 1793, the poet wrote to Deborah Duff Davies without any sign that he had changed his views or been silenced by the January investigation into his sentiments by the Excise –

> ...ascend that rock of Independence ... Make the worthless tremble under your indignation....

> Out upon the world! say I; that its affairs are administered so ill! - They talk of REFORM - My God! what a reform would I make among the Sons, & even the Daughters of men!

> Down, immediately, should go FOOLS from the high places where misbegotten CHANCE has perked them up, & through life should they skulk, ever haunted by their native insignificance, as the body marches accompanied by its shadow. (CL 556A)

This final line is certainly more radical than the statements of most reformers during the 1790's, since it talks about throwing unidentified political leaders from office. It is a highly seditious comment. By no account could this letter be viewed as "apolitical".

A week later, in a letter to Erskine of Mar, the poet reflects on the embarrassing Excise enquiry into his personal ideals and shows quite clearly that his employers had merely forced him to bite his lip in public. In referring to himself he comments "..I will say it! - the sterling of his honest worth, no poverty could debase; and his independent British mind, *Oppression might bend, but could not subdue*! (CL 558) Here we have stunning evidence that the poet was forced to "bend" his principles due to "oppression" but the final note is defiant, that he will not be subdued. Given the culture of oppression during this period, this statement by Burns is a forceful remark on the political situation. He had been instructed to keep out of politics, to be "silent and obedient". The tone of this letter suggests he had no intention of following the petty directive of his employers.

A further letter of April 1793, to Peter Hill, reveals the same radical voice, sounding off at the contemporary political situation: the "unlucky blast" is a reference to the start of the British war against France, which began at the end of January -

> I hope and trust that this unlucky blast which has overturned

so many, & many worthy characters who four months ago little dreaded any such thing - will spare my Friend. -

O! may the wrath & curse of all mankind, haunt & harass these turbulent, unprincipled misc[reants] who have involved a People in this ruinous business!!!. (CL 553)

The angered indignation in this letter is surprisingly similar to the sentiments expressed in the new poem, *Lines on Ambition*, signed A. Briton, which was written later in the year. The words "wrath", "curse", "haunt" and "harass" are strongly emotive in the way they are employed, to describe the poet's feelings towards the "misc[reants]", or government, who "involved" the British people in the war. As MacKay comments, the poet believed the administration of Pitt and Dundas was taking the country down the road to ruin, a view which is itself another side-swipe on the government.[5]

Scanning through the misnamed *Complete Letters* for the 1793 period, we find another Burnsian "side-swipe" at the contemporary situation. The bard goes into indignant mode in a letter to George Thomson -

Have you ever, my dear Sir, felt your bosom ready to burst with indignation, on reading of, or seeing, how these mighty villains who divide kingdom against kingdom, desolate provinces & lay Nations waste out of the wantonness of Ambition, or often from still more ignoble passions? ...the tyrannical strides of some Public Destroyer; & overwhelmed with private distresses, the consequence of a Country's Ruin. (CL 566)

A further letter to Thomson from July 1794, reveals yet another commentary by Burns at Britain's involvement in the war against revolutionary France. It is tongue-in-cheek, with clever wit:

...is your work to be at a dead stop untill these glorious Crusaders, the Allies, set our modern Orpheus at liberty from the savage thraldom of Democratic Discords? Alas the day! And woe is me! That auspicious period, pregnant with the happiness of Millions ... these days of sweet chords & concords seem by no means near! (CL 632)

So, it is clear the radical voice of the poet was not subdued during 1793 and into 1794.

Then again, in 1795, a letter to Patrick Heron of Kirroughtree, shows Burns's radical verve in a flight of free-flowing fury, aimed directly at the Pitt government -

> To pillory on Parnassus the rank reprobation of character, the utter dereliction of all principle, in a profligate junto which has not only outraged virtue, but violated common decency; which, spurning even hypocrisy as paltry iniquity below their daring; - to unmask their flatigiousness to the broadest day - to deliver such over to their merited fate, is surely not merely innocent, but laudable; is not only propriety, but virtue... I swear by the lyre of Thalia to muster on your side all the votaries of honest laughter, and fair, candid ridicule. (CL 660)

No-one could misunderstand the frustrated anger of these lines and what they are about. In fact, there is more than a hint that the poet intended writing poetry to "ridicule" the political leaders of the time. Phrases such as "rank reprobation", "utter dereliction of all principle", "a profligate junto", "outraged virtue", "violated common decency", and so on, are testament to the fact the poet spoke the truth, that he was not subdued by the Excise reprimand.

Further, to Mrs Dunlop, there are several examples of the poet's continued radical voice. On 25th June 1794 he wrote of a new poem, "The subject is Liberty: you know, my honoured friend, how dear the theme is to me."(CL 628). Then, on 29th October 1794, Burns wrote, "My Enemies may dislike (for they dare not despise me) & I can repay them in kind". (CL 645). The "enemies" Burns refers to were those who disliked his radical politics. In a letter of 12th January 1795, also to Mrs Dunlop, the poet's strident radical tone makes the Excise investigation and his obsequious apologia to Graham of Fintry of 5th January 1793, seem like a faded memory from another lifetime -

... you know my Politics; & I cannot approve of the honest Doctor's whining over the deserved fate of a certain pair of Personages. What is there in the delivering over a perjured Blockhead & an unprincipled Prostitute into the hands of the hangman, that it should arrest for a moment, attention, in an eventful hour, when, as my friend Roscoe in Liverpool gloriously expresses it -

"When the welfare of Millions is hung in the scale
And the balance yet trembles with fate!"

But our friend is already indebted to People in power ... so I can apologise for him; for at bottom I am sure he is a staunch friend to liberty. - Thank God these London trials have given us a little more breath, & I imagine that the time is not far distant when a man may freely blame Billy Pitt, without being called an enemy of his Country". (CL 649)

This letter shows unequivocally the poet's continued support for the cause of "liberty" and "democracy" at a time when Britain was at war with France. Pitt's government sought to extinguish all domestic democratic reform agitation. The poet clearly identifies with the London reform radicals, Horne Tooke and others, who were acquitted on a charge of High Treason in January 1795. The notion that there is only a single "side-swipe" among the poet's letters after mid-1793 is so wrong it is bewildering.

A further example from 31st January 1796, also to Mrs Dunlop, tells how the political and economic predicament of Britain contributed to periodic famine in Dumfries:

...but here, we have actual famine, & that too in the midst of plenty. - Many days my family & hundreds of other families, are absolutely without one grain of meal; as money cannot purchase it. - How long the *Swinish Multitude* will be quiet, I cannot tell: they threaten daily. (CL 688)

A footnote in *The Complete Letters* explains that this letter refers to Meal riots of "12th-14th March 1796".[6] Although Burns did remark that poets of "nature's making" were second-sighted, it is simply not possible for him to write about meal riots which had yet to occur, in a letter of 31st January! Burns obviously suffered hunger and malnutrition between January and the end of March 1796, which would have exacerbated his illness. He knew there was "plenty" of food around, but meal was often shipped to other parts of Britain from Dumfries or hidden to force up prices. Grierson, as his diaries from this period show, did not go without food. So, certain areas of Dumfries went hungry while others did not.

Even as late as 1st June 1796, the poet's unbowed, independent mind is evident, in a letter to Maria Riddell -

> ...if I must write, let it be Sedition, or Blasphemy, or something else that begins with a B, so that I may grin with the grin of iniquity, & rejoice with the rejoicing of an apostate angel. (CL 697).

So, until almost his last breath, the poet's continued radical voice is as clear and as loud as a church bell on a frosty winter morning. Thus, there is ample evidence within the letters of Burns to show that from mid-1793 through until June 1796 the poet was still true to his radical views. Therefore, within the poet's letters, there is considerable contextual evidence to support the continuity of the bard's pro-democratic beliefs. The idea that he became "remarkably apolitical" in his last years and made only one remark on the political situation is itself a remarkable conclusion in the teeth of considerable evidence to the contrary.

There are also several reminiscences about the poet during his last years which confirm his continued radical thought and poetic output. An eye witness to the poet's undiluted radical views was Professor Josiah Walker of Edinburgh who visited Burns in November 1795. Walker was a leading establishment figure of the literary world and no reformer. He later related, somewhat condescendingly, how the poet had read him

> ..his fragments of an *Ode to Liberty*, with marked and peculiar energy, and shewed a disposition which, however, was easily repressed, to throw out political remarks, of the same nature with those for which he had been reprehended.[7]

Walker's rather pompous commentary is revealing, particularly his view that the bard's political expressions were "easily repressed". The implication of "easily repressed" is quite clear. Burns, in late 1795 still maintained the principles and values which underpinned his radical beliefs, but had grown cautious of cavalier public expression. The "peculiar energy" of Burns in talking about the political wrongs of the Pitt government roused him to such a fury, according to John Syme, that his eyes "glowed like burning coals". While Syme may have exaggerated a little, he confirms the poet's profound indignation and serious feelings on issues of a national level, notably his detestation of tyranny.

So, the charge of "remarkably apolitical" does not apply to the Scottish bard between 1793 and 1796. In fact, the evidence from his letters tell us he was an ardent supporter of democratic ideals until his death. Precisely because such ideals were driven "underground" and subject to fierce anti-radical oppression by Pitt's paranoid government, it is certain that recorded or unrecorded pro-democracy poetry from Burns would have been anonymous or pseudonymous. The political and cultural forces which lost us many letters by Burns were the same forces which, logically, would have led to the later suppression of radical poems by Burns. A realistic understanding of the history of the period would lead any open-minded scholar to conclude that missing and suppressed letters, equal missing and lost poems. This means that if letters are unrecorded, then poems must be unrecorded. To accept one and deny the other is not a rational position. Indeed, the most seditious letters and poetry written during these years were unlikely to survive.

It is perplexing that some scholars peddle the view that Burns *did not*, and *would not*, write controversial radical material after early January 1793. Of course, he would not have been foolish enough to compose such poetry and let the world know he was the author. Both *A Man's A Man* and the *Washington Ode* are powerful, pro-democratic works penned in the post-1793 period. Moreover, *The Tree of Liberty*, which mentions the execution of the King of France, an event which occurred in late January 1793, was clearly written sometime after the Excise inquiry of early January 1793. A brief consideration of the *Washington Ode* and *A Man's A Man* is enough to dismiss the deliberate de-radicalisation of the poet's so-called "apolitical" years.

The *Irregular Ode for General Washington's Birthday* was written during 1794. The final stanza was sent to Mrs. Dunlop in June 1794. Her reaction did not dwell much on the poem, but focused on how the letter had traveled to her and the surprisingly small writing employed by the poet:

> I received some time ago, after many devious paths through which it has wandered on its way from Castle Douglas since the 25th June, a little line so very diminutive in its size that I thought it must have come from Oberon the fairy..[8]

This tells us Burns did not trust the normal postal system which was known to be monitored by the spy network of Pitt and Dundas. Burns describes the topic of the *Washington Ode* as the "degeneracy of kingdoms", that is, the collapse of Liberty across Europe into warring factions. Burns did not trust the first section of the Ode to Mrs. Dunlop. MacKay records the fact that Mrs. Dunlop received only the last stanza from Burns[9]. He then goes on to imply, in error, that she received the entire poem by scoffing that Mrs. Dunlop might have been impressed by "the panegyrics to William Wallace" but her gratification "was set at naught by her "Dear Burns" daring to condemn the present conflict".[10] Burns did not send the first stanzas because he was aware that the family of Dunlop were involved in the war against France. The entire poem was not known until it turned up in manuscript in a London auction room in 1872, seventy eight years after it was written. The Ode is proof that at least one democratic poem of Burns was "lost" and then found during the late 19th century.

It is worth looking at in detail. It shows that the poet was more than capable of selecting a style and language which would not have been immediately recognized as his by contemporaries. The first stanza celebrates the freedom of the American colonies from British tyranny. It employs bold, strident language,

> No Spartan tube, no attic shell,
> No lyre Aeolian I awake,
> 'Tis Liberty's bold note I swell:
> Thy harp, Columbia, let me take!
> See gathering thousands while I sing,
> A broken chain, exulting, bring

And dash it in a tyrant's face,
And dare him to his very beard,
And tell him he no more is fear'd,
No more the despot of Columbia's race!
A tyrant's proudest insults brav'd,
They shout a People freed! They hail an Empire sav'd!

Had this stanza been published in a newspaper of 1794/5, it is certain that no-one would have guessed Burns as the author.

The second stanza turns from the specific case of America to a general context of individual morality. It calls to those who would "dare maintain The Royalty of Man", a reference to supporters of liberty, strongly influenced by Young's *Night Thoughts,* which Burns called his favourite quote in 1788: "On Reason build Resolve, / That column of true majesty in Man":

Where is Man's godlike form!
Where is that brow erect and bold,
That eye that can, unmoved, behold,
The wildest rage, the loudest storm,
That e'er created fury dared to raise!
Avaunt! thou caitiff, servile, base,
That tremblest at a Despot's nod,
Yet, crouching under th' iron rod,
Canst laud the arm that struck th' insulting blow!
Art thou of man's imperial line ?
Dost boast that countenance divine?
Each sculking feature answers, No!
But come, ye sons of Liberty,
Columbia's offspring, brave as free,
In danger's hour still flaming in the van:
Ye know, and dare maintain, The Royalty of Man.

This stanza verges on rage forged into art. It scorns the man who would be a slave, who could be beaten, subordinated and still feign admiration for the oppressor. It is effectively a statement that liberty is based on the rational independence of each individual. Liberty, for Burns, during 1794, demanded courage of conviction and a fixed, honest, fearless disregard to face oppression eye-to-eye. Yet, in expressing such views, he was forced to keep this type of poetry secret for fear of persecution.

The third stanza focuses on Britain. Its tone and language is unequivocally seditious and treasonable. It contrasts King George III with King Alfred, a King Burns saw as honourable and just - Alfred was responsible for setting up the Jury system and beheaded 44 corrupt judges during his reign:

> Alfred, on thy starry throne,
> Surrounded by the tuneful choir,
> The Bards that erst have struck the patriot lyre,
> And roused the freeborn Briton's soul of fire,
> No more thy England own.
> Dare injured nations form the great design,
> To make detested tyrants bleed?
> Thy England execrates the glorious deed!
> Beneath her hostile banners waving,
> Every pang of honor braving,
> England in thunders calls - "The Tyrant's cause is mine!"
> That hour accurst, how did the fiends rejoice,
> And hell thro' all her confines raise th' exulting voice,
> That hour which saw the generous English name
> Linkt with such damned deeds of everlasting shame!

Is this "apolitical"? Muir, Palmer, Skirving and Margarot, who were sentenced to Botany Bay for their reformist comments, never composed anything as treasonable as these lines. The final lines of the stanza are a seering indictment of Britain's war policy against France. If the Ode had been published by Currie, it would have crushed the chances of raising a subscription for the poet's family. At a stroke, the *Ode* demolishes the view that Burns had changed his radical principles and turned a loyalist Hanoverian bard.

MacKay describes the *Washington Ode* as similar to *Scots Wha Hae*, saying it "waxed lyrical on the golden age of Scottish history when William Wallace ... fought for freedom".[11] The final stanza has little to do with Scotland's past. It had everything to do with Scotland's contemporary scene, the demise of liberty and the collective acquiescence to oppression -

Thee, Caledonia, thy wild heaths among,
Famed for the martial deed, the heaven-taught song,
To thee, I turn with swimming eyes.
Where is that soul of Freedom fled?
Immingled with the mighty Dead!

Reference to Wallace is employed to contrast the historic martial bravery of Scots with the timidity of the present:

Beneath that hallowed turf where WALLACE lies!
Hear it not, Wallace, in thy bed of death!
Ye babbling winds in silence sweep;
Disturb not ye the hero's sleep,
Nor give the coward secret breath.

(*The Complete Poetical Works of Burns* contains a typing error which has the word "weep" instead of "sweep"). The poet then asks, in despair and angst at the problems faced by his country, is this really the Scotland I know? He goes on to picture a Miltonic image of Wallace's arm, falling like a symbol of liberty across Scotland, a broken country –

Is this the ancient Caledonian form,
Firm as her rock, resistless as her storm?
Shew me that eye which shot immortal hate,
Blasting the Despot's proudest bearing:
Shew me that arm which, nerved with thundering fate,
Braved Usurpation's boldest daring!
Dark-quenched as yonder sinking star,
No more that glance lightens afar;
That palsied arm no more whirls on the waste of war.

This poem is probably one of the most powerful historical Odes ever penned. It brims over with indignation at the wrongs of the age. Its language is striking, complex and abstract. Its imagery is stunning. It is, effectively, the condition of Scotland poem for 1794 and a powerful representation of the radical ideals of Burns during 1794.

F. MacKenzie comments in the *Burns Chronicle* that the *Washington Ode* was Burns's most damning indictment of the Hanoverian government.[12] He believed it had been sent to the *Morning Chronicle*, "It is in no way surprising that Perry did not publish the Ode in the *Morning Chronicle*" because of its forceful attack on English tyranny. It is not known whether Burns did send the Ode to Mr. Perry. MacKenzie goes on - "Had the *Washington Ode* been published or traced, as might easily have happened, not only re-examination and dismissal from the Excise, but punishment was inevitable."[13] Thus, it is clear in the Ode that Burns risked his own liberty and life in the democratic cause of reform. Loyalty to liberty was an honourable, but dangerous motive in 1794, when the majority learned to keep their heads down and their mouths shut.

The *Washington Ode* proves that Burns was cautious of the sedition laws, but undeterred in composing powerful treasonable poetry. Its very existence destroys the argument that he could not be the author of any of the new democratic poems which indict Pitt and Dundas as despotic. It displays the intensity of his democratic views and his conviction towards a future world where liberty, equality, and justice would come "yet, for a' that". It is symptomatic of his radical idealist dream to see the "Royalty of Man" placed on every hearth in every household. In considering the new radical poems, it is critical that we focus on the Burns of the *Washington Ode* and not the romanticized Burns drooling over a mountain daisy.

The origin of the Ode is far from being a reaction by the poet to his treatment at the hands of The Loyal Natives Club in Dumfries as MacKay has opined. As early as 1st January, 1790, a song in *The Glasgow Advertiser, Ode for Colombia's Favourite Son,* praised "Great Washington ....Each heart exulting hears the sound, / Thousands to their deliv'rer throng, / And shout him welcome all around!" One strand of influence was probably Washington's series of letters in Scottish newspapers during the 1793/4 period, particularly, his "On the Reciprocal Friendship between States" published in *The Bee* during early 1794. A further link may have been the story of how the Earl of Buchan, a friend of Burns, had sent General Washington a small wooden box, supposedly made from the tree which sheltered William Wallace at the battle of Falkirk. Buchan wrote in *The Bee* that no other man on earth had earned the right to own the box. For Burns, Washington was, in essence, *the* contemporary equivalent of Wallace. So, by 1794 the name "Washington" was almost synonymous with "liberty" among radicals; the established icon of Liberty long before the Statue of Liberty was erected.

The link to Washington, though, goes deeper. The "Sons of Liberty" mentioned in the Ode refers to a radical American Masonic group who counted the famous Paul Revere as a member. Washington, like Burns, is one of the most famous sons of Freemasonry. Around 50 leading members of Washington's first presidency were Freemasons. The slogan of Freemasonry during the period was "Liberty, Fraternity and Brotherhood". It is unfortunate that one or two writer on Burns have tip-toed around the Ode, pretending it does not exist. There are many strands of influence within the poet's radical worldview and the ideals of Freemasonry are important.

The song *A Man's A Man* is also a powerful democratic work, which, in its time, was a searing political indictment of the elitist political order. It was published without the poet's name in the *Glasgow Magazine* of August 1795, another fact missed by modern biographers. In 1795 it was undoubtedly a "seditious" and treasonable song, despite the accolades and panegyrics to its brotherhood of man this century The first version published is markedly different from the final version which has come down to us. It was first published without the first verse which contains the well known "The rank is but the guinea stamp, / The man's the gowd for a' that", which was obviously composed sometime in late 1795:

> What tho' on hamely fare we dine,
> Wear hodden grey, and a' that:
> Gie fools their silk, and knaves their wine,
> A man's a man for a' that.
> For a' that, and a' that,
> Their tinsel shew, and a' that;
> An honest man, tho' ne'er sae poor,
> Is chief o' men for a' that.
>
> Ye see yon birkie ca'd a lord,
> Wha struts and stares, and a' that,
> Tho hundreds worship at his word,
> He's but a cuif for a' that.
> For a' that, and a' that,
> His ribband, star, and a' that;
> A man of independent mind,
> Can look, and laugh at a' that.

The king can make a belted knight,
A marquis, duke, and a' that,
But an honest man's aboon his might,
Guid faith, he manna fa that!
For a' that, and a' that,
His dignities, and a' that;
The pith o' sense, and pride o' worth,
Are grander far than a' that.

Then let us pray, that come it may,
As come it shall, for a' that;
When sense and worth, o'er a' the earth,
Shall bear the gree, and a' that;
For a' that, and a' that;
It's coming yet, for a' that;
And man, and man, the world o'er,
Shall brothers be, and a' that.

It is interesting that the word "King" was later changed to "Prince" and the phrase "chief o' men" is found in the new poem, *The Ghost of Bruce*, version two. This celebrated song vividly displays the radical views of the poet which he was forced to publicly suppress as anonymous during his life.

The historical and cultural context of the song is important. Scotland still had many working people who were bonded to a master and Scottish "slaves" worked in the early mines of Fife. The Scottish reform movement was effectively crushed during 1793 and 1794. So, the air of democratic triumphalism within the song is a vision of the eventual victory of reason and humanity over the oppression of a tyrannical government, set in the future. The song concludes as a humanitarian prayer, "Then let us pray, that come it may". Caught within the cob-web of ideological tumult and oppression during the 1790's, the only real solace for the poet was a historical victory which put faith in human progress. Its message, therefore, to contemporary political leaders such as Pitt and Dundas, is simple, forceful and positive - no matter what oppression might be dished out to control, cowe or dupe the public, it was "coming yet, for a' that" that the democratic revolution, "humanity", would eventually win the day.

The song sets the "honest man" above the throne - a "king can make a belted knight" but "an honest man's aboon his might". This sentiment is republican and fits with Burns's wider radical philosophy emphasized in the *Washington Ode*, concerning "The Royalty of Man" - man's ability to reason and reflect. The poet takes the term "Royalty" out of the Palace and levels it to describe everyday experience, with the qualification that it applies only to the honesty and independent person. *A Man's A Man* paints the world of pomp as a sham, a superficial "tinsel shew" lacking substance. It is quite clear that Burns opposed all forms of institutionalized subordination and therefore would have wished to see a more egalitarian society. In the mid-1790's that made him an "evil Jacobin" enemy of Britain and he was accordingly persecuted by elements of Dumfries society for his views.

It is unhistoric to think Burns would have allowed Thomson to publish *A Man's A Man* with his name if he had lived after 1796. As long as the sedition laws were in force, Burns would have kept his authorship anonymous. The song was eventually published by Thomson in 1803, eight years after he received it from Burns. Thomson subsequently dropped the song from later editions of his *Select Collection of Scots Songs*. It is more than possible that the *Washington Ode* and *A Man's A Man* were only two of the "many democratic effusions" which surfaced from the oppressive anti-radical culture of the period.

There are many other examples of radical composition after early January 1793. The song *Logan Braes* closes with insurrectionary lines. The *Inscription for An Alter to Independence*, written in 1795 for Patrick Heron, is couched in defiant language from a passionate radical whose views are far from cowed. Moreover, the *Heron Ballads* pointedly attack almost every prominent Tory figure in the south west of Scotland. They prove that Burns had not hung up his satirical quill. The fact that he dared to write the Scots vernacular *Heron Ballads* indicates that by early 1795, his tightrope walking had become more daring and dangerous. Burns did not formally publish and acknowledge the *Heron Ballads*. They testify that he was undeterred by the sedition laws and risked his Excise career by penning satirical verse in the vernacular which were readily recognizable as his work. Thus, it cannot be argued against the new poems that Burns would not have composed such democratic work, afraid of prosecution. He was already half-way across Niagra on the tightrope of controversy with the

Washington Ode, Scots Wha Hae, A Man's a Man, and moved into very dangerous territory with *The Heron Ballads.*

So, in both his letters and poetry, the radical voice of Burns continued after 5th January 1793. This makes the new poems a realistic possibility. The alleged single "side-swipe" turns out to be a host of overtly radical comments. A serious reading of the poet's work, from *The Twa Herds, Holy Willie's Prayer, Man Was Made to Mourn, Scotch Drink, The Author's Earnest Cry and Prayer, The Address of Beelzebub, Ode for the Departed Regency Bill, Birthday Ode for the 31st December,* to the *Washington Ode* should be sufficient to confirm that there has never been a more stubborn, independent-minded radical poet in Scotland than Robert Burns. The *Washington Ode* seems to suggest that the enquiry by the Excise fired and enhanced the radical views of the poet, although they were driven "underground" in anonymity. Mrs Dunlop was clearly aware of the poet's continued radical support for the French revolution and the democratic cause in Britain during 1794 when she wrote

> your goddess has behaved in such a way as to injure her reputation, and acquire so very bad a name.... she is too much attached of late to the society of butchers to be admitted among ladies ... her handkerchief spotted with the sanguine stains of the guillotine ... May it not prove fatal, as I greatly fear it may ... By the by, we had a story here that you had lost your office and were gone to London.[14]

The fundamental building block for the new poems is firmly laid - Burns *did* continue to write radical material after early January 1793.

Footnotes

[1] MacKay, *A Biography of Robert Burns*, p.541, Headline, 1992.
[2] MacKay, op cit., p.541.
[3] MacKay, *The Complete Letters of Robert* Burns, p.639, Alloway Publishing, 1987.
[4] Thomas Crawford, *Political and Protest Songs in Eighteenth Century Scotland*, Scottish Studies, Vol 14, 1970, p.124.
[5] MacKay, op cit.,p.539.
[6] MacKay, C.L., op cit., p.215.

[7] Josiah Walker, quoted in Robert Fitzhugh, *Robert Burns, His Associates and Contemporaries*, p.360, Boston, 1943; also quoted verbatim in T. Crawford, *Boswell, Burns and The French Revolution*, Saltire Society, 1990. In MacKay, *A Biography*, p.609, the words "political remarks" are changed to read "peculiar remarks".

[8] Mrs Dunlop to Burns, on 8th Sept 1794, in W. Wallace: *Correspondence Between Robert Burns and Mrs Dunlop*, p.406, Edinburgh, 1898.

[9] MacKay, *A Biography*, op cit., p.569.

[10] MacKay, op cit., p. 570.

[11] Op cit., p. 569.

[12] F. MacKenzie *Burns Chronicle*, 1977, p.6-11.

[13] F. MacKenzie, op cit., p.10.

[14] Mrs Dunlop to Robert Burns, 8th September 1794, p407-409, W. Wallace op cit.

Chapter 3

The Promise

"I have come forward with my services, as poet-laureate to a highly respectable political party" Robert Burns, 1795, (CL 662)

Important evidence which supports the case for the new poems is found in a promise made by the poet during 1794. A letter from Burns to Patrick Miller Jnr., dated mid-March 1794, declines an offer of a full-time job writing for *The Morning Chronicle*, a radical London broadsheet. However, the poet promises to compose and send poems and prose essays to the editor, a fellow Scot, from Aberdeen, Mr James Perry. Burns begins the letter with a rejection of a formal salary to write for the paper -

> Your offer is indeed truly generous... in my present situation, I find that I dare not accept it. You well know my political sentiments... were I an insular individual, unconnected with a wife and a family ... with the most fervid enthusiasm I would have volunteered my services: I then could and would have despised all consequences that might have ensued. (CL 620B).

Miller and Mr. James Perry, both supporters of the Whig opposition party and the pro-democracy movement, contrived to help Burns increase his income (it had declined after the British-French war began in late January 1793) by offering him a paid position as a regular columnist for the *Chronicle*. The bard rejected a formal arrangement, but did not reject the idea of writing for the paper.

The poet agreed to let *Scots Wha Hae* be published, but cautioned against his authorship being made public -

> ... they are most welcome to my *Ode*; only let them insert it as a thing they have met with by accident, & unknown to me. - Nay, if Mr. Perry, whose honor, after your character of him I cannot doubt, if he will give me an Address & channel by

which any thing will come safe from the spies with which he may be certain that his correspondence is beset, I will now & then send him any bagatelle that I may write. - (CL 620B).

Burns regularly uses the French word "bagatelle" to refer to his radical poetry. Here the poet promises to send poetry for the newspaper, but cautious of intrusion by informers, he requests a special channel and address to allow safe passage of material to London. It is highly unlikely Burns would have asked for a safe channel and not take advantage of it. He had a track record of publishing radical poetry in newspapers. So, the promise to write for the *Chronicle* was nothing new for Burns. It is remarkable that this promise has never been researched until now.

The bard even spells out that in the political tumult of the period, only controversial political poetry would be relevant -

In the present hurry of Europe, nothing but news & politics will be regarded, but against the days of Peace, which Heaven send soon, my little assistance may perhaps fill up an idle column of a Newspaper. I have long had it in my head to try my hand in the way of little Prose Essays ... to these Mr Perry shall be welcome.. all my reward shall be - his treating me with his paper...(CL 620B).

The thrust of the letter is clear. Burns did not want a paid relationship with the *Chronicle* but asked for a covert "underground" channel to send poetry that would be anonymous or pseudonymous.

There is a strong hint of such covert radical activity in a letter Burns wrote to Alexander Cunningham around a week after the promise to send material to London. The bard refers to a secret "plot" he cannot tell Cunningham about in his letter -

I will tell you a plot which I have been contriving: you and he (George Thomson) shall ... meet me half way ... at the Beild Inn; & there we will pour out a Drink Offering before the Lord, & enter into a Solemn League and Covenant, never to be broken nor forgotten. (CL 620).

Culturally, this letter is revealing. The "Solemn League and Covenant" is suggestive of the secrecy oaths sworn by Covenantors a century previous when their religious practices were banned across Scotland. Writing and publishing radical poetry was a dangerous pastime, to be practiced with extreme caution. It would have been sensible for Burns to keep such plans under wraps and only let his closest friends know. The letter to Cunningham, although deliberately vague, would probably have been delivered by personal carrier. It is known that many activists of the Scottish reform movement employed secret oaths and pen-names which only other activists recognized. There is no evidence to link Burns's "plot" to anything other than his plan to send radical poetry to London, so it is fair to make the connection with the promise to write radical poetry for Perry.

An interesting comment was made by historian Michael Donnelly on Radio Scotland during January 1996, that paper marked with a water-margin "Pykes and Paine" was found in the bard's desk after his death: this water-margin was a known badge among radicals when passing information to one another.[1] The government spy network monitored leading reform activists, but like most known examples of British intelligence gathering, it is certain that the pro-democracy supporters were often one-step ahead, or used channels and means of communication unknown to the government.

The channel and address were arranged by May 1794. In the issue of 8th May, *Bruce's Address to his Troops at Bannockburn* appeared, albeit anonymously. The manner in which the song was introduced by the newspaper was likely to have alerted readers to Burns being the author:

> If the following warm and animating Ode was not written near the time to which it applies, it is one of the most faithful imitations of the simple and beautiful style of the Scottish bards we ever read, and we know but of one living Poet to whom to ascribe it.[2]

This complimentary description was followed by a minor printing error which read: "Scene - Lewis Garden" rather than "Tune - Lewie Gordon" . The correction was entered in the *Chronicle* of 10th May 1794, "Erratum - In the Ode of *Bruce's Address to his Army* - for "Scene - Lewis Garden" - read - "Tune - Lewie Gordon". This insertion was immediately below the known "Scots Song, by Robt. Burns", *The Sutor's*

Dochter. So, by inference, it would have been clear to any reader that the likely author of *Scots Wha Hae* was Burns. In these circumstances it would have been unwise of Burns to immediately utilise the safe address to send potentially seditious works to the newspaper. The new works now being ascribed to Burns are almost all from the 1795 and early 1796 issues of the newspaper.

A few issues previous to *Scots Wha Hae's* publication saw the appearance of *Sonnet on the Death of Glenriddel* by Burns. Robert Riddell died in April 1794, which tells us that Burns sent the sonnett to the newspaper after the mid-March letter to Patrick Miller. *The Sutor's Dochter* and the sonnet contain no controversial remarks, so Burns's name appears as author. No extant letter mentioning the poem and song to Perry has survived. To date, the only work known to have been sent and published anonymously in the *Chronicle* is *Scots Wha Hae.* These are the only three works of Burns, according to assumed knowledge, which were published in the *Morning Chronicle.*

It is quite clear no Burns scholar has searched through the pages of the *Morning Chronicle* to examine the 1790's period. Henderson and Henley document all the known publications of the poet's works in newspapers or journals. Likewise, Professor Kinsley provides extensive footnotes which indicate all known publications and dates for any work of Burns. Neither mention a Burns epigram, *On Seeing Mrs Kemble in the Part of Yarico at Dumfries Theatre* which appears in *The Morning Chronicle* in February, 1795. Henderson and Henley tell us it was first published in 1801. Kinsley does not record its publication. However insignificant, the publication of the *Mrs Kemble* epigram is proof Burns was still sending material to London in January, 1795. The notion that Burns, a prolific writer, would merely send an epigram on its own is surely questionable - he never sent merely four lines to anyone. Thus, it is likely that the epigram was accompanied by a letter or even several other pieces of poetry to Perry, which are now lost, or were published later in the year. Given that the poet sent three works in early 1794, it is surely possible he would have sent at least two or three compositions with the epigram. Any such works, if controversial, would have been published anonymously.

A failure to record the publication of the Kemble epigram is a trivial oversight. What cannot be explained away as trivial is the cache of Burns' poems published in *The Morning Chronicle* after his death in 1796. Almost every month for well over a year a poem or song by

Burns is featured. A few publications are maybe historically insignificant, such as *On Seeing A Wounded Hare, To Ruin, A Bard's Epitaph,* the song *The Groves o Sweet Myrtle* and several verses of *The Vision.* Not one of these publications has ever been documented by Burns scholars. The regular appearance of poetry by Burns in a London newspaper might not be significant if other newspapers did likewise. We might expect such a feature in a Scottish newspaper. A few tributes to the bard, yes. Poetry, no. It is a startling fact that of all British newspapers, the *Morning Chronicle* stands out as the standard bearer of Burns's writing after his death.

It is remarkable that the *Chronicle* was the first British source to publish both *Scots Wha Hae* and *A Man's A Man,* where Burns is listed as the author. They were not published during the poet's lifetime under his name. *Scots Wha Hae* appears under the banner "By the Late Robert Burns" on October 13th 1796, while *A Man's A Man,* inscribed the same, appears on 23rd May 1797. So, contrary to the footnotes in Henderson and Henley and in Kinsley, these songs were not first published in 1799 and 1803 in Thomson's *Select Collection.* Moreover, the first historical publication of *Scots Wha Hae* and *A Man's A Man* which indicates the bard's authorship, has went unrecorded for 200 years. This tends to knock flat the idea that newspapers of the period have been scanned during the last two centuries by Burns scholars, as mooted in Scottish newspapers of January 1996.

There are many reasons why the bard would have sent radical compositions to London. He ceased to send poetry to his Edinburgh publisher William Creech from 1793. Creech had purchased the poet's copyright and was opposed to the radical movement. What letters or poetry the bard did not want intercepted or read, the evidence suggests, he despatched by personal carrier. Moreover, the *Chronicle* had *safety in numbers.* It contains between 12 and 20 poems monthly during 1794, rising to around 30 per month during 1795 and 1796. Among the contributors were radical poets such as Peter Pindar (Dr John Walcot), William Roscoe and Helen Maria Williams - all friends of Burns.

Moreover, a letter written by Burns in 1795 to Richard Alexander Oswald may be of significance in relation to potential lost poems unearthed in the London *Morning Chronicle.* Burns sent Oswald, a liberal minded Ayrshire Whig, a few songs and boldly announced

I have come forward with my services, as poet-laureate to a highly respectable political party, of which you are a distinguished member. The enclosed are, I hope, only a beginning to the songs of triumph which you will earn in that contest. (CL 662)

The letter probably contained a few of the *Heron Ballads*. It is burlesque to think Burns would call himself the "poet laureate" of one man, his new found patron, Patrick Heron. The *Heron Ballads* were localised to the south west of Scotland. The revealing part of the letter is the poet's comment that he was now the poet laureate of the Whig opposition Party. The main newspaper which supported the Whigs was, of course, the *Morning Chronicle*, the very newspaper Burns had promised to write for. So, if we take the bard at his word - that he did take on a more pro-active role on behalf of the Whig party from the spring of 1795 - it would be expected that he would write poetry on behalf of the party, its leaders and put his shoulder fully behind the progressive wheel of democratic change. Burns, as the self-declared "laureate" of the Whig Party would have been likely to publish writings in the Whig newspaper, the *Morning Chronicle*.

The foundation of Burns' new "laureate" role had already been laid. The 1792 song *Here's A Health Tae Them That's Awa* eulogised many leading Whigs, while, *Sketch - Inscribed to C J Fox*, was dedicated to the leader of the Opposition in 1789. Burns pondered to Mrs Dunlop in 1789 how long his attachment to the Whig "buff and the blue" would last. It seems that his support for the Whigs was galvanized by the political oppression of Scottish radicals during 1793 and 1794 and became stronger in his last years. It is more than probable that the *Heron Ballads, The Washington Ode* and *A Man's A Man* are only a fragment of what survived from the 1793-1796 period.

Aware that there is continuity in the poet's radical sentiments between early January 1793 and through until the composition of *A Man's A Man* in 1795, the possibility that he continued to send radical poems to *The Edinburgh Gazetteer* is worthy of serious investigation. After all, he needed only a safe channel and address to indulge in radical composition. Also, it was probably easier to arrange such a channel between Dumfries and Edinburgh, than Dumfries and London. It has already been shown that the poet did not abandon his radical principles after being chastised by his employers in early 1793.

From *The Cottar's Saturday Night, Epistle to Davie, Man Was Made to Mourn, A Winter Night* to *A Man's A Man,* there is an unbroken thread of passionate humanitarian sentiment. Moreover, it has only been *assumed* that Burns stopped writing for *The Edinburgh Gazetteer* during 1793, it has never been proven *fact.*

It is an interesting and rather apt coincidence that the closure of the *Edinburgh Gazetteer* occurs only six weeks prior to the poet's request for a "safe" channel to send controversial works to London. The Edinburgh newspaper was forcibly closed at the end of January 1794. So, the poet's promise to send material to the *Chronicle* follows timeously the closure of the *Gazetteer.* It does appear that the bard had lost one platform to publish radical works and soon after, sought another. In this light, the letter to Miller reveals Burns's desire to *continue* publishing radical works covertly.

The manner and enthusiasm in which the poet embraced the launch of *The Edinburgh Gazetteer* in November 1792 is striking. He considered it to be the foremost radical paper of the late 18th century: he wrote to its editor Captain William Johnston, in a rhapsody of enthusiasm -

> ...If you go on in your paper with the same spirit, it will, beyond all comparison, be the first Composition of the kind in Europe......Go on Sir! Lay bair, with undaunted heart & steady hand, that horrid mass of corruption called Politics and State-Craft! Dare to draw in their native colors these "Calm, thinking Villains whom no faith can fix" - whatever be the shibboleth of their pretended Party. (CL 515)

This strident language is not the tone of a normal subscriber to a newspaper by any stretch of the imagination. Burns quickly despatched *Extempore Stanzas on Some Late Commemorations of the Poet Thomson* and *The Rights of Woman* to the newspaper. Whether he sent and saw *Here's A Health Tae Them That's Awa* published is not known as fact, since it is missing from the extant newspapers. The poet's endorsement of Johnston's editorial stance is probably the most supportive eulogy ever penned to a newspaper. The poet's vivid enthusiasm for the *Gazetteer* would not be easily broken.

To date it has been assumed that the poet stopped writing for the newspaper after the inquisitorial investigation by the Excise. If we recall the words of the bard himself on the issue of the investigation, that "Oppression might bend, but could not subdue!" his "independent mind", and acknowledge the existence of the powerful democratic *Washington Ode* and *A Man's A Man*, written in 1794 and 1795 respectively, it is clear the bard did write radical material after the milestone of 5th January 1793. The poet may have been intimidated by the Excise directive to be "silent and obedient", but it does not mean he was a coward during his last years. So, the point that Burns was still engaged in radical composition after early January 1793 is sufficient evidence to make it possible that he would send additional material to the *Gazetteer* - albeit anonymously or under a pen-name.

Without doubt, the Excise investigation made Burns extremely cautious of being detected as the author of radical writings from early 1793 onwards. It is somewhat incongruous that the author of *Scots Wha Hae* - a song on the theme of "Liberty" - would bow the knee to oppression, then drop from the sky a forceful poem like the *Washington Ode*. In fact, the evidence shows that on receipt of his formal chastisement by the Excise, Burns was not cowed, but was angered enough to write seditious poetry. Robert Ainslie, a close friend of the poet, wrote in 1834:

> The Commissioners of Excise, irritated at his opinions, wrote him a formal, official letter, sealing with the large seal of office, informing him that a "petty officer" had "no business with politics". The proud heart of Burns did not like this humbling; after a few wrathful words in secret to one of his friends, he took a pencil and wrote these lines on the envelope:

> In politics if you would mix,
> And low your station be,
> Keep this in mind - be deaf and blind,
> Let great folk hear and see.[3]

Ainslie's letter, written from the more politically relaxed period of 1834, tells us the four lines, known as *The Creed of Poverty* were written by Burns on the very envelope he received from the Excise which rebuked him for involvement in radical politics. (The letter from

Ainslie shows that Kinsley was in error to guess that the *Creed of Poverty* was written in The Globe Inn[4] sometime in 1795 or 1796). The words quoted by Ainslie are, of course, different from the final version of *The Creed of Poverty* and may have been the first version penned extempore by Burns. So, contrary to the view the bard was silenced by the Excise, the formal reprimand received by the poet actually provoked him to write radical, seditious lines. Having composed anonymous and pseudonymous poetry from 1789-1792, which were published in newspapers, the door is wide open to the possibility that he did write and publish additional, unrecorded material in the *Gazetteer*.

Only one Burns scholar is on record as having looked at *The Edinburgh Gazetteer* this century. In 1940, J. C. Ewing wrote a brief article on the subject of Burns and his known correspondence with the editor of the *Gazetteer*, Johnston.[5] Ewing's article records the publication of two poems, *The Rights of Woman* and *Stanzas on Thomson*. He confirms that *The Rights of Woman* was published anonymously while the poem on Thomson was printed under the pen-name Thomas A Rhymer. The brief article focuses purely on the known poems sent by Burns to the newspaper and does not consider the possibility of unrecorded anonymous poetry in the 1793 issues. It seems obvious from the brevity of Ewing's 5 page article that he had only a cursory dip into the newspaper.

Ewing certainly did not scan the weekly issues of 1793 and January 1794 - no serious Burns scholar could have read both versions of *The Ghost of Bruce* without being struck by the astonishing coincidence that the second version was published around the same time that Burns composed *Ode - Bruce's Address to His Troops at Bannockburn*. Also, the known Burns pen-name A. Briton would have stopped him in his tracks if he had read *Lines on Ambition*. If these poems had been seen by Ewing, he would have mentioned them *at the very least*, and would have written a more substantial article. Furthermore, Ewing clearly did not scan the *Gazetteer* for lost works of Burns because the notion of missing works did not occur to him. So, the claim in the Scottish press in January 1996 that the controversy over anonymous poems by Burns in newspapers of the period was not new and had been dealt with before, is simply wrong.[6]

Ewing rightly states that the song, *Here's A Health Tae Them That's Awa*, cannot be traced in the extant copies of the newspaper.[7] However, he fails to state that a large half page is torn away from the Supplement in the issue of 21st December 1792. The torn page is the back page where almost every poem or song was featured weekly. It is somewhat surprising that over the first months of the newspaper, only one half page is neatly torn away from the poetry page - coincidentally, in an issue dated a few days before Burns's investigation by the Excise. The two known works of Burns feature in late November issues of the newspaper, so it is clear they were not the spark which led to the Excise Investigation. We cannot, therefore, conclude with Scott Douglas and MacKay, that the song was definitely published. Nor can we be absolutely certain that it was *not* published. The matter is likely to remain unresolved.

Due to the fact that the newspaper only became available for scholars in 1925[8] and Ewing's is the only piece by a Burns scholar since then, it is the case that no-one has rejected any of the new poems from the *Gazetteer* as works of Burns. MacKay's dismissive comment in early 1996 "How is it, I ask myself, that this stupendous body of Burns material has been under our noses for almost 200 years, and no-one until this very year ... has had the percipience to recognise the fact"[9] is answered simply: no-one looked for it. The biographer went on, wading further into the mire of assumption "People have been studying these newspapers' poems for almost 200 years - it is an obvious place to look, but they have been rejected on stylistic grounds".[10] What "people"? When? There is no supportive evidence, nor has there been previous research into possible anonymous or pseudonymous poems lost to the canon. To reject the new poems wholesale on the assumption that some imaginary person, at some unknown time in the past *must* have rejected the poems is to dismiss *The Lost Poems* on mumbo jumbo. The new poems are printed here for the first time since they were published during the poet's life.

In peroration, there is concrete evidence to show that the poet promised to send hitherto unrecorded poetry to London. Given his request for a safe channel to send material; given his flamboyant support for Heron and the Whig party; given his known radical and pro-democratic works, published under various pen-names or anonymously; given his continued radical views; given his ability to write in almost any style and adopt language which few contemporaries would have recognised as his, it is almost certain that he did send material to London. It follows, if Burns arranged a safe channel to London, *just after* the demise of the *Edinburgh Gazetteer*, it a likely that he had such a channel in operation between January 1793 and 1794 to see poetry published in the *Gazetteer*. The time-scale of one door closing and another opening, suggests a continuity in radical composition. The fact that the first historical publication of *Scots Wha Hae* and *A Man's A Man* which mention Burns as the author has been unrecorded for two centuries makes a mockery of the claim that newspapers which were only available to the public this century, have been looked at for two hundred years by Burns scholars. The real surprise is that no-one has researched these newspapers. Thus, it is *evidence found among the poet's own letters* which point to "lost" poems from the 1793-6 period.

Footnotes

1. Michael Donnelly, Radio Scotland broadcast: Discussion on Burns, January 24th 1996.
2. *The Morning Chronicle*, 8th May 1794.
3. Robert Ainslie, 3rd September 1834, quoted in Cunningham's *The Life and Works of Robert Burns*, p.725, 1834.
4. James Kinsley, *The Poems and Songs of Robert Burns*, Vol III, p.1494, Oxford, 1968.
5. J. C. Ewing, *The Burns Chronicle*, 1940.
6. Featured in most British daily newspapers, particularly *The Scotman*, between 9th and 12th January, 1996.
7. In *The Lost Works of Robert Burns*, in *The Edinburgh Review*, 1996, I made the error of accepting MacKay's view that *Here's A Health Tae Them That's Awa*, was published *in The Edinburgh Gazetteer* and criticised Ewing's article in the BC. Ewing's article made me double check this point and he is correct.
8. The front inside cover of the bound copies of *The Edinburgh Gazetteer*, housed in The Mitchell Library, Glasgow, contains a note about the donator and when it was donated. Only a handful of issues are extant in The National Library, Edinburgh.
9. James A MacKay, quoted in *The Herald*, January 12th 1996.
10. James A MacKay, op cit. During conversation for the BBC's Omnibus programme, *The Ploughboy of the Western World*, the biographer remarked that he did not have enough time to travel to Edinburgh and check through the extant copies of the *Gazetteer*. The only complete set in Scotland is in the Mitchell Library, Glasgow. The handful of issues in Edinburgh did not contain the poems we discussed. Stewart Hunter of the Mitchell library calls the Burns Collection, "A Neglected Treasure House", BC, 1977. It still is.

Chapter 4

Burns as Poet X

It is essential to look at the radical poems of Burns, particularly those he composed and published in newspapers, if we are to judge the new poems properly. Of all the poet's writings, it is his radical effusions which are most likely to reveal similarities with the new poems. We need to know the range of poetic techniques and language which Burns employed in such poems. Intuitive reactions to, or "gut-feelings" about the new works, after a cursory perusal, prove nothing. An obvious feature of the bard's radical writing, which is of significance, is the fact that he used the pen-name A. Briton in 1788 which is used again in two of the new poems. The only known poet to use this pen-name during the 1788-1800 period was Burns. In fact, between 1788 and 1792, he was a regular contributor to newspapers.

There is a general tendency to view the poetry of Burns as purely Scots vernacular work. In annual celebration of his work, we often focus exclusively on his Scots poems. In delighting in the irreverent satire *Holy Willie's Prayer*, it is rarely noted that this immortal work was not widely known as a work of Burns during his lifetime. It seems that Burns was almost destined to dash controversy into most of his writing given that even four lines from *Tam O'Shanter* were suppressed as libelous to lawyers and priests. Naturally, his best works are in the Scottish language, but as Daiches and Crawford have shown, even the best of his Scots work is marbled through with English. Aware that the bard drew inspiration from English and Scottish poets, top academics rightly view him as the poetic synthesizer of the late 18th century.

So, it is an over-simplification of Burns to equate him solely with Scots poetry. In fact, the varying brew of Scots vernacular, Scots-English and English poems, written in a myriad of styles from *Epistle to Davie, To A Young Friend, Parcel o Rogues, Strathallan's Lament, A Red Red Rose,* to *Ode for The Departed Regency Bill,* reveal the many different "voices" within his writing. There is a range of "voices" in Burns like an emotional radio frequency band, which stretches from the gentle, tearful beauty in *Ye Banks and Braes,* to the fiery indignation of the *Washington Ode.* There is no singular *"the voice of the bard"*. Hence, a proper assessment of the new works, must take into account a full appreciation of the range of the bard's poetic techniques.

The diverse range of voices in Burns is seen in microcosm within the genre of his radical works. In a general sense, the apparently uncontroversial *The Twa Dogs* is a radical poem. The term is used here to mean poetry or songs with more satirical controversy than *The Twa Dogs*, such as *A Dream.* Burns printed *A Dream* in the Kilmarnock edition and refused to omit it from the Edinburgh edition, spurning advice to drop the irreverent poem which described "God Save the King" as a "cuckoo song". His core radical works include *Stanzas on Psalmody, Sketch to C. J. Fox, Ode for the Departed Regency Bill, The Address of Beelzebub, The Author's Earnest Cry and Prayer, On Scotch Drink, The Jolly Beggars, The Twa Herds, The Kirk's Alarm, A Man's A Man, Scots Wha Hae, On Glenriddell's Fox, The Tree of Liberty, The Heron Ballads* and the *Washington Ode*. In fact, if the term "radical" is widened to include poems with a social commentary and the mockery of hypocrisy, the bard's radical works amount to more than half the canon. So, Burns was predominantly a radical, satirical poet with a bent towards controversial topics.

After joining the Excise, the poet was forced to seriously examine his indulgence in controversiality. On taking the Oath of Allegiance to the crown, he effectively agreed that he would no longer engage in topics like religion and politics. So, when he wrote "Politics is dangerous ground for me to tread on" (CL 326), he was not referring to the sedition laws, which were only passed in 1792. He was saying quite simply that, due to his professional work, he was supposed to avoid controversy. Yet, as he remarked to Mrs Dunlop, he could not resist *having a go* on controversial issues. (CL 326) In not wishing to be identified as the author of radical poems, he generally chose a style and language which would not be immediately associated with him. The dominant public image of Burns was that of a "heaven-taught ploughman poet" who composed in the Standard Habbie form of *Ode to A Mouse*. Clearly, it was a style he would avoid like the plague in radical poetry.

In one specific case, *Stanzas on Psalmody*, the poet went as far as pretending that his song was written in a chapel in Kilmarnock by a Duncan M'Leerie. In sending the song to a London newspaper, he wrote, "Mr. Printer "

In a certain chapel, not fifty leagues from the market-cross of this good town, the following stanzas of Psalmody, it is said, were composed for, & devoutly sung on, the late joyful Solemnity of the 23rd... (CL 335)

This was the poet simply covering his back, distancing himself from the controversial sentiments of the piece. The song, which pillories the thanksgiving-day for King George's recovery from a bout of insanity is certainly not in the mould of the bard's better known works:

> O, sing a new song to the Lord!
> Make, all and every one,
> A joyful noise, ev'n for the King
> His restoration!
>
> The sons of Belial in the land
> Did set their heads together.
> "Come, let us sweep them off," said they,
> "Like an o'erflowing river!" ...

After criticising the Prime Minister, William Pitt, the song goes on to remark on Lord Thurlow:

> And him, among the Princes, chief
> In our Jerusalem,
> The Judge that's mighty in Thy law,
> The man that fears Thy name.
>
> Yet they, even they, with all their strength,
> Began to faint and fail;
> Even as two howling, rav'ning wolves
> To dogs do turn their tail.
>
> Th' ungodly o'er the just prevail'd;
> For so Thou hadst appointed,
> That Thou might'st greater glory give
> Unto thine own anointed!

And now Thou hast restored our State,
Pity our Kirk also;
For she by tribulations
Is now brought very low!

Consume that high-place, Patronage,
From off Thy holy hill;
And in Thy fury burn the book
Even of that man McGill!

Now hear our prayer, accept our song,
And fight Thy chosen's battle!
We seek but little, Lord, from Thee;
Thou kens we get as little!

Other than the Scots word "kens" in the final verse and the mention of the Rev. Dr McGill, an Ayrshire cleric and friend of Burns, there is little in the song which would have led contemporaries of the poet to suspect him as the author. Indeed, to London readers, he was obviously not the author. Duncan M'Leerie was the author. Readers of *The Star* would have been stunned to find out this song was composed by Burns. Obviously they would have thought the author was a Scot from Kilmarnock who was Catholic. The revealing features of this radical song relevant to the new poems are its language and the deliberate false locus of composition. It is almost certain that if the song had recently been uncovered from a newspaper of 1789, a few modern commentators might have been quick to dismiss the poet's authorship, fooled like the bard's contemporaries. Fortunately, the manuscript survived along with supporting evidence in a letter to Mrs. Dunlop.

In the same year, 1789, Burns sent to a London newspaper the poem *Ode for the Departed Regency Bill*. Once again, the poet employed a style which would not be immediately recognised as his. He signed the poem Agricola (Latin, for rustic or rural countryman) and dated its composition as April 7th 1789. MacKay fails to mention Agricola as a pen-name used by Burns, although it is in Kinsley, Carswell and Chambers-Wallace. Burns inscribed it as a poem written in Edinburgh, to throw suspicion on poet X from Edinburgh, away from him at Ellisland. So, in looking at some basic facts about two radical poems, we see a pattern emerging. The poet often changed his pen-name, and gave a clue in Latin about the type of author in one example. More important, though, is the fact that he employed a false place of composition, or place of posting, to keep his authorship unknown.

The *Ode on the Regency Bill* reveals very little comparison with the poet's Scots vernacular work and surely any contemporary who thought it by Burns would have been scoffed at:

> Daughter of Chaos' doting years,
> Nurse of ten thousands hopes and fears!
> Whether thy airy, unsubstantial shade
> (The rights of sepulture now duly paid)
> Spread abroad its hideous form
> On the roaring civil storm,
> Deafening din and warring rage
> Factions wild with factions wage;
> Or under-ground, deep sunk, profound,
> Among the demons of the earth,
> With groans that make the mountains shake,
> Thou mourn thy ill-starr'd, blighted birth,
> Or in the uncreated Void,
> Where seeds of future being fight,
> With lighten'd step thou wander wide
> To greet thy mother - Ancient Night,
> And as each jarring, monster-mass is past,
> Fond recollect what once thou wast:
> In manner due, beneath this sacred oak,
> Hear, Spirit, hear! thy presence I invoke!
> By a Monarch's heaven-struck fate!
> By a disunited State!
> By a generous Prince's wrongs!
> By a Senate's strife of tongues!
> By a Premier's sullen pride,
> Louring on the changing tide!
> By dread Thurlow's powers to awe,
> Rhetoric, blasphemy and law!
> By the turbulent ocean,
> A Nation's commotion!
> By the harlot-caresses

Of borough-addresses!
By days few and evil!
Thy portion, poor devil!
By Power, Wealth, Show! the gods by men adored!
By Nameless Poverty! their hell abhorred!
By all they hope! By all they fear!
Hear!!! And Appear!!!

The Ode goes on to pillory the expedient posturing of ministers in the constitutional crisis caused by the King's insanity from mid-1788 until early 1789. Burns first swipe at Dundas is seen in the line "Paint Ruin, in the shape of high Dundas / Gaping with giddy terror o'er the brow". The abstract Miltonic language of the poem bears little comparison to the "heaven-taught ploughman poet" image of Burns. There is a force, energy, intellectual strength and radical power in the Ode which many contemporaries of Burns would have considered alien to his "style". In fact, up until 1872, when the Ode first became public as a work of Burns, literary experts had no idea that the dust-gathering Ode which lay unnoticed in a London newspaper signed "Agricola", apparently from Edinburgh, had any connection with Burns. Today, we are surely smarter and know it is his Ode, mainly because it is printed in every edition of his works and it is mentioned in his letters. Without this contextual evidence to prove his authorship, how would a Burns scholar prove the bard wrote this Ode?

With this question we begin to consider the case of *The Lost Poems* with the seriousness they merit. To argue that we know that poem X is by Burns simply because it is in a book and experts say it is by Burns, is to abdicate a wholesome understanding of the complex range of styles in the poet's writing. The simple conclusion, if the *Regency Ode* were one of the new works, would be to say he did not write it, because it is the work of an Edinburgh poet who employed the pen-name Agricola. Case closed. Would expert commentators have said that *this word* and *that phrase* in the Ode are really nothing like Burns? Clearly they would have been wrong. On balance, the Ode would probably have been rejected.

A further controversial work from 1789, *Sketch - Inscribed to C. J. Fox*, is dedicated to the leader of the Whig party, Charles James Fox. The style of the poem is based on a popular form of satirical verse employed by the poets Shenstone, Swift, Prior and the Della Cruscan

poets in *The Oracle*. Again, there are several words and phrases which
no contemporary of Burns would have linked to him -

How Wisdom and Folly meet, mix and unite;
How Virtue and Vice blend their black and their white;
How Genius, th' lllustrious father of fiction,
Confounds rule and law, reconciles contradiction,
I sing: if these mortals, the critics, should hustle,
I care not, not I - let the Critics go whistle! ...

... Good Lord, what is Man! For as simple he looks,
Do but try to develope his hooks and his crooks,
With his depths and his shallows, his good and his evil,
All in all, he's a problem must puzzle the Devil.
On his one ruling Passion Sir Pope warmly labors,
That, like th' old Hebrew walking switch, eats up its neighbours;
Human Nature's his show-box - your friend, would you know him?
Pull the string, Ruling Passion, the picture will show him.
What pity, in rearing so beauteous a system,
One trifling particular, Truth, should have miss'd him!
For, spite of his fine theoretic positions,
Mankind is a science defies definitions.

Some sort all our qualities each to its tribe,
And think Human-nature they truly describe.
Have you found this, or t'other? There's more in the wind,
As by one drunken fellow his comrades you'll find.
But such is the flaw, or the depth of the plan
In the make of that wonderful creature called MAN,
No two virtues whatever relation they claim,
Nor even two different shades of the same,
Though like as was ever twin brother to brother,
Possessing the one shall imply you've the other.

But truce with abstraction, and truce with a Muse,
Whose rhymes you'll perhaps, Sir, ne'er deign to peruse:
Will you leave your justings, your jars and your quarrels,
Contending with Billy for proud-nodding laurels?
(My much-honor'd Patron, believe your poor Poet,
Your courage, much more than your prudence you show it;
In vain with Squire Billy for laurels you struggle;
He'll have them by fair trade - if not, he will smuggle;
Not cabinets even of kings would conceal 'em,
He'd up the back-stairs and by God he would steal 'em!
Then feats like Squire Billy's you ne'er can atchieve 'em,
It is not, out-do him, the task is, out-thieve him).

Once more, if we strip away the contextual proof of manuscript evidence and the supportive comments in the poet's letters, the radical English *Sketch* would struggle to be accepted as a work of the bard, if it had been recently uncovered as an anonymous piece. It does not "ring" of many known works of Burns. It displays the coy wit of the bard, but he had no monopoly on humour. On close inspection there are several phrases and key words which point to Burns's authorship, but on stylistic evidence alone, the case is not strong. Were this one of the new works, it would be quite understandable if a few experts questioned the words "th' old Hebrew walking switch", "show-box"; the phrase "proud-nodding" and the spelling of "develope" (as listed in Kinsley but not MacKay) with an "e" at the end - they are not found anywhere else in the bard's writings. It may have been judged as a turgid Augustan poem of poor quality, unworthy of Burns. Once again, such a dismissive "gut reaction" would have been wrong.

On the issue of the *Washington Ode*, already considered in detail, there can be little doubt that the poet's peers would have assumed there was not a chance it could be Burns. The final stanza which mentions William Wallace might have raised a few eyebrows in cautious skepticism, verging on a "maybe". Without concrete proof of the poet's authorship, it would be predictable today that some of the dismissive comments hurled at my attributions in January 1996, would apply to this Ode. Words such as "Aeolian", "attic shell", "babbling" and "dark-quenched", which do not occur in his other works, might have been taken as evidence he did not write the Ode. The first few stanzas are distinctively unlike a lot of the poet's work. So, it is clear that the problem of proving the authenticity of any work of the bard, without manuscript evidence, is fraught with many difficulties - even with supportive manuscript evidence, as in the case of *A Revolutionary Lyric*, provenance may still be denied.

The real puzzle, therefore, is not so much that we should be surprised to think the poet composed additional, "lost" poems, in the 1793-1796 period, but that there we have so few poems by Burns from his last years. It is stunning incongruity that the poet would write only a handful of radical works during this period. The cache of radical work from 1788 until 1792 is not in dispute. More important, a lifetime's radical views do not vanish overnight. We have seen in the *Washington Ode* that his views were sharply galvanised, not diminished. So, it is reasonable to expect that the bard would have managed to see additional pro-democratic poems published during his last years, precisely as Pattison suggested and Chambers believed. If any Scottish poet eschewed the skill to outfox the sedition laws and write in a myriad of styles which spies and informers would not detect, it was Burns. He had fooled his employers before 1793. Given his passionate democratic views, it is entirely predictable that he would continue to do so, albeit, more careful not to be caught. In fact, we know he did, with the anonymous publication of *A Man's A Man* in August 1795.

So, given the overt government suppression of radicals from 1793 onwards, given the tightrope of controversiality walked by the poet in the *Washington Ode* and *A Man's A Man*, given the poet's forceful radical opinions in letters and poetry during his last years, given his habit of using pen-names, given his deliberate *modus operandi* of employing a false locus of composition in political satires, given the bard's promise to write radical poetry in his last years which would be anonymous, it seems pretty clear that Burns was more than capable, willing and indeed, planned to write additional radical material which would have been anonymous or pseudonymous. Moreover, since the poet's fame during his own life relied upon only seventy odd poems and a few dozen songs, there can be little doubt that with the anonymous and pseudonymous works which came down to us, Robert Burns was the quintessential, prolific unknown poet X of the late 18th century. Many works from behind the mask of the heaven taught ploughman poet surfaced after his death; others did not.

Chapter 5
Research Methodology

In previous chapters, extensive contextual evidence was outlined to show that pro-democratic poems from Burns's pen were either withheld, lost, or destroyed during the post-1796 period. Obviously, within this mix of unknown manuscripts there would be a few which were bawdy songs, but it is certain that the majority would have been radical works as suggested by Pattison and Chambers. After all, the bard promised radical works for *The Morning Chronicle.* The evidence of lost or destroyed manuscripts within an anti-radical milieu firmly support the concept of the "lost" poems. The notion of "lost" poems did not drop from the sky in January 1996. The facts show that there are "lost" poems. The problem is *how* do we decide on the provenance of the new poems?

Intuition, as Brian Morton remarked on this very subject, is not enough.[1] The judgement and opinion of *literary experts,* however, is of great value. Recognised experts on the poet's writings are more likely to be accurate in judging the authenticity of the new poems than biographical experts. A parrotorial regurgitation of biographical minutiae, giving the where-when-who-and-how list of events and people in the narrative story of the bard's life is no substitute for in-depth understanding of the poet's *poetry.* Obviously, Daiches, a renowned literary expert, is more qualified than MacKay to judge the new poems. Likewise, the views of literary authorities such as Crawford or Noble should take precedence over biographers. Readers, though, ought to make their own judgements on the poems and maintain a *questioning* irreverence towards authorities. "The man o' independent mind" is not a peddler of second hand views.

It was mooted in the Scottish press during January 1996 that the provenance of the poems could be settled by computer-driven stylometrics which would provide the equivalent of a linguistic "D.N.A." test.[2] Explained simply, stylometrics creates a picture of an author's use of words, such as the incidence and pattern of verbs, and matches the results in template or graph form, to the anonymous work. If there is no match, then the attribution is rejected.

Ironically, in the London press of the January 1996, as I was being *hoggwashed* as a nobody, Professor Don Foster of the U.S.A was being pummelled for his attribution of *A Funeral Elegy* to Shakespeare - the object of derision being Foster's "computer".[3] So, during one week in Scotland, computer-based analyses were the silicon panacea of objective truth, while the following week in London, the same approach was blasted as useless. Neither press view is correct. Stylometric testing is a complex tool of immense value in the case of attributing anonymous writings. As a linguistic science, it is still in development. As yet, no agreed standards of protocol exist among practitioners to assist in anonymous attribution.

Scotland's stylometric expert, Morton, is noted for "proving" at a conference at Stirling University that Burns did not write *The Tree of Liberty*. His conclusion is not shared by the majority of modern Burns scholars, who accept its provenance. Having read almost every Scottish newspaper from the period and afterwards for a possible alternative poetic voice for *The Tree of Liberty*, I can find no other poet capable of its composition. Foster's computer analyses, in the shape of his sophisticated "Shaxicon" rare-words system,[4] is markedly different from the linguistic logic approach of Morton. So, the stylometric science is as yet, not quite the magic "D.N.A." wand to unravel the mystery of anonymous writings from the late 18th century.

Despite caution on the imperfection of stylometric analyses, Foster's rare-words approach proved itself in tracking down the anonymous author of the novel *Primary Colours* recently published in America.[5] Despite two denials by the author, Joe Klein, Foster put the writing of over a dozen candidates under the microscope and concluded that only Klein could have written *Primary Colours*. When Foster explained his case, he provoked Klein into admission of authorship. Foster's approach was to list the many rare adjectives and adverbs within *Primary Colours* and compare them to the rare adjectives and adverbs employed by each author. The results showed a regular pattern of overlaps in rare key words between Klein's writing in *Newsweek* and *Primary Colours*, a feature which did not occur with the other possible authors. Given that Foster's full-blown system of analyses is not available to researchers, it is not yet possible to apply his system to the new poems.

Before considering the topic of textual analyses, the obvious area to consider is the question of poetic imitators. The bard, after all, remarked that his fame spawned a shoal of imitators in the Scots vernacular.(CL 319) In 1786 the poet's success provoked a burst of Scots poetry from other lesser writers. Most imitators, though, latched onto only one form of poetry which Burns effectively made his own, the Standard Habbie of *Ode to A Mouse*. Their outpourings were monotonous in this form. They included Janet Little, Alexander Wilson, David Sillar, Thomas Telford and many others.[6] Not one of the poet's so-called impersonators composed a radical poem in Standard Habbie. No-one imitated the English based poems or songs of Burns. So, the dominant theme of imitation was the use of Scots words in purely *Ode to A Mouse* style poetry. The fact that the majority of the new poems are in English and not one was found in Standard Habbie, quashes the notion that I have collated merely the dross of the bard's imitators.

In the various attempts at mimicry in the Scots style, there are certain obvious differences in language between Burns and his amateurish poetaster following. The gulf in quality between Burns and "the many" is epitomised in stanzas about *The King's Birthday* in 1792 –

> Like ither bards right fain I'd sing
> The great birthday o' Britain's king;
> But that it will me right sair ding
> I've cause to fear;
> For book-lear'd chaps wi high flown wing
> Sings't ilka year.

> When Musie kend o the affair,
> She grew as mad as a March hare;
> Quo she ye are half daft an' mair,
> Ye senseless coof;
> That subject's worn, just as thread bare
> 'S a body's loof.

> It to my heart gade wi' a dunt,
> To think the cuttie had the strunt;
> Says I, ye crabbit mislear'd runt,
> Gif I draw breath,
> This day ye sall Pegasus munt,
> As shure as death.

When that she heard me crack sae crouse,
She grew as caum as ony mouse;
Syne look'd sae pleasant and sae douse,
      An' nae mair snarl'd;
That now I dinna care a louse
      For a' the warld.

Come then, my winsome, dautit lamb!
An' I'se gie you a gude Scots dram
O' aquavitae; just the sam
      I tak mysell;
Whether it mend your milk or dam,
      You need na tell.[7]

The confidence, clarity, and ambience of a major poetic voice is not
found in this little fun poem. From a reading of Scottish newspapers
from 1788 to 1800 this is, surprisingly, one of the best imitations. It
does not say a lot for the remainder There are a host of spellings
and a few words in the poem which the bard never used. "Sings't"
and "caum" are clear examples. Poems of this level do not need to be
stylistically tested. They are obviously not by Burns. Overall, the ring
of the poem is distinctively one of a jovial rhymer, hidden beneath
the shadow of the bard's stature. No-one would dare stand forth and
claim this could be by Burns.

    A detailed reading of the published poems in the Scottish vernacu-
lar from this era reveal a pattern of distinctive regional word usage
and spellings alien to Burns. This makes it relatively easy to spot a
work in the Scots tongue which Burns *did not write*. For instance, if we
consider the following poem *The New-Year's Morning*, it is easy to see
the words and a turn of phrase unfamiliar to Burns (in italics) -

The bard wha sang o' hallow fair,
      The daft days at Leith races,
Wha's cantie sangs *dis kill* our care
      In mony *funny places*,
Forgat tae sing the morning air,
      Whan lassies shaw their faces,
Wi guid *het pints* maist ilka where,
      Ye'll kep them gau'n in braces,
        Fu' soon that morn.

Hail *hogmenai*! hail *funny night*!
　　For daffin' an' for drinkin';
For makin' a' thing right an' tight,
　　For *killin' care* an' thinkin';
For *rinnin' through the streets like drift*,
　　For kissin' an' for clappin';
For clearin' up the mind an' sight,
　　Wi' a weel made *het chapin*,
　　　　Fu' strang that morn....

.....A wee drap drink is unco guid
　　As lang's we keep frae anger,
It pits ane in a merry mood,
　　An' keeps them *oot o' langer*.
But troth I'm *fly'd* that some daft chiel,
　　To some wrang place will stammer,
An' fair against his will atweel
　　He'll see the council *chammer*,
　　　　For it next morn.[8]

Compared to *The Holy Fair* from Burns, or the new radical work, *The Dagger*, this piece is the work of another feeble rhymer. The word "forgat" is found three times in Burns, while "kep" and "atweel" are found only once. The word "het" is found six times, although not linked with "pints". The words "Hogmennai" (a curious spelling), "fly'd", "rinnin'", "chapin" or "chammer" are not in Burns. It would appear that "chammer", meaning chamber, is a parochial spelling based on regional dialect. There are no echoes in the use of language to any Burns work. The poem does not get past the first hurdle. It is clear the use of regional spelling based on parochial dialect, plus non-Burnsian adverbs and adjectives make the poem blatantly unlike Burns.

It is clear that the majority of would-be Scots vernacular poets were not steeped in the *ouvre* of Scottish poetry like Burns. The "many" imitators regularly peppered their writings with regional spellings and words which cannot be found in the bard's works. An essay on Scottish poetry in *The Bee* in 1791, obviously in reference to the imitators stirred to poetry by Burns, remarked -

For about five years past (1786) we have been amused by the booksellers with an incessant chorus of verses in the Scottish dialect. Every county in Scotland has a number of words and phrases peculiar and intelligible to itself only, and it is usual for the bard to borrow, without selection, the provincial vulgarisms to which he has been accustomed.... The fame of such poetry can hardly be extensive or lasting. But besides, these writers commonly deform their pages with every antiquarian phrase which perverted industry can discover...

When a man of sense intends to publish in rhyme, he will first make himself familiar with at least a few of the best and more popular English poets ... he will either learn the art of elegant composition, or the propriety of silence...[9]

This is a polite way of saying the bulk of Scottish vernacular poetry printed during the 1786-1791 period is rubbish. Due to the lack of standardisation in the Scots language during this period, the writer in *The Bee* is mostly correct - regional dialects meant parochial spelling and various turns of phrase characteristic of different cultural traditions. The poems on *The King's Birthday* and *The New-Year Morning* reveal ample proof of this pattern. So, in the vernacular Scots poetry from the 1786-1790 period, the easy way to exclude Burns as the author is to check for a combination of regional spellings and words the bard never used. In the consideration of the provenance of the new poems, it is invaluable to be able to exclude other writers are possible candidates by spotting rare regional words or spellings alien to Burns.

By the early 1790's, the rarest feature in Scotland's newspapers and journals is Scottish vernacular poetry. During the 1790's the fashion of cleansing poetry of "scotticisms" - those awfully *un*English Scottish words - regained a dominant posture in newspapers and periodicals. If there had been a mystery poet around who was almost as good as Burns in Scots, it is certain he or she would have published a few poems in the newspapers or journals of the period and their poetry would have been evident after the bard's death. Even if this had been the case - it was not - the different use of spellings or regional words, plus close analysis of adjectives and adverbs, would have given away the mimicry of a mystery poet X. No poet who wrote in

Scots during the 1790's whose work was as good as Burns has ever been identified. This research set out to find anyone close to Burns in the Scots vernacular and could trace no-one.

Of course, the possibility of other potential poets for the new works must to looked at seriously. From 1792 until 1796 the majority of poems within Scottish journals and newspapers are written in English. English based poems are a more difficult subject than Scots poems for several reasons. The first is sheer numbers. There were more people writing in English. This group can be cut down to those who wrote mainly radical poems. When considering the new poems from *The Edinburgh Gazetteer* the timescale is from 1792 until January 1794 and the lexical field is purely Scottish radical poets. There seem to be no more that five or six authors or poetic voices writing for the newspaper. Only a handful of issues went over the border and there is little sign of poetry being copied from English newspapers. So, in looking at excluding other authors in poems from *The Edinburgh Gazetteer*, the poet X factor is down to a handful of poets.

In the case of *The Morning Chronicle*, from 1794 until 1796, a greater range of possible authors opens up. There appear to be around twenty radical voices sending their work to the *Chronicle*. The *Chronicle* has an average of just under 20 poems per month in 1793, rising to around 21 per month in 1794, then it peaks at around 30 per month for much of 1795 and 1796, only to fall back a little during 1797 and again in 1798. This is far greater than the number of poems in Scottish newspapers. So, textual stylistic testing is more problematic in the attribution of the new radical poems from the *Chronicle*.

The stylistic procedure employed here is similar to Professor Foster's approach, but is less complex. It is based on a detailed word analysis using *Burns: A-Z, The Complete Wordfinder* which lists most of the commonly used words of Burns as found in the poems and songs. This is an excellent reference resource, but it is not a definitive lexical base. It does not include all the important words from the poems, such as "haughty" from *The Dumfries Volunteers*, or "frae", "ayont", "yont", and so on. So, if a word is found in one of the new poems and cannot be traced in the *Wordfinder*, it would be foolish to jump to the conclusion that Burns is not the author or did not use the word. The *Wordfinder* does not contain a listing of the many distinctive adjectives or adverbs used by Burns throughout his letters. A few examples of words found in the poet's letters which are not listed in the

Wordfinder, are - "frigid", "distend", "approbation", "contumelious", "salutary", "torpitude", "sublunary", "puling", "horrent", "lucurbations" and "lugubrious". There are many, many more such words. So, a robust comparative analyses of the new poems against the poet's word usage must include *The Complete Letters and* the songs and poetry before it can be concluded that Burns did not use specific words.

It was found that the incidence and nature of nouns in Burns is largely determined by the subject and theme of a poem. So, names such as Xerxes, Semiramis, Reynard, and Nimrod, who all appear in *On Glenriddell's Fox Breaking his Chain,* occur only once in the poet's writings, in that very poem. Obviously, if this poem had been one of the new poems, there would have been several words we could not find in the *Wordfinder.* Therefore, in reading through the new poems, readers should be alerted to the fact that nouns new to Burns are to be expected and cannot be viewed as evidence against the poet's authorship. Nouns provide no gauge of authorship. However, as Foster's work shows, adjectives and adverbs do tend to give away their author, especially *rare* adjectives and adverbs.

In a detailed consideration of around twenty radical poems of Burns, it was observed that many contain two or three rare adjectives or adverbs which are not found in other poems. Also, no poem by Burns looked at in the sample reveals more than four rare adjectives or adverbs. This pattern is significant. It means that in writing a new poem or song, the poet did not stick to using the same old stock of words, but creatively added to his imagery and poetic vocabulary. It was found that the bard might add up to a maximum of four new adjectives or adverbs per poem. In most works, it is less, if any. We can deduce, therefore, that if this pattern was repeated with the new radical poems, we should expect to see a limited addition of new adjectives and adverbs per poem. So, an assessment of the differences between accepted radical works of the poet tells us that he kept adding to his usage of adjectives or adverbs. This means we can set a toleration level of up to four new adjectives or adverbs for any potentially new poem by Burns. Therefore, if one of the "lost" poems reveals a cluster of four or more adjectives or adverbs which are not found in Burns at all, it is unlikely that Burns could be the author.

For instance, in the *Washington Ode,* Burns uses the words "babbling", "swimming", "dark-quenched" and "nerv'd", plus the word "tottering" in his first draught of the Ode. These words are not found elsewhere in his works. The word "nerv'd" is the past tense of "nerve" which is found 8 times in Burns. He used "quenched" twice. The original draught of the *Washington Ode* employs "quenched" on its own, followed by "darkness", so "dark-quenched" is a modification of language that is easy to understand. Burns used the words "dark-raging" and "dark-muffled" and included variants of darkness: "darkling", "dark", "darker", "darkest", "darkly", "darken'd", "dark-ening" and "darksome". The incidence of hyphenated adjectives or adverbs may also be a significant lexical trait in Burns. Thus, "dark-quenched" is a finely honed improvement from a stock of used imagery. So, there are 3 key words in the Ode which the bard did not use in other poetic works. Clearly, a poet whose stock of adjectives and adverbs is far greater in his letters, will use *new* descriptive language in most new poems.

In *On Glenriddell's Fox Breaking His Chain*, there are also 3 words which the bard only used in that one poem - "staunchest", "reaping" and "bowing". Of course, the words "staunch" and "reap" are found in Burns, so there is nothing alien in modifying previously used words. In the *Address Spoken by Miss Fontenelle* Burns used the words "ter-rific", "sluggish", "temptingly" and "jiltish" for the first and only time. The word "temptingly" can be easily over looked since the poet employed "tempt", "temptation", "tempted" and "tempting" in other works. So, there are two key words in the poem which cannot be found elsewhere in Burns. In *Scots Wha Hae*, the word "lour" is only found in one other example. In *The Tree of Liberty*, the words "glad-den" and "vicious" are new to Burns. The word "gladden", though, is a modification of "glad", "gladdening", "gladly" and "gladness" which are found in poems. The word "viscious" is an addition to the poet's stock of poetry words. Also, the word "cracked" is merely the past tense of the verb to "crack" which is found six times in Burns. There-fore, in the overall sample of radical poems which were considered there is not one with more than four new, or once only occurring, adjectives or adverbs. So, taking this as a pattern and expected norm, the new poems which reveal more than four adjectives or adverbs (not nouns) alien to Burns have been rejected. This method is not definitive, but it provides a lexical template to map onto a given poem and decide if it might be by Burns.

For example, a poem which contains many words used by the bard but displays a cluster of adjectives and adverbs alien to Burns, is *On the African Slave Trade*. The poem contains a high incidence of words commonly found in Burns, but a quantitative word count tends to only measure the intertexuality of commonly used language *shared* by radicals during the period. It is rare adjectives and adverbs that are the stuff of authorship -

> Ye Friends of Liberty! come lend your ear,
> The voice of pity calls you to appear,
> And in the gen'ral cause yourselves exert
> With feeling mind and sympathising heart.
> What gen'rous breast but shudders at the thought
> Of fellow-creatures basely sold and bought!
> What man, whose sentiments are brave and just,
> Can calmly hear, without a great disgust,
> The crimes committed on wild Afric's shore
> By cruel tyrants, to encrease their store -
> The many hardships, and the many woes,
> The dreadful suff'rings the poor Negro knows.[10]

The words which Burns did not use and which give away the fact he could not have written the poem, are "basely", "calmly", "disgust", "committed", "sympathising" and "encrease". The words "sentiments", "shudder" and "exert" are only used in Burns once. Moreover, there are other words further into the poem such as "traffic" and "recital" which he never used. There is an indignation in this poem akin to the radical posture of Burns, but the use of language is not his.

Another work *On African Slavery*, written in blank verse and published in the *Glasgow Courier*, displays a similar lexical pattern of *rare* words which confirm Burns is not the author -

>   - My ear is pain'd,
> My soul is sick with ev'ry day's report
> Of wrong and outrage with which he earth is fill'd.
> There is no flesh in man's obdurate heart,
> It does not feel for man. The nat'ral bond
> Of brotherhood is sever'd as the flax
> That falls asunder at the touch of fire.

He finds his fellow guilty of a skin
Not colour'd like his own, and having pow'r
T' enforce the wrong, for such a worthy cause
Dooms and devotes him as his lawful prey. -
Thus man devotes his brother, and destroys;
And worse than all, and most to be deplored,
As human-nature's broadest, *foulest* blot,
Chains him, and tasks him, and exacts his sweat
With stripes, that Mercy with a bleeding heart
Weeps when she sees inflicted on a breast.
Then what is man?...[11]

The words never used by Burns in this worthy piece, are "obdurate", "enforce", "colour'd", "devotes", "deplored" and further into the poem, "stripes", "broadest", "exacts", "ferried" and "inflicted". The words "pain'd", "asunder" and "foulest" are found only once in Burns.

The next poem, titled *To the People of Scotland* contains many words used by Burns and would have certainly incurred the wrath of Dundas and his spy network:

While every bosom glows with gen'rous flame
To rescue from disgrace the British name -
While from her azure throne Heav'ns fav'rite Isle
Surveys around her, with benignant smile,
The Rights of Nations bursting into birth,
And Freedom's fire wide spreading o'er the earth,
Shall Scotia's Sons endure the galling chain
Of servitude, and beg redress in vain? -
Curst be the thought too abject for the slave!
How much repugnant to the enlighten'd brave,
Whose ancestors would ne'er deign to yield,
Bur drench'd with patriot blood the well-fought field.
In Freedom's glorious cause! - Then rouse for shame!
By ev'ry lawful means assert your claim,
Which once denied will lay that sacred trust,
Brittania's bulwark, level with the dust.[12]

The words not found in Burns are "well-fought", "drenched", "re-pugnant", "rescue" and "servitude" and from later in the poem, "overboiling", "absurdities" and "respectfully". Burns never used "Scotia's Sons" as a phrase nor did he use the word "lord" as a verb, a clumsy description found later in the poem, "With sway tyrannic *lord* it o'er the land". The poem shows the influence of Thomas Mercer who was dead by the time it was written. It is probably the work of Walter Callander who was prosecuted for seditious libel in January 1794.

A further example, taken from the *Edinburgh Gazetteer*, is *Ode to Liberty*. It is filled with intertextual language, the words Burns shared with other radical writers. However, the use of language in imagery to describe the Miltonic feminine "Liberty" is wildly out of kelter with Burns -

> Hail, more resultant than the morning star!
> Gay Queen of Bliss! fair daughter of the Sky!
> I woo thee, Liberty, and hope from far
> To catch the brightness of thy raptured eye,
> While not unseemly streams thy zoneless vest,
> Thy wild locks dancing to the frolic wind
> And, borne on flying feet, thou scorn'st to rest,
> Save where meek truth her modest seat may find.
> Hail radiant form divine, blest Liberty!
> Whene'er thou deign'st to rove, oh let me rove with thee!
>
> Say, dost thou chuse to tread the mountain's brows,
> Or haunt meand'ring streams, or wanton plains?[13]

Burns, of course, used words such as "Gay", "Queen" and "Bliss", but did not over-indulge such words in flowery Augustan imagery. Line 5 rings out of key with anything Burns wrote. The words "unseemly", "zoneless", "resultant" and "brightness" are not in Burns. The adjective "streams", like the word "vest" are found only once in Burns. There are other words throughout the poem which are not used by the bard, such as "shaven" in "shaven green". The image of Liberty and her "flying feet" is cumbersome and unlike the more focused portrayal of "Liberty" in *On Glenriddels Fox Breaking His Chain* or in the *Washington Ode*. Clearly, the bard was not the author of *Ode to Liberty*. So, the methodology is sufficiently robust to pinpoint poetry which we can safely conclude is *not by Burns*.

The *Ode to Liberty* epitomises the poems in English which may possess many of the ubiquitous words of liberty Burns shared with his radical contemporaries, but the turn of phrase and imagery are distinctively unBurnsian. The poet did not have a monopoly in describing the forces of nature in terms of abstract personage, such as "Spring" in, "Thou young-ey'd Spring", from his touching sonnet to Glenriddell. However, even in this line we see a notable feature of his use of adjectives and adverbs in the hyphenated "young-ey'd", to describe Spring. There are many such hyphenated words in his works. So, the manner of his language in Miltonic allusion can be studied and the peculiar traits found only in Burns can be identified and cross-checked in the new poems.

Another distinct feature of Burns is his use of capitals for emphasis, such as "FREEDOM", rather than "Freedom", or "freedom". During the 1788-1800 period, most anonymous writers employ capitals only for a name, such as "BURNS" and do not capitalise other words. So, even if one of the new poems fits the bill and does not have more than four new adjectives or adverbs, it must contain a phraseology and imagery which is consistent with the poet's writing, or display features only found in Burns, before there is any chance that he might be the author. Moreover, it is only in examples where there is very close comparison with Burns in every stanza or even every line, that it is possible to attribute a poem to the bard. Ideally, such a stylistic case would be supported by contextual evidence such as a pen-name like "A. Briton" which we know was used by Burns.

A poem, sent to me by post in 1996 by A. M. Mitchell of Blairgowrie, is found, with slight modification, in MacKay's *Wordfinder* Appendix B, number 90. It has the ring of the 20th century forgery *Look Up and See*. It begins "My Lord, I wadna fill your chair / To be the proudest noble's heir" and goes on to use words such as "translate", "bandy", "loan", "pedigree", "tax-paid", "buffoon" and "fox-hunting", all alien to Burns. Like *Look Up and See*, this imitation is a good attempt to show that the bard was truly a religious man during times when he was painted as an irreligious monster. The poem captures the essence of the radical sentiments of Burns, but under close examination, there is an excessive cluster of key word not used by the poet. A poem may carry the sentiments of Burns and not be his, due to clearly identifiable language differences with his known works. Burns is not the author.

There are examples of poetry by Burns which are "lost" to the general public due to editorial decisions. One such example, not included in the modern *The Complete Poetical Works* is the lengthy dedication to John Ballantine in a manuscript of *The Brigs of Ayr*.[14] Its manuscript is now lost, but the lines are collated in Appendix A of MacKay's *Wordfinder*, as alternate lines for *The Brigs of Ayr*. Since every published version of *The Brigs of Ayr* records that the poem is dedicated to Ballantine, is there not a case that the dedication should be featured as an introduction to the poem? By no stretch of the imagination is the dedication *alternate lines*. So, although the lines cannot be described as a "lost" poem of Burns, they are generally known only to scholars who purchase the costly *Wordfinder*. Arguably, the dedication ought to be part of the canon.

A further example which lingers in a literary no-man's land, is a fragment called *Sketch*. It is quite probable that very few enthusiasts would immediately recognise in its language, the hand of the bard:

> A LITTLE, upright, pert, tart, tripping wight,
> And still his precious self his dear delight;
> Who loves his own smart shadow in the streets,
> Better than e'er the fairest she he meets.
> A man of fashion too, he made his tour,
> Learn'd *vive la bagatelle, et vive l'amour*;
> So travell'd monkeys their grimace improve,
> Polish their grin - nay, sigh for ladies' love.
> Much specious lore, but little understood;-
> Veneering oft outshines the solid wood:
> His solid sense - by inches you must tell,
> But mete his cunning by the old Scots ell;
> His meddling vanity, a busy fiend,
> Still making work his selfish craft must mend.[15]

This was written as one of several fragments intended as part of a larger work *The Poet's Progress* which was abandoned.(CL 297) Most of the other related fragments were eventually woven into *To Robert Graham of Fintry*. MacKay includes a slightly different version of *Sketch*, in Appendix A of his *Wordfinder*, as alternate lines to the poem on Fintry.[16] Strictly, the fragment is not *alternate* lines to the Fintry work since it was intended as part of a larger, different poem. There are no lines in *To Robert Graham of Fintry* which supersede *Sketch* or are an improvement to it. It does not fit anywhere in the poem and probably should stand separately among the many fragments left by Burns.

It is interesting that the poet told Douglas Steward that he had not "shown" this fragment to anyone and cautious of publishing satirical libel, he went on, "if it appear at all, (it) shall be placed in a variety of lights". (CL 297) This remark by Burns is an interesting insight into his thoughts regarding libelous poetry and how he would go about employing his masterful chameleon skills to dazzle readers with a *variety of lights*. How many modern Burnsians would have recognised the hand of the bard in this fragment were it not known as his work? A few "experts" might have decided the first line was bad poetry, very unlike Burns, "A LITTLE, upright, pert, tart, tripping wight". Maybe the *Sketch* tells us about this type of critic?

In sum, the stylistic methodology applied to the new poems is a detailed comparative cross-reference to the language found in known works of Burns. The most important aspect is a consideration of adjectives and adverbs in the new poems. In looking at a sample of the poet's radical works, it was found that he did not employ more than four new adjectives or adverbs in any new poem. This pattern, if taken as a rule, suggests that Burns would be highly unlikely to employ more than four such words in any new poem. This rare words template was tested on several Scots and English poems from newspapers of the period, by known poets who wrote in a style akin to Burns. As a control sample, the poems tested had to be works we know the bard did not write, to see what results were thrown up. The results indicate that it is possible to use this approach to identify poems the bard did not write. Even poems which are very similar to Burns can be rejected with confidence. So, among the "lost" poems, those which display a cluster of more than four adjectives and adverbs alien to the bard, excluding nouns, have been rejected. It was essential to consider the poems *and poets* of the age as though they formed part of a literary identity parade: once every possible suspect or style has been identified as *not Burns* and only one suspect remains, that is, Burns himself, then it follows that he is the most likely author. So, if it can be proven that no one other than Burns could be the author of poem X and the poem stands up to very close scrutiny with the poet's distinctive use of language *and* it is supported by additional contextual evidence, the case for provenance is surely over-whelming.

On a cautionary note, it is obvious that more rigorous, scientific linguistic analyses will be required from senior international literary academics before any of the new works can formally enter the canon. The poems numbered A1, A2, and so on, are the works now provisionally ascribed to the bard, while those numbered B1, B2, are a selection of poems which *may be* by Burns, although I have included a few works I do not believe are his. The first category of "A" poems contain several works where the evidence for provenance is very strong indeed.

Footnotes

[1] Brian Morton, Radio Scotland interview of 24th January 1996.

[2] Reference was made by a freelance journalist in *The Herald* that I had presented a report on the new poems to Dumfries & Galloway Council in April 1996 and that the poems could be tested for authenticity by Dr. Andrew Q. Morton, Glasgow University.

[3] See *The Observer*, 14th January, 1996, and *The Times*, 15th January, 1996.

[4] This is partly explained on the Internet from "Shaxicon Home Page", Online, World Wide Web, at http://faculty.vassar.edu/~foster/shax.

[5] An article *Primary Culprit: An Analysis of a Novel of Politics*, written for *New York* magazine, by Vassar Professor Donald Foster, on *Primary Colours*, an anonymous novel, Random House, 1996.

[6] See *Robert Burns and His Rhyming Friends*, John D. Ross, Stirling, 1928.

[7] *The Bee*, September 19th 1792.

[8] Signed ADSE, from *The Bee*, January 19th 1791.

[9] Timothy Thunderproof, pen-name of James Thompson Callander, "On Allan Ramsay", *The Bee*, 21st September 1791.

[10] *On the African Slave Trade*, signed "W. Y." is from *The Glasgow Advertiser*, March 9th 1792.

[11] This poem from the 1780's by Willaim Cowper is reprinted, *The Glasgow Courier*, 1789.

[12] *To the People of Scotland* is signed W. C., from *The Glasgow Advertiser*, March 23rd 1792.

[13] *Ode to Liberty* is by G. Dyer, from *The Edinburgh Gazetteer*, 1793.

[14] From *The Burns Chronicle*, 1926 and reprinted in Appendix A, MacKay's *Wordfinder*.

[15] William Scott Douglas, *Poetical Works of Robert Burns*, The Kilmarnock Edition, Vol. II, p.276, Thirteenth Edition, Glasgow, 1938.

[16] James A. MacKay, *Burns: A-Z, The Complete Wordfinder*, Appendix A, p.689, Alloway Publishing, 1990.

Chapter 6

Poems from The Edinburgh Gazetteer, 1793-1794

A1. On the Year 1793

Thou, who from dust alone couldst man create,
And bade th' immortal soul his being animate!
At whose command sub-marine mountains rise,
And towering Aetna's smoke obscures the skies!
Thou, who canst check the comet's wild career,
To FREEDOM consecrate the new-born Year!
O Thou, that form'dst old Ocean's briny waves,
Its strange productions, its unfathomed caves!
Thou, at whose bidding lightning's dire arrest
The life of man, and death invades his breast!
At whose decree ev'n Time itself stands still,
And all created things perform thy will!
Say but the word, and despots shall no more
With *human blood*, empurple ev'ry shore!

Hark! sacred Liberty's persuasive voice
Calls all mankind, and bids the poor rejoice!
See how she ushers in the auspicious year,
And bids the trembling Tyrant learn to fear!

Hail, wond'rous Year ordain'd to renovate
The cause of Man, and smile on human fate!
Men now are rous'd, and that to sleep no more;
Their long deluding dream's for ever o'er:
Can cruel despots bid their shackles bind
The reason'ng pow'r, and chain the human mind!
Can they o'erturn Truth's ever sacred cause,
By barb'rous precedents, or barb'rous laws?

31st December 1792 - Aratus.

Grant me, indulgent Heaven, that I may live
To see the miscreants feel the pain they give
Deal Freedom's secret treasure free as air
Till Slave and Despot be but things which were.

These last 4 lines *are* by Burns.

Aratus and the Quatrain by Burns

This poem is found in The Edinburgh Gazetteer of 8th January, 1793. The final lines appended to *On the Year 1793*, were written by Robert Burns. They are placed next to the poem to illustrate a simple point - that Burns composed four lines which are in the same poetic form, language and sentiment of *On the Year 1793*. The bard's lines are the only poetry from the period of the 1790's which bear any resemblance to *On the Year 1793*. There can be little doubt that Burns's lines bear a striking similarity in style and language to the new poem. Hunter, a highly respected Galloway lecturer in Scottish literature, describes the continuity between the two pieces as a "seamless dress". They fit together, as though they were written by the one author. This does not mean to say they were meant as part of the same poem. The similarity between the two pieces of poetry *is* significant by the very fact that there is no other poetry for the entire 1790's which match the style, language and sentiment of *On The Year 1793* so closely. So, the first factor in trying to establish the author of the new poem, is that the only known poet to write anything akin to the poem, was Burns.

The lines by Burns were not printed in the *Gazetteer* with the poem. They were written on two separate occasions and in two separate places. They were only published after 1800, when it became a fashion to collect and print any snippets by Burns. The lines were found in the fly leaf of a Lady's *Pocket Book;* and also in a book of poetry, *The British Album,* owned by John Syme. It has been claimed the lines were penned extempore, that is, on the spur of the moment. It is logically impossible that the four lines, a quatrain, could have been composed extempore by Burns on two separate occasions. So, which story is correct, if any?

The story of why Burns penned the quatrain in a Lady's pocket-book is highly suspect. The words were allegedly written in response to the horrors of the French Revolution. What "horrors" of the French revolution? In 1793, when the King and Queen of France were beheaded, Burns was far from horrified. He took a stoical viewpoint of the event and stated to Mrs. Dunlop that when the social justice of millions hung in the balance, the death of a "Perjured Blockhead" and an "Unprincipled Prostitute" was insignificant. (CL 649) It seems clear that this quatrain was cleansed of its political edge and explained away in a politically "correct" manner in the anti-radical years after its composition. So, the first story is wrong.

The second story tell us the lines were penned in the *British Album* as an extempore remark on a poem. The holograph quatrain on page 21 of *The British Album* is certainly by Burns. There is an asterisk, though, with a note which reads "see below", adjacent to a piece of poetry by Della Crusca. The note is clearly not in Burns's hand. It may be by John Syme. It was, after all, his book. The asterisk and note have been taken to indicate that Burns wrote the quatrain purely as a response to reading a verse of poetry. This implies, of course, that the words have no contemporary political context. The verse, from *Elegy, On the Plain of Fontenoy*, which allegedly provoked the quatrain, was:

> For War is Murder, tho' the voice of Kings
> Has styl'd it Justice, styl'd it Glory too!
> Yet from worst motives, fierce Ambition springs,
> And there, fix'd Prejudice is all we view.

Even if the lines by Burns were written in response to reading the stanza by Della Crusca, it does not follow that they have no contemporary political context. The quatrain by Burns is clearly not a judgment on the poetic style of the *Elegy*, nor a criticism of the poem. In fact, the lines by Burns have nothing to do with the *Elegy per se*. It was Syme who suggested the quatrain was written purely in relation to the *Elegy*. It is understandable that Syme would explain the lines had no political context to prevent the lines from being seen as seditious libel. It *may be* correct that the Elegy sparked Burns's quatrain. Beyond doubt, the message of the quatrain is a judgment on the political oppression of 1793, in the manner of the new poem.

The sentiment of the lines by Burns are clear. It is a religo-political prayer for vengeance, against an increasingly dictatorial government who declared martial law in December 1792 and oppressed reform activists. The line "Grant me indulgent heaven that I may live" is the start of the poetic prayer. The phrase "indulgent Heaven" is used in Ferguson, one of the bard's favourite poets. The wish "To see the miscreants feel the pain they give" is echoed strongly in a letter of April 1793, to Peter Hill:

> O! May the wrath and curse of all mankind, haunt & harass these turbulent, unprincipled miscreants who have involved a People in this ruinous business!!! (CL 553)

The poet was vehemently opposed to the war. The quatrain is also a religious plea to God for the end to tyranny and social inequalities in Britain, evident in the lines, "Deal Freedom's secret treasure free as air / Till Slave and Despot be but things which were". The juxtaposition of opposites, "slave" and "despot" or "slave" and "tyrant", is found in Burns's *The Song of Death, Their Groves o Sweet Myrtle, Scots Wha Hae* and lines for an *Alter To Independence*. There can be little doubt that the quatrain is authentic.

There is a tone of frustrated anger in *On The Year 1793*. In fact, the poem is an articulate burst of anger by a poet who has been personally distraught at the prospect of the loss of liberty to speak freely. There are overtones of *Scots Wha Hae* in the poem which might not be obvious on a first reading. *Scots Wha Hae* refers to "chains and slavery" in the stark choice Bruce lays out to his men at Bannockburn. In *Scots Wha Hae* the political overtone of "chains and slavery" is a reference to the imposed laws and oppression of a foreign power. It is a fascinating coincidence that on the day *On the Year 1793* was written, 31st December 1792, Burns was informed that the Excise had ordered an investigation into his political sentiments. It is particularly significant that the Excise began a process on that very day to place "shackles" which would "chain the human mind" and curb "The reas'ning power" of Robert Burns. So, *On the Year 1793* is on the same theme as *Scots Wha Hae*, Burns's favourite theme of liberty.

It is certain that *On the Year 1793* was composed by a poet who felt enraged at the oppression of the period. It is known that Burns was moved to a lather of radical frustration, "surprised, confounded & distracted" that he was to be investigated. The threat of possible prosecution under the sedition laws had hung over active radicals for almost a year. No-one in Scotland was prosecuted in late 1792. Although on the statute books, the draconian laws were yet to be put into practice until early 1793, after the composition of this poem. So, there is no evidence to show that a radical poet other than Burns was personally affected by the oppression of the period on 31st December 1792. Moreover, since the poem was written on that date, and the first radical Scot fingered by the authorities was Burns on that very day, we need look no further for a powerful motive to compose *On the Year 1793*.

Obviously the poet was not eventually charged under the sedition laws. However, on the evening of 31st December 1792, he did not know what the outcome of the investigation might be. He wrote in panic to his patron Graham of Fintry to ask for his support. It is almost certain, as Burns later wrote, that without Fintry's intervention, he would have been turned out of his job. The view from within the poet's shoes, was serious. On the evening of 31st December 1792, Burns wrote to Mrs. Dunlop, but did not complete the letter. In the continued missive dated 2nd January 1793 there are a few very interesting remarks. It is not so much what is written in the letter but what was *torn*, or *edited out* of the letter. The misnamed *Complete Letters* mention two parts of the letter which were torn away. The missing parts amount to one and a half pages missing. Just before the passages that have been torn away, there is an indication of what they contained -

> ... some envious, malicious devil has raised a little demur on my political principles ... I have set, henceforth a seal on my lips as to these unlucky politics; but to you, I must breathe my sentiments... I shall shew the undisguised emotions of my soul. - War I deprecate: misery and ruin to thousands, are in the blast that announces the destructive Demon. But...(CL 529)

And here, just as Burns was getting into full swing and obviously did state his political sentiments, someone - possibly Currie - edited out his views. The inevitable conclusion is that these passages contained comments that were "seditious" - anti-government, or pro-democracy. One thing is clear - Burns was perturbed by the investigation and let rip his feelings to Mrs. Dunlop. The missing sections of the letter cannot be explained away in a dismissive view that it was merely "folds in the paper" which made the letter unreadable as MacKay suggested in interview for *Omnibus*. The notes within *the Complete Letters* record "Three quarters of a page cut away here" and is followed by "Three quarters of a page missing".(CL 529) The problem with the letter of the 2nd January 1793, is that it seems to have carried sentiments which match perfectly those so powerfully displayed in *On the Year 1793*. If the poem had been written into the letter and edited out by Currie, it would explain why one and a half pages were "cut away" and "missing".

That the edited-out passages were "seditious" can be proven. The latter part of the letter which survived was left as mumbo-jumbo. Although fragmentary, it indicates that the sentiments expressed were in the form of an angry, personal religo-political rant:

> ... the wisdom of their wickedness, & wither the strength of their iniquity! Set this seal upon their unrighteous resolves, "Behold, whatever you do, it shall not prosper". That destruction THOU hast already begun to deal unto them, may it be the for ..(CL 529)

The last sentence makes it certain that the poet was not merely rambling about the informer who spied on him. The bard was clearly writing about God "THOU" and how things on the grander political scale were in the process of changing. This is reinforced by his following letter to Mrs. Dunlop:

> ... as to these inquisitorial Informers, Spies, Persecutors, & c may the devil & his angels be let loose to - but hold! I was *praying most fervently in my last sheet, & I must not so soon fall accursing in this.-* (CL 529)

The interesting point here is that there is no indication of fervent "praying" in the letter of 2nd January, nor the letter of 31st December 1792. Taking the reference literally, it refers to the 2nd January 1793 letter which has one and a half pages missing. So, we can confidently infer the "praying" referred to by Burns was couched in strong political overtones, although the exact context has been left blurred.

The fragmentary sections are of a religo-political language, a fervent religo-political prayer. This confirms that the poet's letter to Mrs. Dunlop dovetails precisely with the tone and language of *On the Year 1793*. Therefore, Burns was writing in the exact same language and indignant religo-political tone of *On the Year 1793* more or less on the same day the new poem was written. This is powerful evidence to support the case for his authorship, whether we like the poem or not.

The pen-name also points to Burns. "Aratus" means "ploughed" in Latin. It is derived from "arator", which means *the ploughman*. This certainly suggests Burns, whose reputation was that of a "heaven-taught ploughman poet". A reference to *ploughing, ploughed*, or *ploughman* would have been associated with Burns during the 1790's - by those who understood Latin and read the *Gazetteer*. The only other poem to appear in print during the poet's lifetime, signed "The Ploughing Poet" was in a London newspaper of 1789, and caused a public controversy. It was the work of Henry Dundas, written to slight Burns in the eyes of the Duchess of Gordon, who favoured the poet over Dundas. The incident is revealing. Only one poet of the age was associated with *ploughing*. This suggests Aratus, or "ploughed", can only point to Burns.

Indeed, even if Burns was minimal in Latin, he had previously used *Praeses* as part of a pen-name and the pen-name *Agricola*. Despite the fact that there are quite a few Lain pen-names to be found in news-papers, most notably, English newspapers, there is no great usage of Latin pen-names to imply a rural, rustic persona. It would seem natu-ral to assume that there might have been many pen-names like "Aratus" in the age when Ramsay's *The Gentle Shepherd* was hailed as the greatest Scottish poem. Latin pen-names to indicate rural, rustic or ploughing motifs were a rarity. A rural pen-name which can be found in Scotland at this time is "The Norland Shepherd", a poet who wrote only in *The Bee* and who did not write radical poetry. The only other Latin pen-name akin to Aratus is Agrestis, found with the new poems *The Ghost of Bruce* - Agrestis means rural or rustic country-man and is synonymous with the bard's pen-name Agricola, and sits adjacent to it in any Latin dictionary. So, employing a Latin pen-name would have been nothing new for Burns.

During conversation filmed in January 1996 for *Omnibus*, MacKay suggested that the pen-name seemed to be so obvious a link to Burns, that it could not be Burns, and commented that the poem was a possible attempt to frame the poet. He further claimed that most spies or informers who worked for Dundas in Scotland would have been well versed in Latin and would have known who "Aratus" was. There is no evidence to show that spies and informers were trained in Latin, the *sine qua non* of aristocratic learning. Spies were often themselves peasantry or people desperate for money or loyalists caught up in the propaganda war against the pro democracy movement. Had the identity of Aratus been known to Dundas, "Aratus" would have been arrested and tried for sedition. As newspaper evidence shows, no such arrest or trial occurred. If the poem was a ploy to set up Burns, there would have been a contrived trail of evidence which would have led to Dumfries. The simpler, more rational explanation for the mystery surrounding Aratus is that the name baffled informers - if they even noticed the poem at all, or understood it. The poem does not criticise the King nor openly attack specific political leaders. So, it is more than likely that the poem was hardly even noticed in the *Gazetteer* by Dundas's troop of radical busters.

Informers would have foolishly expected Scots vernacular poetry in the style of *Ode to a Mouse* from Burns. Moreover, in the wake of the bard's humiliating investigation, no-one would have expected him to write and publish such a poem. What the poet was forced to write and confess as his political sins, under duress to keep his job, has little connection with his keenly felt views; indeed, it is very likely that his being forced to write such a letter infuriated the poet. It probably sparked the composition of the poem.

Upset, angered and frustrated at the investigation by the Excise, he would not have written a poem he would have honed into a masterpiece. Political broadsides have never been works of art. As Noble has commented, the poem is linguistically weak - in the same way that the strikingly similar quatrain of Burns is not in his best hand. In the glance and decide atmosphere of January 1996, it is interesting that the American scholar, McGurk, commented in *The Herald* that the new poem was modeled on the style of the bard's *To Robert Graham of Fintry*. Although the poem on Fintry was composed in 1791 as confirmed in the Glenriddell manuscripts, it was not published until the Edinburgh edition of 1793, *after On the Year 1793*. So, the only person who could have modeled *On the Year 1793* on the Fintry poem was Burns himself.

McGurk may be right that *To Robert Graham of Fintry* is the model for *On the Year 1793*. If so, it effectively clinches the case that Burns was its author. However, in searching for possible influences and trying to find any other poet who might have been capable of writing the new poem, the model appears to the *Epigoniad*, from *The Death of Hercules*, by William Wilkie, Professor of Natural Philosophy at St. Andrews University. In this poem, Wilkie, dubbed "the Scottish Homer" by David Hume, wrote "Sovereign of heaven and earth, whose boundless sway / The fates of men and mortal things obey!" Further on, it reads "Here me, dread Power, whose nod controls the skies, / At whose command the winged lightening flies". This is stunningly similar to *On the Year 1793* and might even prompt the thought that Wilkie wrote the new poem. Wilkie died in 1772. In fact, throughout Wilkie's long poem there are phrases which are strikingly akin to lines in several poems by Burns. It may be surprising that the influence of this poet has not hitherto been highlighted in Burns, but it is well known that the bard's reading was extremely eclectic. Wilkie published the *Epigoniad* in 1757 and it is certain that Burns would have read it. So, it is almost certain that the model for *On the Year 1793* was Wilkie's *The Death of Hercules*.

Stylistically, the poem does not immediately ring of the better known works of Burns. However, there are many echoes from his lesser known works. Many poems of Burns begin with the word "Thou" and contain religious descriptions of the powers of God over the earth. For instance, in the final lines of *Stanzas on the Prospect of Death*, (titled *Stanzas, On the Same Occasion*, in MacKay) the link between the natural forces of the world and God, as witnessed in *On the Year 1793*, are vivid:

> O Thou great Governor of all below!
> If I may dare a lifted eye to Thee,
> Thy nod can make the tempest cease to blow,
> Or still the tumult of the raging sea:
> With that controlling pow'r assist e'en me,
> Those headlong furious passions to confine,
> For all unfit I feel my pow'rs to be,
> To rule their torrent in th' allowed line;
> O, aid me with Thy help, Omnipotence Divine!

In this early prayer epistle, the powers of God over the sea are mentioned just as they are in the new poem. In *The Ninetieth Psalm Versified*, Burns mentions the rising mountains at God's "command" in the second and third stanza -

> Before the mountains heav'd their heads
>> Beneath Thy forming hand,
> Before this ponderous globe itself
>> Arose at Thy command.

> That Pow'r which rais'd and still upholds
>> This universal frame,
> From countless unbeginning time
>> Was ever still the same

In addition, the Burns poem refers religiously to "the word", an echo found in line 13 of *On the Year 1793*. In *To Ruin*, Burns wrote "All hail, inexorable lord! / At whose destruction-breathing word, / The mightiest empires fall!" Also, *A Prayer in the Prospect of Death* begins "O Thou unknown, Almighty Cause" and goes on in the third stanza "Thou know'st that Thou hast formed me". The language of the new poem, couched in religious metaphor, is, therefore, echoed in several works of Burns. It turns out that the language of *On the Year 1793* is not so alien to Burns after all.

There are a few apparently trivial features in the new poem which may point to the author. In the description of death in *On the Year 1793*, the word "lightnings", in the plural, can only be found in *Tam O'Shanter* during this period, "The lightnings flash from pole to pole". A scan of the complete 18th century poetry database housed in the Mitchell Library and a reading of newspaper poetry reveals the use of only "lightning" in the singular, not plural. So, Burns was the only person to use "lightenings" in the plural. Also, a trait in the bard's poetry which cannot be found in any poems of the period published in newspapers or journals, is word capitalization other than for proper names. This means that other poets, if they fully capitalized a word, would only do so in the case of a surname, but not in the case of a word like "FREEDOM" as seen in *On the Year 1793*. If we scan through Kinsley's edition of the poems, which meticulously records all word capitalization, it is clear that it was a habitual practice of the poet, employed for emphasis. In addition, there is no book or newspaper poetry from a poet who used exclamation marks so liberally as Burns, a feature found prominently in poems like *Ode for the Departed Regency Bill* and now evident in *On the Year 1793*. These three factors are all indicative of a poet's writing habits and reinforce the case for the bard's authorship of the new poem.

The first stanza of *On the Year 1793*, lines 1-14, reveal echoes of the poet William Cowper. Burns was familiar with Cowper's writings and adored his religious poem *The Task*. Cowper's lines, "Shall burning Aetna, if a sage requires, / Forget to thunder, and recall her fires?" is akin to lines 3 and 4 of *On The Year 1793* - "At whose command submarine mountains rise, / And towering Etna's smoke obscures the skies!". The use of "sub-marine", for *under the sea*, is similar to the "sublunary sphere" (CL 619) and "Sublunary state" (CL 570) from the poet's letters. There is also an echo from *Ode on The Departed Regency Bill* which refers to "under-ground" forces "With groans that make the mountains shake". There are other similarities between *On the Year 1793* and *Ode on The Departed Regency Bill*, where Burns's line "And bid him check his blind career" finds its echo in "Thou, who canst check the comet's wild career". The words "check" and "career" are found in both. The rhyme of "waves" and "caves" in lines 7 and 8 are the same rhyming words in lines 7 and 8 of *On the Death of Lord President Dundas*. Moreover, it is characteristic of Burns to use the word "old" in the manner of "old Ocean's briny waves". He uses "old", for instance, in "old Solomon", "old Satan", "old Scotia's", "old Scotland", "old landlord", "old Colia" and "old Britain". The words "mountains", "rise", "towering", "obscures", "Ocean", "briny", "strange", "decree", "invades" and "created" are all found in Burns. There are at least 11 lines of Burns's poetry which begin with the word "Say", seen in line 13 of the new work. The phrase "the life of man" is used in the first verse of the song *Green Grow the Rashes, O* and in a letter to Mrs McElhose (CL 217). So, the first stanza is steeped in Burnsian language and contains many echoes from his works.

A striking echo from a known Burns song is found in the phrase "...bids the trembling Tyrant learn to fear!" in *On the Year 1793*. In *The Song of Death*, Burns wrote "Go, frighten the coward and slave! / Go, teach them to tremble, fell tyrant, but know, / No terror hast thou to the Brave!" The sentiment of the song and the poem are identical. The context which describes tyrants is different. In the

Song of Death the *tyrant* makes others *tremble* in *terror*, while the poem turns *fear* on the tyrants themselves. It is the combination of key words used around "tyrant" in both works which is revealing. Anyone could have used the word "tyrant". However, when we compare "trembling Tyrant" in the one work with "tremble, fell tyrant" in the other, an overlapping matrix of language begins to appear. The matrix is "trembling" with "tremble"; "Tyrant" with "fell tyrant"; "fear" with either "frighten" or "terror"; and "learn" with "teach". The unexpected overlap is "learn" and "teach", which are synonymous. So, what we have is an astounding combination of four like words employed to describe the same thing. Two or three very similar words in a phrase would have been a tenuous link. Four such words is striking and surely defies probability. If there were merely a few echoes of Burns' poetry, the lexical overlap could be put down to coincidence. Similarities which include words, adjectives and phrases prominent in Burns, are more difficult to explain as coincidence. So far, there are too many "coincidences" to dismiss the case of Burns as the most likely author.

The poem does appear to contain a few words which would rightly question Burns's authorship. Although the word "animate" is not found in the bard's poems, the past tense of "animate", "animated" is. In a reference to God in a letter to Mrs Dunlop, Burns used "animated" similar to the first line of *On the Year 1793*, "..the All-Good Being animated a human form" (CL 374). Also, the word "unfathomed", referring to uncharted areas of the sea, is not listed in the *Wordfinder*, but is used in the present tense, in a letter of the poet's in the exact context of *On the Year 1793*, "..deep as the unfathomable abyss of the boundless ocean" (CL 505). The word "empurple" is not common to Burns, but it is found in *On Castle Gordon,* "From tyranny's empurpled hands". The line "Hail, wond'rous year ordain'd to renovate" contains the word "renovate" which seems unlike Burns, until we notice his reference to the "renovating year" in a letter to Alexander Cunningham (CL 620). It is significant that the word "renovate" or "renovating" in relation to the changing year is only found in Burns *and* within *On the Year 1793* during the 18th century. So, even the words which appear at first to detract from the case, are words used by the bard.

There are three words spelt in old Biblical English, in *On the Year 1793*, "couldst", "canst" and "form'dst". They might seem alien to

Burns. If we look closely at his writings, many such words, couched in Biblical English are found. It is interesting to note that he used three similar spellings - "hadst", "madest", and "might'st" - in the radical, pseudonymous work *Stanzas on Psalmody*, signed Duncan M'Leerie. Other examples from various poems include "canst", "sleep'st", "wauk'st", "tremblest", "erst", "accurst", and "left'st". This type of word usage is common and distinctive in the bard's letters, in passages where he lets rip his feelings about political matters. So, it was a trait of the poet's, when expressing his strongest held views, to partly couch his language in high Biblical English. If *On the Year 1793* is viewed as a political broadside, then this type of language is certainly reflective of Burns "headlong passions" to use his own words.

The word "auspicious" cannot be found in the poetry of Burns, but is seen in the radical polemic signed A Briton published in the *Edinburgh Evening Courant*, which refers to "that auspicious event" of the 1688 Revolution. Moreover, the same letter has echoes of the final lines of *On the Year 1793*, "barb'rous precedents, or barb'rous laws", in the phrases "emerging from the dark ages of ignorance and barbarism" and "beyond historic precedent" (CL 283). So, "barb'rous" and "precedent" do not detract from his potential authorship. Overall, the poem fulfils the criteria set out in the methodology and stands up to a detailed scrutiny with the poet's writings, reinforced by contextual evidence from his letters written around the same time as the poem and his known quatrain in the same meter.

If an unknown poet X wrote *On the Year 1793*, this leads us into a maze of nowhere coincidences. What can we tell about poet X? Poet X was in a similar frame of mind to Burns on the evening of 31st December 1792, the date of composition. Unlike the majority of people who would have celebrated the New Year, poet X sat down to write poetry in a rage. Poet X was a radical who sent material to the *Gazetteer*. Poet X was concerned about the liberty of free expression being taken away, precisely at the time Burns was told to be *silent* and *obedient* by the Excise: "Can cruel Despots bid their shackles bind / The reason'ng pow'r, and chain the human mind!" Poet X used a pen-name and cultivated an image associated with "*ploughed*" or ploughing, or ploughman. Poet X never used the same style or pen-name again and managed to stay anonymous, similar to the bard's use of Agricola in *Ode on The Departed Regency Bill*. Astonishingly, the style of poet X was imitated by Burns in the quatrain he penned in

Syme's *The British Album.* Poet X also had the ability to write in a religo-political style employed by Burns in a letter to Mrs Dunlop on the same day the poem was written. By the very fact that *On the Year 1793* is far from being in the fashion of period poetry, there can be little doubt that the many coincidences form a pattern; that pattern strongly implicates poet X as one Robert Burns.

Indeed, it is quite possible that the page and a half torn away from the poet's letter of 2nd January 1793 did contain a holograph copy of *On the Year 1793.* Strong circumstantial evidence, particularly the similarity between the accepted quatrain and the new poem, reinforce the strong textual evidence to enhance the case for attribution. It is somewhat ironic that the Excise board thought they had silenced the Scottish bard after reading his supposedly humiliating letter to Fintry - they were unaware that the poet threw a party at his home in Dumfries during the second week of January 1793, which went on until the wee hours. The poet was celebrating something. Maybe the raucous party mentioned by Chambers just happened to coincide with the arrival of the 8th January issue of *The Edinburgh Gazetteer* which contained the new poem.

A2. The Dagger

When a' the people thick an' thrang
    Disclose their minds sae fully,
Permit me here to sing a sang
    Of Paddy and his gully;
(For Paddy's e'en a dainty chiel;
    Glib gabbed an' auld farran;
An' can busk up a tale as weel
    As onie Lord or Baron)
              I trow this day.

Had ye but seen him in his glee,
    When he drew out his gully,
Ye maist wad swear that he should be,
    The House o' Commons bully:
For when he's warmed in argument,
    An' wants to be a bragger,
He handles weel the instrument -
    The all-convincing DAGGER,
                On onie day.

The DAGGER mode that's been brought in
    By this Hibernian shaver,
Has raised indeed an unco din,
    And muckle clishmaclaver,
An' been a topic o' discourse
    To ilka lass and laddie;
While mony jokes are pass'd in course;
    But fient a hair cares Paddy
                For that this day.

For tho' wi' aspect like a Turk,
    Demosthenes or Tully
Had tried an argument wi' B—ke,
    An' gi'en him but his gully;
In spite o' a' their eloquence,
    Their rhetoric and logic,
Their Lettres Belle and Common Sense,
    'Twad been a fruitless project.
                For them this day.

For tho' a man can speak wi' grace,
    That matters na a spittle -
Can onie man haud up his face,
    An' argue wi' a whittle?
An' Paddy, should the DAGGER fail,
    Before he will knock under,
Can neist apply (to back his tale)
    A twa and forty pounder,
                Wi' birr some day.

But trouth I fear the Parliament
    Its ancient splendour fully,
When chiels man back an argument
    By waving o' a gully:
Yet some there are, wi' honest heart,
    (Whose courage never swaggers)
Will ne'er the public cause desert,
    For cannons or for daggers,
                By night or day.

Now Paddy be nae langer rude,
    But lay aside your storming;
And shew the "Swinish Multitude"
    The folly o' reforming.
Convince them that their cause is wrang,
    An' tell how sair they grieve ye;
But swine are aye sae damned headstrang,
    They'll aiblins no believe ye
                In that this day.

May peace and plenty bless our isle -
    May placemen ne'er oppress us -
May Grey and Erskine's gracious smile
    O' grievances redress us.
May Fox and brave McLeod exert
    Their power with due attention;
And never from our cause depart
    For sake o' post or pension,
                Like some this day.

God bless our King, lang may he reign
    Owre subjects free and happy -
May ilka loyal British swain
    Toss off his health in nappy -
May War be banish'd from our land,
    Wi' a' its dreadfu' thunder; -
And may our Constitution stand
    The warld's pride and wonder
                Ilk coming day.
Ane O' The Swine.

Of Cannons and Daggers

The Dagger was published in *The Edinburgh Gazetteer* of 25 May 1793. The first few stanzas appear, at first, to be good impersonation of Burns' eight-line stanza with refrain, employed in *The Holy Fair, Halloween* or *The Ordination.* The subject is Edmund Burke's speech of 28 December 1792 in the House of Commons. During debate of the Alien Bill, Burke condemned the campaign to raise a subscription to manufacture daggers to assist the French war effort against Poland and Prussia. During the speech he brandished a dagger, to the shock and raucous hilarity of sitting M.P.'s The poem uses this incident to develop a brilliant satire on the wider subject of parliamentary reform, which dominated British politics during the winter of 1792-3.

The man behind the dagger campaign was William Maxwell of Kirkconnel. The incident does not feature in *The Dumfries Weekly Journal.* It was reported in *The Edinburgh Gazetteer* on 1st January, 1793. It is known Burns was a subscriber to the publication that was the broadsheet of the pro-democracy group, the Friends of the People in Scotland. Burke was reported as saying "... every man in France has murder in his heart and in his face", although his colleague, Lord Loughborough, pointed out that less than 200 people were involved in the bloodshed of the 2 September 1792 in France. William Maxwell earned himself the label Britain's "No 1 Jacobin" in the London *Sun* newspaper for his efforts to raise a subscription to manufacture daggers for the French. Dr Maxwell, of course, became the poet's doctor and intimate friend.

Burns was aware of the famous dagger incident. He mentions it in two letters: to Mrs Dunlop, he wrote of "the Dr. Maxwell whom Burke mentioned in the House of Commons about the affair of the daggers", (CL 638) as though it was Maxwell's claim to public fame. To George Thomson, he boasts of his friend, describing him as "the identical Maxwell whom Burke mentioned in the House of COMMONS". (CL 637) Having reputedly dispatched four carronade cannons to aid the French war effort himself earlier in 1792, it is no surprise the bard identified with Dr Maxwell.

In the issue of the *Gazetteer* on 1st January 1793, a short didactic catechism savaged Burke. It is written in the same style as Burns' "catechism" beginning "What is Politics?" and "What is a minister?" sent to Cunningham.(CL 536) Burke was obviously a target for many radicals given his defection to the Tory party. In a way it would be surprising if Burns had not risen to Burke's infamous description of those who did not have the right to vote, the so-called "Swinish Multitude" - the definition, by implication, included the poet. Burns was always quick to react to public figures and their statements by penning radical satire. We know exactly how the poet felt towards the father of modern Conservatism and the principal protagonist of Thomas Paine's two-part pamphlet, *The Rights of Man*. In an epigram which has not amused the recent biographer, McIntyre, the bard mocked venomously:

> Oft have I wonder'd that on Irish ground
> No poisonous reptile has ever been found:
> Revealed the secret stands of great Nature's work:
> She preserved her poison to create a Burke!

So, if we are looking for the bard's personal and political motivation to compose *The Dagger*, they are not difficult to find.

Burns, however, had personal reason to be behind *The Dagger*. His close and intimate friend Robert Riddell, of Glenriddell, was far more than an antiquarian-come-musician. He wrote several powerful political pieces under the pen-name of Cato. Recent research shows that Glenriddell locked horns with Burke in a fierce constitutional debate in *The Glasgow Journal* during the 1790-1 period when Burns was his neighbour at Ellisland. The feud between Glenriddell and Burke would have been well known to Burns, who remarked that he spent more enjoyable conversation with Glenriddell than with all the other gentry of Scotland put together. So, one of the poet's closest friends, the passionate Whig, Glenriddell, had a track record of bashing Burke and had published material in the *Gazetteer* in late 1792.

Evidence suggests that the poem was written shortly after the incident, but for whatever reason, it was not published until the end of May 1793, a gap of almost five months. The editor of *The Gazetteer* printed an explanation: "The following piece of original Poetry was received by the Editor soon after the dagger scene in the House of Commons, but by accident mislaid until now". Is this to be accepted at face value? If Burns was indeed the author, the time delay might reflect the same caution he showed when planning to send copies of

The Kirk's Alarm to "both sides" of the religious debate in Ayrshire. He believed he might be "suspected" as the author of *The Kirk's Alarm*. As a poet famed for his Scots vernacular poetry, he was probably right. After the Excise investigation, a poem published in broad Lowland Scots of high satirical quality would have pointed the finger of suspicion at him immediately. No other Scottish poet was actively publishing any satirical verse in Scots of worthwhile quality. Augustan English ballad or Shakespearian blank verse might have been safe poetic styles for Burns to employ. So, if he had penned the poem in early January, it would have been wise of him to hold it back for a few months.

Before 1793 there is only one other poem on Burke in Scottish periodicals and newspapers. It occurs in Dr. James Anderson's weekly literary and scientific journal, *The Bee,* of 1791. It does not refer to Burke as "Paddy Burke" and, written in standard English, it bears little comparison with *The Dagger.* The only known reference to Burke as "Paddy" in poetry occurs in, *When Guilford Good,* by Burns: "For Paddy Burke, like ony Turk". Here is a clear echo of the first line of stanza 4 of *The Dagger* where "Burke" and "Turk" are the chosen rhyme. It is surely an important fact that the use of "Paddy" to describe Burke's Dublin origin is only recorded in the poetry of Burns.

There is certainly nothing weak about this metrically balanced and carefully structured poem. Close reading discovers many Burnsian connections. Stanza 1 bears strong language and form similarity with *The Holy Fair,* in stanza 18, "While thick and thrang and loud and lang". There is also an echo of *A Dream,* where in stanza 2, the line "I see ye're complimented thrang", finds its rhyme with "sang" as in *The Dagger.* The descriptive phrase "a dainty chiel", in line 5, stanza 1 of *The Dagger* can also be found in *On A Scotch Bard.* The last lines of stanza 1 are also strikingly close to stanza 13 of *The Author's Earnest Cry and Prayer,* which refers to

> Demptster, a true blue Scot I'se warran
> Thee, aith detesting, chaste Kilkerran;
> An' that glib-gabbet Highland baron,
> The Laird o Graham;
> An' ane, a chap that's damn'd auldfarran,
> Dundas his name.

This simple overlap is peculiar because it was no longer fashionable in Scotland to use such old Scots words such as "Glib-gabbet" and "auld farran" in 1793. The "shoal" of imitators Burns "spawned" after the Kilmarnock edition in 1786 generally all fell into the trap of employing an excess of easy to spot parochial dialect words and spelling throughout their poems - a featured outlined in the chapter on methodology. By mid-1793 there are very few Scots vernacular poems to be found anywhere in print which are not peppered with words and spelling alien to Burns's poetry. It is a characteristic of the bard's supposedly vernacular poetry, that it is often a subtle blend of Scots and English words. The example in the final stanzas of *The Dagger*, which alternate from an English rhyme to a Scots rhyme is common to Burns Scottish poetry. It is precisely because *The Dagger* uses older words found in Scottish traditional poems, such as Ramsay and his predecessors, that indicate the author of *The Dagger* was intimately familiar with the *ouvre*. Burns most certainly was.

From stanza 2 onwards, Burke is presented as an idiot. He is a "bully", a "bragger" who brandishes with "glee" his "all convincing dagger" to dramatise his argument. By stanza 3 the episode has become legend throughout Britain, and although the entire population has laughed at him, "fient a hair cares" Burke. A similar boisterous poetic demolition had already been dished out by Burns to *Holy Willie*, the hypocrites who never see the joke become bigger jokes themselves. Burke's criticism of the reform movement is cleverly mocked and turned back on him. Stanza 3's use of words such as "clishmaclaver" and "Hibernian" might appear, initially, to be alien to Burns poetry, but the former is found in *A Dream*, the *Libel Summons, The Brigs of Ayr* and the latter, in *From Aesopus to Maria*.

Stanza 4's mock-heroic invocation of Cicero (colloquially termed "Tully") and Demosthenes, famed for logic and rhetorical oration in ancient Rome, can only also be found in *The Author's Earnest Cry and Prayer*, stanza 14, "Whom auld Demosthenes or Tully/ Might own for brithers". Here, the classic authorities of logic and rhetoric ironically reduce Burke further in the suggestion that neither could have talked Burke out of his impetuosity. This pinpoints swiftly the hyperbole of Burke's rantings, and his exaggeration of the issue of Maxwell's subscription. The majority of the daggers manufactured did not find their way to France. "Common Sense" is literally lost to Burke, a description very similar to *The Holy Fair*, stanza 16 "While Common-

Sense has taen the road,/ An aff, an up the Cowgate". There is also the same use of "rhetoric" in relation to debates in the House of Commons, found in stanza 12 of *The Author's Earnest Cry and Prayer*, "An with the rhetoric clause on clause", echoing line 6, stanza 4, *The Dagger*. The number of similarities with Burns' poetry in this one stanza is itself striking. Generally, most other poems found in newspapers of the period just do not stand up to the level of detailed overlapping cross-reference with works of the bard. In fact, most struggle to provide even one stanza which is not immediately suspect. Thus far, the Burnsian imprint is abundantly clear.

In stanza 5 there is an echo of Burns' *Death and Dr Hornbrook*, which mentions "See there's a gully"", then describes a foolhardy, stubborn creature like Burke, prepared to fight to defend a point of view:

> Gudeman, quo he, "put up yer whittle,
> I'm no design'd tae try its mettle;
> But if I did, I wad be kittle
> To be mislear'd:
> I wadna mind it, no that spittle...

This lexical similarity is reinforced by the mocking humour which pillories Burke for attempting to force his listeners into agreement. It concludes with the threat that Burke would go as far as getting a "four and twenty" pound cannon to blast a consensus through force, if necessary.

This description of how Burke might "apply" a cannon to "back his tail" in the House of Commons is ludicrous, perfectly in keeping with Burns' reputed and distinctive dry wit. However, the progression from the mentions of daggers to the use of a cannon is unexpected and certainly not inevitable. It raises an interesting question: does the association of Maxwell's daggers with cannons perhaps refer to that infamous episode when Burns supposedly purchased four carronade guns from the ship *Rosamond in* early 1792 and sent them, as Maxwell hoped with his daggers, to aid the French war effort? Surely this link between Maxwell's daggers and Burns' cannons is much more than mere coincidence - Maxwell's notorious episode was well known, but Burns' exploits on behalf of French Liberty were not. So, it is highly improbable that any other poet would have made this association at the time, suggesting inside information. No poet of the time, other than Burns, was known to have dispatched cannons to France, thus further implicating Burns as author of *The Dagger*.

Stanza 6 repeats the association between cannons and daggers, appearing to bond Maxwell and Burns in a "brotherhood in arms". It suggests, tongue-in-cheek, that the entire fabric of British constitutional freedom could be torn apart by the precedent of an argument being forced through the House of Commons by brandishing a knife. Then follow four lines which, on the surface, appear to refer to those M.P.'s who have resolved to be true to the "public cause" and support democratic reform, but can also be read as referring to Maxwell and Burns' "honest heart", "whose courage never swaggers", who "Will ne'er the public cause desert/ For cannons or for daggers/ By night or day". The poem does not, of course, inform us its author dispatched cannons to France, but there appears to be almost an obsessional link between cannons and Maxwell's daggers. The bond between Burns and Maxwell was underlined when, on his deathbed, the poet pointed to the pistols he had been gifted by the makers Blair of Birmingham, and asked Dr. Maxwell to accept them as they could not be in worthier keeping. If the cannons associated with *The Dagger* incident do not refer to the *Rosamond* affair, then this must be the most mind boggling coincidence in Scottish literary history.

Stanza 7 is vintage Burns. Burke is to stop his "rude" behaviour and his solitary "storming" of the House of Commons - referring, of course, to the storming of the Bastille. In "Now Paddy be nae langer rude, / But lay aside your storming", there is a clear ring of *The Ordination*, where the word "shaver", from *The Dagger*, stanza 3, is also found:

> Now Robertson, harangue nae mair
>   But steek your gab for ever;
> Or try the wicked town of Ayr,
>   For there they'll think you clever;
> Or, nae reflection on your lear,
>   You may commence a shaver.

Burke is advised to use his eloquence to explain - the "folly o' reforming" - why the reform movement is "wrong" from an intellectual standpoint. He is doomed to fail, according to the poet, because having treated the British lower orders as the "Swinish Multitude", he must expect them to behave as such. In fact, the implication is that this is precisely what Burke deserves. The "swine" are "sae damned headstrang/ They'll aiblins no believe ye". This is in the mould of Burns's classic ironic wit.

Moreover, the phrase "... shew the "Swinish Multitude".." in line 3, stanza 7, can be found in a letter Burns wrote to George Thomson, around a month after *The Dagger* was published. The letter goes further than the poem, matching not only the first five words, but is loaded with the same sardonic language "... & shew the swinish multitude that they are but beasts & like beasts must be led by the nose & goaded in the backside". (CL 632) The echoes of a stubborn, "damned headstrang" population, are clear. Thus, the language of Burns' letter is almost a continuation of stanza 7 in prose. By this stage, Burke's fate is that of Holy Willie - his credibility is finished off in a flurry of derisory laughter. Stanza 7, therefore, provides echoes of Burns' poetry and an exact match of words to a letter written by the poet around the same time, thus adding weight to the case for Burns' authorship.

Three of the four politicians mentioned in stanza 8 are names praised in *Here's A Health Tae Them That's Awa,* a known Burns song which had already been printed anonymously in first issues of *The Gazetteer.* Those named - Thomas Erskine, Charles James Fox, Colonel Norman McLeod and Charles Grey - were leading figures in the reform movement. Moreover, in *The Author's Earnest Cry and Prayer,* stanza 14 begins with a mention of Thomas Erskine and compares him with "Demosthenes or Tully" saying Erskine might own them "for brithers". From a detailed scan of newspapers from the 1789-1798 period, no other poet can be found who praised the same pantheon of icons, ancient and modern. Thus, the array of names which Burns held as beacons of liberty, *contemporary and historical,* are employed in *The Dagger.* Either contemporary or historical icons would have added to the case for provenance, but the combination of both groups in the same poem is remarkable evidence. This pantheon of icons, unique to Burns's poetry in the late 18th century, is surely the distinctive brushstroke of the bard.

The gesture of drinking to the success of the reformers who would protect the populace from "placemen" and would not be corrupted by "post or pension,/ Like some this day" is classic Burnsian bombast, almost straight from *A Dream,*

> For me! before a Monarch's face,
>   E'en there I winna flatter;
> For neither pension, post, not place,
>   Am I your humble debtor:

This penultimate stanza is also alive with the anti-rank and anti-pomp ideals enshrined in *A Man's A Man*. (It is worth noting that the "post" and "pension" of Burke, after joining the Tory party, was a pension of around £3000 per annum - compared to the salary of £75 per annum paid to Burns - which declined during his last year). The celebratory posture, the names mentioned and the attack on corruption are at the heart of Burns' political broadsides that have come down to us.

The use of the word "May" six times in stanzas 8 and 9 is distinctively in the Burnsian mould. A search through the *Burns: A-Z, The Complete Wordfinder* might cause the reader to think the bard never used the word "May" as it is not listed. However, in *Here's A Health Tae Them That's Awa*, "May" begins 4 different lines of poetry, in stanza 1 and 2 -

> May never guid luck be their fa'!.../

> May Liberty meet wi' success,
>   May Prudence protect her frae evil!
> May tyrants and Tyranny tine i' the mist
>   And wander their way to the Devil!

A similar tone is employed in the penultimate stanza of *The Cottar's Saturday Night* where "may" occurs on 3 occasions to bless and celebrate:

> ...Long *may* thy sons of rustic toil
>   Be blest with health, and peace, and sweet content!
>   And O! *may* Heaven their simple lives prevent..../
> A virtuous populace *may* rise the while ....

So, Burns used the word "May" in the same celebratory posture in at least two different works, one which is dedicated to the same radical icons as *The Dagger*.

The final stanza is even more convincing. It concludes the round of ironic celebratory toasts by blessing the King and wishes happiness and freedom on his subjects, against a background of sedition laws and the war with France. It is known the bard vehemently opposed the war. (CL 553). The end of the British-French war is toasted and a final call is made to see the British Constitution reformed to become the wonder of the world, some coming day. The echo from *Tam O' Shanter* in "nappy" and "happy" is incidental compared to the striking overlap with the poet's inscription in the copy of Robert De Lolme's *The British Constitution*. Burns placed his copy of the book in the Dumfries Library, September 1793, inscribed: "Mr Burns presents this book to the Library, & begs they will take it as a creed of British Liberty - untill they find a better." The final phrase of *The Dagger*, hoping the Constitution would become the wonder of the world, "Ilk coming day", matches the prose line "Until they find a better". It is a perfect English translation of the last words of *The Dagger*. Here, for the second time, is a matching linguistic overlay confirmed by accepted writings of the poet. Burns did not see the British Constitution as the greatest thing since sliced bread; his genuine view - not written under the cosh of Inquisitorial oppression - was to see it reformed and improved. Clearly, the poem closes in perfect harmony with the poet's beliefs and in vintage Burnsian style.

Can all these factors really be dismissed as mere "coincidence"? The notion which began as incredible and seemed implausible, that there could not be even one Burns poem lost to the canon, has been shown to be superficial assumption, in the face of considerable evidence to the contrary. Surely not even the most prejudiced anti-radical Burns scholar, in the vein of Christopher North, keen to perpetuate the myth of the Hanoverian bard, could dismiss outright, the connected pattern of "coincidences" which suggest the poem's provenance? The pattern that connects is the key to understanding. The pattern of language usage found in Burns' works have been shown throughout this poem and clearly transcend imitation. Moreover, the final few stanzas are *better* than many comparable poems written by the bard in the 1780's. This does not imply the absurd scenario of an unknown Poet X, but reinforces the view that Burns, who was a craftsmith of words, always added to and improved his skill as a poet. Most of *The Dagger* is certainly on a par with the best stanzas from *The Holy Fair*.

In a detailed search of late 18th century Scottish poetry to find works similar to *The Dagger* little can be uncovered other than Burns' works . The closest comparison is found in one stanza by Alexander Wilson, the Paisley weaver, (later a famous American botanist). The comparison is revealing. Wilson's best verses do not stand up to close comparison with even the weakest verses in *The Dagger*. His work is often imitative of Burns but fails in the task. The following stanza is one of his best:

> The Rights of Man is now well kenned,
> And red by mony a hunder;
> For Tammie Paine the buik has penned,
> And lent the court a lounder.
> It's like a keeking-glass to see
> The craft of kirk and statesmen,
> And wi' a bauld and easy glee,
> Guid faith the birkie beats them
> Aff hand this day

There are no echoes whatsoever from Burns in this stanza. He employs regional dialect and spelling alien to Burns. Wilson may have met the bard, but his writings are not the better for it. They are vastly inferior to *The Dagger*. There are virtually no cross-references to the bard's writings from this stanza. In fact, the stylistic case for *The Dagger* is stronger - that is, it contains more similarities - than the case for *The Tree of Liberty*, no longer in manuscript, although accepted as genuine.

In peroration, if we consider the language similarities echoed from known Burns' writings, here shown in abundance, the imprint of the poet's almost unique and notorious satirical wit, the disturbing overtone of the *Rosamond* cannons in stanza 6, the evidence of overlapping references from the poet's letters and his inscription in De Lohme's Constitution, Burns is squarely in the frame as the author of *The Dagger*. *The Dagger* is certainly the best Scottish poem in this poetic form written and published during the 1790's. Moreover, aware that the bard would probably have been suspected of this poem and that he employed a false locus of composition on at least two occasions in 1789 - pretending that *Stanzas on Psalmody* was from a Kilmarnock poet and *Ode for the Departed Regency Bill* was by an Edinburgh poet - the note to indicate "Airdrie" as the bottom of *The Dagger*, does not detract from the case, but adds to it. Under no circumstances would Burns have seen this poem published without a deliberate distraction away from Dumfries. It was his *modus operandi* prior to 1793 to pretend that his compositions were written from a "safe" address. So, this would be expected from Burns. Any high quality poem in Scots was guaranteed to be annotated as somewhere away from Dumfries. Having checked for an Airdrie poet who wrote in the Scots vernacular there is none. In addition, this stunning poem is the only Scots vernacular poem from 1786-1800 signed from "Airdrie". Stylistic testing proves the locus to be a clever, but predictable, red herring. The best Scottish poet of the time was Burns. The poem, therefore, is ascribed to Burns with a considerable degree of certainty, but not with *absolute* certainty. Thus, with this one qualification, it can be argued, *beyond reasonable doubt* Robert Burns was the author of *The Dagger*.

The implications of *The Dagger* being accepted as a work of Burns have considerable significance. If this one poem was lost and is now found, it shows Dr. Chambers was right and the likelihood that there are other "democratic effusions" which have not come down to us is increased. It reinforces our kernel argument, that the poet continued writing, covertly, radical pro-democratic works after his patronizing chastisement by the Excise. He had become an "underground" poet. If he managed to compose and see published *The Dagger*, it is certain he would have seen other similar works published.

A3. The Ghost of Bruce

As late I stroll'd through Bannockburn's proud field,
At midnight hour, close by the *bore stene* stood
A Form Divine illumin'd round with fire,
In ancient armour spendidly array'd:
"Stop passenger," he said; "art thou a Scot?
Does Caledonian blood flow in thy veins?
Art thou a friend or foe to Freedom's cause?"
A friend, aghast I said of Scottish blood.
"Then fear not," he said; "the Ghost of Bruce
Four hundred years and more, in quiet rest,
The shade of Bruce has silent kept the tomb,
But rest no longer can his Spirit have:
His country is in danger; chains anew
Are forging fast t' enslave his Native Land.
Go forth, my Son, for every Scot is mine
Whom brave unconquer'd Caledonia owns;
Go tell my Country that the Shade of Bruce
Is risen to protect her injur'd Rights; -
To reinstate in splendour, as before,
Her Liberty near lost - bid her not fear -
The time approaches fast when Brucian fire
Shall slash destruction on her perjur'd foes.
My broad Egeant Shield shall guard my Sons,
My arm shall bring them Victory and Peace,
And happiness shall crown their honest toils."
Thus spake the Ghost - and in a flame flew south:
Night seiz'd her mantle - and I heard no more.

Signed Agrestis: April 16th 1793.

A4. The Ghost of Bruce

I who erewhile the Ghost of far fam'd Bruce
Made aft the dread and eke the joy to see,
Alone went wandering through his laurel'd field
The other night, revolving all the ills
Our country has endur'd from Pitt, Dundas,
And all their Pension'd Slaves - Curse of our Isle.

O'erwhelm'd with grief, and bursting into tears,
I cried, Indignant, "Oh! dear Native land!"
"My country!" "Is there not some chosen curse,
Some hidden thunder in the stores of Heaven,
Red with uncommon wrath to blast the men
Who owe their greatness to their Country's ruin!"

Scarce had I spoke, when, thick, involv'd in mist,
More awful and more grand than former fire,
The Chief of Men, great minded Bruce appear'd.

"Cheer up your heart, my Son; why grieve you so:
Your Country in her breast still carries Bruce,
And ne'er shall be enslav'd. Trust me (he said)
So far you've done your duty as I bade,
To warn my Country what she had to fear -
And what she had to hope for from my arm.
The time is now arriv'd, when all that's dear
To Briton's shall arouse them from their sleep -
To sleep no more, till each brave Briton's free:
But still it much imports each patriot Scot
To act with prudence, keen and still reserve.
Their foes are wringing out their dying pangs
On Virtue; - but the strife will soon be o'er -
Bid all my Sons be firm; and when the storm
Shall gather thickest, boldly show their front,
United as in One. The work is done".
He only added, When the clouds should burst,
That awful hover'd over Britain's Isle,

He would again appear to stay the hand
Of Vengeance, and bid Mercy take her place.

Dated September 6th 1793 - Agrestis.

Bruce and Scots Wha Hae

There are two poems which are *The Ghost of Bruce*. The first was printed in *The Edinburgh Gazetteer* on 16th July 1793, but symbolically dated as composed on Easter Sunday, April 16th 1793 to give overtones of a resurrection of Scottish patriotism. The second version appeared in *The Edinburgh Gazetteer*, 16th September 1793, but was dated as written, 6th September, 1793. These poems are fascinating in the way they straddle the composition of *Ode - Bruce's Address to His Troops at Bannockburn,* commonly known as *Scots Wha Hae,* a name never used by Burns. *Scots Wha Hae* was written around the end of August or beginning of September, 1793. It may, of course, be mere coincidence that two poems of the same name and on the same theme as *Scots Wha Hae* were written and published around the same period. It is astonishing that these poems with the similarity of theme and sentiment to *Scots Wha Hae* have never been mentioned in literary analyses about the origin of *Scots Wha Hae* during the last two centuries. Thorough analyses of both poems suggest strong links with the bard which implicate Burns as their most likely author.

An analysis of the second version of *The Ghost of Bruce* was presented in an essay in *The Herald,* 25th January, 1996. It was also broadcast on Radio Scotland by Brian Morton on 24th January 1996. Yet, despite media publicity, no-one came forward to point out the first version of the poem had not been mentioned. This surely indicates both poems are new to this century.

The *Bruce* poems are written in Shakespearian blank verse, in iambic pentameter or lines of ten syllables with five stresses. Blank verse had been employed by many of Burns's literary icons such as Shakespeare, Milton, Cowper, Thomson and Young. Obvious first thoughts are that blank verse is not common to Burns. There are two early examples where the bard used blank verse. The first, *Remorse,* is based on introspective thoughts spurred by reading Adam Smith's *The Theory of Moral Sentiments:*

Of all the numerous ills that hurt our peace,
That press the soul or wring the heart with anguish,
Beyond comparison the worst are those
By our own folly, or our guilt brought on:
In ev'ry other circumstance, the mind
Has this to say: - "It was no deed of mine."
But, when to all the evil of misfortune
This sting is added: - "Blame thy foolish self!"
Or worser far, the pangs of keen remorse,
The torturing, gnawing consciousness of guilt,
Of guilt, perhaps, where we've involved others...

We tacitly accept this poem as authentic mainly because we find it in all versions of the *Collected Works*, although nothing in the poem immediately strikes the reader as distinctively "Burnsian". The poem is a lesser known work. It is clear from *Remorse*, the poet had little success with blank verse, bar self-amusement. A second early work, often called *Tragic Fragment*, is also in blank verse. It is not a work of high literary merit, but it rings clearly of Burns' radical idealism:

All villain as I am - a damned wretch,
A hardened, stubborn, unrepenting sinner -
Still my heart melts at human wretchedness,
And with sincere, tho unavailing sighs
I view the helpless children of distress.
With tears indignant I behold the oppressor
Rejoicing in the honest man's destruction,
Whose unsubmitting heart was all his crime.
E'en you, ye hapless crew! I pity you;
Ye, whom the seeming good think sin to pity:
Ye poor, despised, abandoned vagabonds,
Whom Vice, as usual, has turn'd o'er to ruin.

There are clear echoes here of the second version of *The Ghost of Bruce* where "indignant" and "tears" are employed in a similar fashion to *Tragic Fragment*. Indignation on witnessing social injustice was undoubtedly a personality trait of the poet. During his poetic career, Burns did not publish any poem in blank verse which bore his name. So, he was not known as a poet who employed the style. To hide authorship of potentially treasonable, seditious poetry, blank verse would, therefore, have been an ideal style. Who, during the 1790's, would have immediately linked the *Bruce* poems with the popular stylistics of *Ode to A Mouse* from the famed "heaven-taught ploughman poet"? Surely no-one.

It was a remarkable error by MacKay, mentioned in *The Herald*, 12th January 1996, that the second version of the poem is supposedly badly out of meter. It is simply not. Both poems are evenly balanced in syllable count. This shows they are not the work of an amateur. What is surprising among the work of other poets during the early 1790's is the scarcity of radical blank verse. Moreover, there has never been identified another poet of the period who was besotted with Brucian and Wallace imagery in poetry. The bard's passion for Scottish martial heroes is writ large in *The Vision*, probably the poetic milestone in which Burns marked himself out as a poet of Caledonia, "I mark'd a martial race, pourtray'd/ In colours strong:/ Bold, soldier-featured, undismay'd,/ They strode along". It is also reputed that Burns had planned to write a play to be called *The Bruce*. This is supported by the poet's question in *Scots Prologue for Mrs Sutherland*, stanza 2, written in 1790:

> "Is there no daring Bard will rise and tell
> How glorious Wallace stood, how hapless fell?
> Where are the Muses fled that could produce
> A drama worthy o the name o Bruce?"

It is certain he would have read the old ballad *The Life and Actions of Sir William Wallace*, by William Hamilton and John Harvey's *The Life of Robert Bruce: King of Scots*. In the pantheon of historical icons admired by Burns, the *Bruce* came very high on his list.

Neither poem displays the distinctive feature of parochial words and spelling of dialect Scots, found scattered among the works of Telford, Little, Wilson et al, who imitated Burns. Their Scots vernacular is often distinctively unlike Burns blend of auld Scots interwoven with English. Moreover, if there is to a be a case to argue that the *Bruce* poems are imitation of Burns, it is difficult to sustain: Burns was not known publicly as a writer of blank verse. Both poems are predominantly in English. Imitators of Burns tended to chose Standard Habbie form. The characteristic flaws of imitators are not found in either *Ghost of Bruce*. Clearly, therefore, the *Bruce* poems are not imitations.

Both poems employ the Latin pen-name *Agrestis*. Agrestis means a rustic, rural countryman. This is immediately significant. Burns used the pen name *Agricola*, meaning farmer, land tiller or countryman when he published *Ode to the Departed Regency Bill* in a London newspaper of 1789. Agricola not only means virtually the same as Agrestis - rural, rustic or countryman - it sits adjacent to Agrestis in any Latin dictionary. Another simple coincidence? Is it possible two different authors would choose to use Latin pen-names so similar? It seems more likely the same author would employ both pen-names, repeating an old, well worn *modus operandi*.

In light of Ramsay's *The Gentle Shepherd*, it might be argued, such rural, countryfied persona might mask many a poetic guise. The evidence does not support this notion for the 1790's. Setting aside Aratus, used for *On the Year 1793*, which seems also to be Burns, the only other pen-name with a hint of rural persona, is found in *The Bee* of 1792, with a poet called The Norland Shepherd as mentioned in the essay for *On the Year 1793*. It is worth noting that The Norland Shepherd's poetic themes are rural dominated, not political. Agrestis, of course, indicates and relates not to the poetic content, but to the author. Moreover, the pattern which embraces Agrestis, Agricola and Aratus, is the deliberate Latin concealment of a poet who hints at rural, rustic origins. Not until the Ettrick Shepherd, was there another Scottish poet badged so firmly as Burns by their rural, rustic image. Since Burns knew he was viewed as a "heaven-taught ploughman poet" by his contemporaries, who would suspect this supposedly uneducated poet would use Latin pen-names? So, even if Burns was no expert in Latin, he had used Latin in at least one pseudonym prior to 1793. The bard's friendship with Nicol, a teacher of Latin, must have improved the poet's knowledge of the subject.

Research of newspapers after 1796 reveals that there are no continued examples of poetry from Agrestis after the poet's death. To escape the sedition laws, one or maybe two poems might be published under a specific pen-name, then safety would compel a new guise. So, whoever Agricola was, (we know it was Burns with hindsight) would adopt another persona in time. The simplest change from the pen-name Agricola would, of course, be to Agrestis. Moreover, Aratus and Agrestis would also be changed in time.

There are many Burnsian echoes in the first *Bruce* poem. The first obvious connection is the Shakespearian phrase "Stop, passenger!" found in Burns' *Elegy on Captain Matthew Henderson*, "Stop, passenger! my story's brief". From a scan of all 18th century poetry, only Burns, Joseph Mitchell and Alexander Pennicuik employed the phrase "Stop, passenger". Mitchell and Pennicuik were dead by 1793. The question "art thou a Scot?" is found in William Hamilton's *The Life and Heroic Actions of Sir William Wallace*. Hamilton died in the middle of the century. Burns was familiar with his writings.

Moreover, the appearance of the Bruce's ghost is couched in a more powerful nationalistic image than *A Vision*, "When lo! in form of minstrel auld / A stern and stalwart ghiast appear'd". Bruce is a grander figure than the "auld" "minstrel", he is a "Form Divine illumin'd round with fire, / In ancient armour splendidly array'd" who has appeared at the place most symbolic of Scottish freedom, the "bore stene", where Bruce raised the Scottish flag and declared Independence from English tyranny. When Burns told Mrs Dunlop his greatest poetic ambition was to sing and write at leisure on the great patriotic themes of Caledonia, he had just returned from a Highland tour and his visit to Stirling and Bannockburn had filled him with a Scottish "prejudice", akin to the patriotism of Agrestis in the first *Bruce* poem. In a letter to Robert Muir, the poet wrote of his visit to Bannockburn where he "said a fervent prayer for old Caledonia over the hole in a blue whin-stone (the "bore stene") where Robert de Bruce fixed his Royal Standard on the banks of Bannockburn".(CL 131) The visit was a historic and psychological event for the poet.

In the symbolic re-birth of Bruce's "Spirit", or "shade" across Scotland, there are echoes of *Extempore Stanzas on Thomson*, published pseudonymously in the *Edinburgh Gazetteer*, "Dost thou not rise, Indignant Shade? /And smile wi spurning scorn". More significant is the description "brave unconquer'd Caledonia". It is a very distinctive use of language found echoed in Burns' song *Caledonia*, "Thus bold, independent, *unconquer'd* and free". The words "bold" and "unconquer'd" from the song Caledonia are synonymous with "brave unconquer'd". Such definitive nationalistic language was not commonplace among contemporary radical effusions. It is distinctively the ring of Burns' radical, patriotic Scots voice.

A striking passage in the first *Bruce* poem is the use of historical symbolism to represent the rise of Bruce's "shade", returned to protect Scotland's liberty - written, supposedly, on Easter Sunday:

> ... "the Ghost of Bruce
> Four hundred years and more, in quiet rest,
> The shade of Bruce has silent kept the tomb,
> But rest no longer can his Spirit have:
> His country is in danger; chains anew
> Are forging fast t' enslave his Native Land.
> Go forth, my Son, for every Scot is mine
> Whom brave unconquer'd Caledonia owns..."

Agrestis, here, is throwing down the sword of Scotland and speaking for the nation. The statement that the shade of Bruce is risen across Scotland to protect Caledonia's ancient rights is boldly asserted. The return of Bruce's ghost, who could have no rest in a Scotland where "dangers" and "chains" were forging to enslave his country, is an image so indicative of Burns in song and poetry, it is difficult to imagine he would have been beaten to write this poetic imagery. Agrestis, if not Burns, has stolen Burns's clothes and has effectively donned the mantle of the Bard of Caledonia.

Burns lamented the lack of patriotic spirit across Scotland in "Where is that soul of freedom fled" from the *Washington Ode* of 1794 and in mid-1793 rearranged *Logan Braes* and added a final anti-war stanza. No one could doubt Burns took up the mission given to Agrestis by Bruce, to

> "Go tell my Country that the Shade of Bruce
> Is risen to protect her injur'd Rights; -
> To reinstate in splendour, as before,
> Her Liberty..."

In the second *Bruce* poem, the apparition of the Scottish King speaks to the poet, "So far you've done your duty as I bade, / To warn my Country what she had to fear -". The phrase "my Country" overlaps both poems and is followed by instruction from Bruce to the poet to inform Scots to prepare for freedom and to "sleep no more", an expression lifted from Shakespeare's play MacBeth. (This phrase is also found in *On The Year 1793*, signed Aratus) The political raison

112

d'etre of *Scots Wha Hae* is surely to urge Scots to stand forth against oppressive laws. If Agrestis is not Burns, then Burns borrowed Agrestis' theme for *Scots Wha Hae*. The *Bruce* poem of 16th April 1793 is surely the literary origin of *Scots Wha Hae*. Did Burns steal the idea of *Scots Wha Hae* from another writer? Surely, this is highly improbable. Is it not more likely Burns was indeed Agrestis?

The use of the word "danger" in the first poem, is found on several occasions in Burns in reference to bygone Caledonian martial exploits, in precisely the same context. The Scottish "ancestors" in *Address to Edinburgh*, stanza 7, "fac'd grim Danger's loudest roar". Having mentioned "Caledonians" in *Prologue Spoken by Mr Woods*, Burns went on to expiate a semi-religious prayer, hoping the spirit of Caledonia would be a bulwark against all forms of oppression in the future:

> ...to shield the honor'd land!
> Strong may she glow with all her ancient fire;
> May every son be worthy of his sire;
> Firm may she rise, with generous disdain
> At Tyranny's, or dire Pleasure's chain;
> Still self-dependent in her native shore,
> Bold may she brave grim Danger's loudest roar,
> Till Fate the curtain drops on worlds to be no more!

A more striking overlap in the use of language is found in comparison with *Scots Wha Hae*. *Bruce* tells that "chains anew / Are forging fast t' enslave his Native Land, " meaning of course, the oppressive sedition laws and the hunting of radicals - the end of free speech and liberty in Scotland. It is a reference to politically imposed "chains" which will "enslave". Bruce's comments in *Scots Wha Hae* refer to "chains and slavery" which have been *forged*. Thus, the first *Bruce* poem displays the word "danger" in the same historical context employed by Burns and echoes the radical language of *Scots Wha Hae* in reference to chains and slavery.

The final lines of the first Bruce poem conclude after the ghost has ceased to speak and describe its abrupt departure "Thus spake the Ghost - and in a flame flew south: / Night seiz'd her mantle - and I heard no more". A similar abrupt ending occurs in the bard's elegy *On the Death of Sir James Hunter Blair* where it is "Caledonia's trophied shield ... Her form majestic" who spoke then "..vanish'd with the sweeping blast". It may not be significant that the ghost "flew south", but if the bard's imagination was fixed on "bore stene" at Bannockburn, it is southward to Dumfries. Overall, the poem stands up to close scrutiny with the known works of Burns and rings strongly of Burnsian language and imagery.

The first line of the second *Bruce* poem is partly lifted from Milton's *Paradise Regained*, which reads "I who erewhile the happy garden sung". Burns often employed this integration of known writers into his own works, sometimes acknowledging the quote. The first two lines juxtapose "dread" and "joy" in a rich use of language. There is a hint that the author of the poem has seen a vision of Bruce before, "former fire" - a reference to the first Bruce poem - and feels a dread for such an apparition, that the "joy" itself *expands* with the appearance of the ghost. An eerie dramatic sense, pregnant with expectation is set by these lines.

There is an interesting remark in *The Vision* by Coila, the poet's muse, when she refers to the bard's writing habits. She says, "I saw thee leave their ev'ning joys, / And lonely stalk,/ To vent thy bosom's swelling rise/ In pensive walk." This informs us that the poet's habit of courting the poetic muses was during his solitary evening walks. Is it mere coincidence that the second *Ghost of Bruce* begins with a poet "wandering" "alone" during "The other night"? Coincidence begins to evaporate when Burns's letter to George Thomson is considered. The poet told Thomson the notion of *Bruce's Address to his Troops* came to him suddenly and accidentally "in my *yesternight's evening walk*". The key word is "yesternight", synonymous with "the other night" from the Bruce poem. Burns told Thomson he was thinking about the political problems of the period, "..the glowing ideas of some other struggles... *not quite so ancient*". Burns was not courting his poetic Muse like days of old, he was obsessed with the major problems of his period. What he was doing was turning over in his head the various problems of the time, or "revolving all the ills", as described precisely by Agrestis. So, if Agrestis is not Burns, the coincidence is now staggering - both Agrestis and Burns walked alone *and* did so "The other night" or "yesternight", (not last week or tonight) *and* both were thinking over the "ills" or "some other struggles" of the period *and* both suddenly thought on King Robert the Bruce *and* related the story of Bruce to contemporary events. This reveals a stunning overlap between Burns' letter to Thomson and the *Bruce* poem which defies probability that it can be mere coincidence. It makes logical sense to see Agrestis and Burns as the same person.

Surely it is absurd to believe another unknown poet could have experienced the same as the poet and through mere coincidence, described Burns's unique experience in a poem the bard knew nothing about? It is certain Burns would have toned down any radical comments in his letter to Thomson which he sent by normal post - the commentary in the Bruce poem is inferred to Thomson - but would have expressed himself freely in a poem such as *The Ghost of Bruce* which would have been delivered to Edinburgh by a safe personal carrier.

There are many further links between the bard and the second poem. *The Ghost of Bruce* refers to the ruin of the country and names Dundas and Pitt as responsible. Whether or not it would have been wise for Burns to indict such personage is immaterial, the poem was signed Agrestis, not Robert Burns. Moreover, the poem is intensely radical and being critical of government, it is "seditious" but it does not reach the forceful rage of the *Washington Ode*. In *Ode to the Departed Regency Bill*, printed anonymously in 1789, Burns displayed his dislike of Dundas - "Paint Ruin, in the shape of high Dundas/ Gaping with giddy terror o'er the brow". The criticism of Pitt and Dundas is spread between lines 4 and 12 in The Ghost of Bruce:

revolving all the ills
Our country has endur'd from Pitt, Dundas,
And all their Pension'd Slaves - Curse of our Isle.

O'erwhelm'd with grief, and bursting into tears,
I cried, Indignant, "Oh! dear Native land!
"My country!" "Is there not some chosen curse,
Some hidden thunder in the stores of Heaven,
Red with uncommon wrath to blast the men
Who owe their greatness to their Country's ruin!"

Burns was never at ease with Dundas. He had as much liking for Dundas as he had for Edmund Burke. In the Autumn of 1793 the poet believed that the government - effectively Pitt and Dundas -

were ruining the country. Is it mere coincidence again to find Burns' sentiments of this time enshrined in *The Ghost of Bruce*?

The dialogue of the poet, prior to Bruce's reply, from "Is there not some chosen curse".. until " Who owe their greatness to their Country's ruin!" is a clever adaptation taken from Joseph Addison's play *Cato*, (1672-1719). The lines of Addison are spoken by Marcus, son of Cato, referring to his brother Portius:

> Oh Portius! is there not some chosen curse,
> Some hidden thunder in the store of Heav'n,
> Big with uncommon vengeance to blast the men
> Who owe their greatness to their country's ruin.

Did Burns read Addison? W. D. Fisher in *The Burns Chronicle*, 1940, lists the "favourite" poets of Burns by looking at references in the poet's letters and estimates the order of preference as "Thomson, Shakespeare, Pope, Ramsay, Young, Milton, Fergusson, Addison" and lastly, "Shenstone". A numerical count of references in the Index of *The Complete Letters* reveals there are 22 for Addison, but only 21 for Ramsay, 19 for Young, 14 for Milton and 13 for Fergusson. Addison, according to Fisher "holds a distinctive claim in association with Burns" by being the poet who first inspired the young Burns in "*Vision of Mirza*". Burns quotes lines from Addison in his Autobiographical letter to Dr Moore "For though in dreadful whirls we hung / High on the broken wave" and describes them as "music to my boyish ears". The bard also paraphrased a line from Addison's *Cato*, beginning "O Jeany, thou hast stolen away my soul". (CL 37). In fact, the play Cato is quoted 4 times in *The Complete Letters*. Thus, the lines adapted from Addison are almost *business as usual* for Burns.

There is a more significant link between Burns, Addison and the theme of Bruce and Bannockburn which might be labeled just another coincidence. When the bard wrote to Captain Patrick Miller with a copy of *Ode - Bruce's Address to His Troops at Bannockburn*, he introduced the *Ode* with a passage of Addison's poem *Letter from Italy to Lord Halifax,* "O, Liberty - / Thou mak'st the gloomy face of Nature gay, / Giv'st beauty to the sun, & pleasure to the day!" (CL 613) This shows that Burns associated the language of liberty employed by the English writer Joseph Addison, with the story of Bruce - a specific context also found in the second *Bruce* poem. The probability that Burns and another radical poet would associate Bruce and Scotland's struggle for Independence in the 14th century with lines from Addison is pretty remote. The works of Thomson and Ramsay were the public favourites of the day. It also seems very unlikely that Burns would have made the Bruce-Addison association after composing *Scots Wha Hae*. If the bard's association was triggered by reading the second *Bruce* poem - assuming he did not write it - he would first have to be familiar with the play *Cato* to know the lines were adapted from Addison, so this option can be excluded. The language of liberty might have been ubiquitous during the late 18th century, but an association between Bruce and the poetry of Addison was not. The only known example belongs to Burns. This further binds the authorship of the poems to him.

More coincidences appear when the language of the Bruce poem is examined in detail. For instance, there is an interesting lexical similarity between Burns song, *The Ruined Maid's Complaint*, (line 1, verse 7) which reads "But heaven's curse will blast the man" and lines 9-12 of the second *Bruce* poem. The old song, polished up by Burns, "bears the impress of Burns genius", as Scott Douglas commented. It is agreed that verse 7 of the song was written by Burns. The use of "heaven's", "curse", and "blast" and "man" is a distinctive use of language. In the second *The Ghost of Bruce* these words are ordered differently to read "curse", "Heaven", "blast" and the plural of man, "men". The context of the song is the moral dictate that a father should admit fathering his children or be condemned, a point Burns certainly knew about. In fact, the likelihood that these words should be employed in *The Ghost of Bruce* in the same manner, mixed with "thunder", "red", "wrath" and "ruin" suggest a strong link to Burns. A lexical overlap of two or three words might be explained as coincidental and dismissed, especially if the phrase was common parlance of the period, but an overlap of 4 key words is not so easy to explain away.

The use of language employing religious terminology within a context of a moral-political view, as in lines 9-12 of *The Ghost of Bruce*, is witnessed many times in Burns' writings. In paragraph 5 of Burns' well known letter addressed *appropriately* to the co-accused in *The Ghost of Bruce*, William Pitt, a biblical image is employed. A further clear example is the end of *The Election Ballad to Graham of Fintry* -

I pray with holy fire:
Lord, send a rough-shod troop o' Hell
O'er a' wad Scotland buy or sell,
And grind them in the mire!!!

This language is consistent with the sentiment expressed in the *Ghost of Bruce* where a "chosen curse" or "hidden thunder in the stores of Heaven" to "blast" Pitt and Dundas is posed as a question. In *Lines on Ambition,* signed A Briton, a new work being attributed to Burns, the anger of the poet is seen in the line which wishes *"curses"* to *"*visit them to the grave", those who would ruin their country for glory. The religo-political sentiment of Burns' idealist anger is a subject which many biographers do not meet head on.

A more specific example where Pitt and Dundas are again blamed by Burns was written in April 1793, to Mr Peter Hill. Burns carefully couches his criticism of the British war with France in the letter. Cautious of possibly being prosecuted under the sedition laws, he describes the war as an "unlucky blast which has overturned so many... four months ago" then veils his attack on Pitt and Dundas "O! may the wrath & curse of all mankind, haunt & harass these turbulent, unprincipled miscreants who have involved a People in this ruinous business!!!" (CL 553) In *The Ghost of Bruce,* this sentiment is put in stronger and more controlled words which ring like a hammer on an anvil. The words used in Burns' letter and the *Bruce* poem are "curse" and "wrath", but it is obvious that "a People" is equivalent to "their Country's" and "ruinous" is the adjective of "ruin" as used in the poem. It is of significance this overlap in language occurs in a letter written in the same year as the *Bruce* poems.

There is a distinctive Burnsian ring to the phrase "Pension'd Slaves" in *The Ghost of Bruce.* It sounds like the voice of the bard in *The Author's Earnest Cry and Prayer,* stanza 5, "Let posts an' pensions sink or soom/ Wi' them wha grant them;" and echoes *A Dream,* stanza 3, "For neither pension, post nor place,/ Am I your humble debtor". The use of the word "tears" in line 7 is indicative of Burns, the *Man of Feeling* in his characteristic semi-dramatic poetic posture. Burns had been unfairly criticised in his life for "bursting into tears" at the drop of a hat, when moved by poetry or a work of art. In the short piece, *Tragic Fragment,* Burns' burning sense of social justice "With tears indignant..." is echoed in *The Ghost of Bruce* " O'erwhelm'd with grief, and bursting into tears, / I cried, Indignant, "Oh! dear Native land!" From "pension'd slaves" to "tears" and "Indignant" a distinctive indignant voice of the bard comes through.

In addition, the change in the poem from the general use of "Britons" to "each Patriot Scot" in lines 22-25 is a specific shift in emphasis echoed in Burns' 1788 letter published in *The Edinburgh Courant*, "...*let every Briton, and particularly every Scotsman*...", (CL 283). So, even this subtle change in emphasis in the *Bruce* poem echoes the prose of Burns.

A more distinctive use of language is the description of Bruce appearing "thick, involv'd in mist" which rings of "thick mists obscure involv'd me round" from, *Lament for James, Earl of Glencairn*. The three words "thick", "mist" and "involv'd" occur in each work. Such a phrase is peculiar because of the key word "involv'd" which is used exactly in both cases with the "e" taken out. An amateur might have written "Bruce appeared in mist", or "In the thick mist, appeared Bruce." The adjective "thick" to describe "mist" would be commonplace. However, the word "involv'd" is unexpected. It paints a cinematic picture of an unnatural mist, almost other worldly, which suits the apparition of Bruce. The language sets dramatic expectation. Moreover, the words from *Lament for Glencairn* are used in a similar context to *The Ghost of Bruce*, to develop an image where an apparition has appeared. Again, this example of language and imagery add to the case for provenance. The word "involved" employed in relation to weather or natural elements is regularly found in Milton, Thompson, and other favourite poets of the bard.

In the second poem, Bruce is hailed as "The Chief of Men" on his appearance, and although this phrase does not immediately ring of Burns's poetry, the phrase "chief o' men" is employed by Burns in the first version of *A Man's A Man*, the "...honest man, tho' ne'er sae poor,/ Is chief o' men for a' that". Here again, we enter the possibility that Burns lifted the phrase "chief o' men" in his first anonymous draught of *A Man's A Man*, from Agrestis. Yet another coincidence?

When the poem describes Bruce's "arm" as a symbol of hope, the image is a very distinctive Burnsian image. In the *Irregular Ode for General Washington's Birthday*, it is Wallace's arm - "Show me that arm which, nerv'd with thundering fate,/ Crush'd Usurpation's boldest daring!/ ..that palsied arm..." The *Ode* symbolises the fall of Scottish liberty in his "arm". *The Ghost of Bruce* is more optimistic. Bruce promises to "stay the hand of Vengeance" which is similar to Burns's *Birthday Ode for the 31st December, 1787* where it is "Vengeance's arm.." rather than "hand". It would have been characteristic of his thinking to appeal to such icons in moments of solitary thought when considering the contemporary political condition of 1793, as evident in *Bruce's Address to His Troops*. Did Burns, as Agrestis, develop the Brucian theme onto a more overtly radical basis than has hitherto been known?

Moreover, there is a strong Burnsian ring to the use of "the storm" as a political storm with religious portent, described as "awful" in lines 29, and 32-33 of the second poem. The word "awful" carries connotations which imply the wrath of God lingers behind the clouds ready to "burst" "over Britain's Isle". An example from Burns is found in *Ode to the Departed Regency Bill*, "Spread abroad its hideous form/ On the roaring Civil Storm,/ Deafening din and warring rage/ Factions wild with factions wage". The image of how the "storm shall gather thickest" at the end of *The Ghost of Bruce* echoes the use of imagery developed to the level of breath-taking genius in *Tam O'Shanter*. Kate's wrath is likened to the "gathering storm". The word "thickest" in relation to storms or the natural elements is distinctively Burnsian. For instance, "Thickest night, surround my dwelling" from *Strathallan's Lament*. In a letter to Robert Aitken Burns wrote of "the storm of mischief thickening".(CL 53) The storm of the second *Bruce* poem, though, is more akin to the gathering battle in *Scots Wha Hae*, where the phrase "See the *front* o battle *lour*" describes the impending battle of Bannockburn as an ominous storm coming towards the Scottish troops. The word "lour" is critical to the cross-reference. Also, the word "front" is used in the song *and* in the poem, "boldly show their *front*" within the same context of an oncoming battle. This lexical similarity is stunning from a poem written around the same time as *Scots Wha Hae*, long before *Scots Wha Hae* was published. Thus, the poem contains imagery strikingly similar to *Scots Wha Hae* which is also consistent with other radical works of Burns.

Storm imagery is a dominant feature of Burns' poetry, often used as a background canvas to social comment poetry. He had a peculiar fascination with storms, as explained in his autobiographical letter to Dr Moore (copied from his *Commonplace Book*), "...scarcely any earthly object gives me more... pleasure ...enraptures me - than to walk in the sheltered side of a wood or high plantation, in a cloudy winter day, and hear the stormy wind howling among the trees, and raving o'er the plain...". This eloquent passage explains the semi-religious awe Burns felt for winter's wildest weather as though the raging elements represented the powers of God on earth - a point developed in a letter to Mrs Dunlop. The ominous religious overtone of the *thickest storm* and *awful* clouds which would *burst* across Britain in the second *Bruce* poem conveys distinctively, the semi-religious awe Burns saw in the forces of nature.

Probably the most important message concerning the sentiment of the Bruce poems is that they are anti-violent. If a possible rebellion in Britain is the pregnant, underlying theme of the poems, then it is not to be a bloody rebellion of vengeance. Bruce, in the final poem is not the sword wielding hero. He is to be the peacemaker and will "stay the hand / Of Vengeance, and bid Mercy take her place". The poems are, by implication, opposed to any British equivalent of the French Jacobin "terror". Burns may have supported the revolutionary ideals associated with France, but he was not an advocate of political murder.

Had the *Bruce* poems not been by Burns, there should have been obvious gaps where there were no language echoes and a cluster of words he did not use, as evident in the poems looked at in our earlier methodology chapter. The only word which troubled me for a while was "import" in the second poem, until it was found in *The Complete Letters*, to Dugald Stewart. (CL 297) Moreover, in checking many examples of blank verse, it became obvious that Shakespeare and Milton regularly employed this word, thus giving its origin. In fact, the shades of Milton, Shakespeare and Addison in the second poem were not mentioned by any of the press critics of last January who were so quick to round on this poem as a "bad" work. Maybe Milton, Shakespeare and Addison are bad models to emulate? Thus, there are consistent echoes and phrases from Burns throughout both poems, in almost every line and strong echoes from poets we would expect to find echoed in Burns.

Therefore, taking all the evidence into consideration, there is clearly a very strong case that Burns was Agrestis, alias Agricola. The first *Bruce* poem has a distinctive Burnsian ring to it. Taken together, the poems reveal many apparently coincidental echoes and overlaps from Burns's writings which suggest a pattern. Is it really possible another writer could have mirrored Burns's ideals, language and style - on a theme so close to his heart - with adapted phraseology from a poet (Addison) who fired Burns' poetic career in its youth? No two poems not written by Burns stand up to such close comparison with his known works. Probability points to the conclusion that it is very unlikely any poet other than Burns could have written the poems. Burns certainly had the ability and radical motive to write both poems.

It is surely the rich radical language which gives him away and in particular the lifting of words from Addison and Milton. Burns was writing powerful radical material in June 1794 asking of Scotland "Is this the ancient Caledonian form", in angst and dismay at why the legendary fire of his martial ancestors could not be stirred among contemporary Scots to oppose oppression. Surely only a poet who had tried to stir patriotic feelings in July, late August and September 1793, would have asked such a question in June 1794? The buoyant optimism and patriotic focus of the *Bruce* poems is interwoven in the passionate anthem *Scots Wha Hae* - the victorious Bruce. It is almost beyond possibility that Burns was not Agrestis. A consistent pattern of contextual and textual "coincidences" combine to reinforce their provenance. The notion that these poems merely reflect several dozen "coincidental" links to Burns is surely now far more fantastic and ridiculous than the rational conclusion, that they are, beyond reasonable doubt, from the bard.

A5. The Scotian Muse: An Elegy

The Muse unwilling leaves the sacred shore,
Where every virtue held its peaceful reign -
Hangs with regret on scenes she lov'd before;
The last sad wand'rer from the pensive plain.

She views where once the Sons of Freedom stray'd
Whose hard misfortunes claim the sigh sincere:
She saw fair Genius fly his native shade,
And pour'd the parting tribute of a tear.

But why, sweet maid, so fondly dost thou cling
To rugged rocks, where no soft verdure grows,
While climes more grateful court the tuneful string,
And point to vales of pleasure and repose?

Haply thou lov'st to soothe the afflicting smart
That tears the breast, by misery doom'd to mourn;
To gild the gloom around the victim's heart;
Or bend with pity o'er the partiot's urn.

Or haply, where beneath the iron hand
Of stern Oppression, youth's fair flow'rets fade,
Kindly, with Sympathy's endearing band,
And bright ey'd Hope, thou cheer'st the dungeon's shade.

For him, who warm'd by Freedom's genial fire,
With soul unfetter'd, drags the despot's chain,
Perhaps thy hand attunes the living lyre
To soothe his woes by music's magic strain.

And thou, gay Fancy, bless his languid hours!
Each flattering phantom let thy care bestow;
To strew his lonely path with fairy flowers,
And pluck the noxious nettles as they grow.

Say (and, ye Powers of Truth, accordant join!)
"The time will come - that fate has fix'd the doom -
"The friends of suffering virtue shall combine,
"And hurl each blood-stained Despot to the tomb!"

Signed Lysander.

Where the Scottish Muse Immortal Lives

The Scotian Muse was published on October 1st 1793 in *The Edinburgh Gazetteer*, a few weeks after the second *Ghost of Bruce*. It is a stunning poem of the highest literary quality and would fit within the genre of Burns's laments with ease were it not for the fiery radical rage of the final stanza, which some readers might find repugnant. It is almost certain the tone of the last stanza will prove to be a stumbling block in the poem being authenticated, given the ambience of anti-radicalism evident in the work of some modern writers. Whatever reactions are drawn by the poem, it is a very strong contender to be from the pen of the bard. In the first 12 lines of the poem there is an astonishing density of key Burnsian words, used more than 20 times by the poet - 31 in total. In the final 12 lines of the poem there are also 31 such keywords. This is significant because few known radical works score more than 18 such words in a 12 line block of poetry.

The subject of the lament is the transportation of Muir and Palmer to Botany bay for their political activities. The laden overtone of the poem is one which depicts the spirit of freedom departing Scotland, in sorrow, with the exiles.

The first line finds an echo with "And leave auld Scotia's shore" *from Will Ye Go to the Indies, My Mary*. Over ninety lines of poetry from Burns begin with the word "Where". One poignant example, in the mould of *The Scotian Muse*, is "Where haply, Pity strays forlorn" from *Elegy of Captain Matthew Henderson*. The phrase "the last sad" is used exactly in *Poor Mailie's Elegy*, and in *A Dedication to Gavin Hamilton*, "The last, sad, mournful rites bestow". The tone of the poem is very similar to *On the Death of Lord President Dundas*, "Sad to your sympathetic glooms I fly". It also has the distinctive ring of Burns's works *Elegy On the Death of Sir James Hunter-Blair*, written in the same meter as *The Scotian Muse*, and *Sonnet on the Death of Robert Riddel of Glenriddel.*

In the second stanza the description "Sons of Freedom" is strongly echoed in *The Tree of Liberty*, "For Freedom, standing by the tree, / Her sons did loudly ca', man" and is synonymous with "Sons of Liberty" from the *Washington Ode*. The line "She saw fair Genius fly his native shade" is similar to "I saw fair Freedom's blossoms richly blow" from *On the Death of Sir James Hunter-Blair*. In fact there are lines from the *Elegy* on Hunter-Blair which could fall into the poem with ease as though written on the same subject, such as, "Her form majestic droop'd in pensive woe". Both "native" and "shade" are used by Burns in many different contexts. The word "native" is employed to describe "native skies", "native air", "native shore", "native plain", "native land" and "native sons". The line "And pour'd the parting tribute of a tear" finds its echo in "The tearful tribute" and "This humble tribute, with a tear, he gives" from *Lines to Sir John Whitefoord* and *Inscription for the Headstone of Ferguson the Poet*. A further echo similar to stanza 4's "the patriot's urn" is found in the bard's Inscription to Ferguson, "No storied Urn nor animated bust". Thus, in language, tone and imagery, the first stanzas fit the lexical pattern of Burns's elegiac poetry like a perfect template.

Stanzas 3, 4, and 5 also reveal many echoes from Burns. The phrase "gild the gloom" is seen exactly in Burns's *The Lament* which closes "And not a wish to gild the gloom". The phrase "rugged rocks" is echoed in *Elegy on the Late Miss Burnet of Monboddo*, "Ye rugged cliffs". The same *Elegy* employs the word "accord", the present tense of "accordant" seen in the final stanza of *The Scotian Muse*. The words "soothe" and "gloom" in stanza 3 are found in Burns's song *And Maun I Still On Menie Doat*, "Thy gloom will soothe my cheerless soul". The phrase "court the tuneful string" is similar to "who court the tuneful Nine", from *Epistle to Robert Graham of Fintry*. The phrase "the iron hand" is found in Burns's *The Days Returns*, while "iron hands" is used in *From Aesopus to Maria*. In *Lines on Ferguson, The Poet*, the line "Beneath the iron grasp of Want and Woe" is very similar to the phrase "the iron hand / Of stern Oppression" from the new Elegy. Moreover, the same phrase is almost matched perfectly in "See stern Oppression's iron grip" from *A Winter Night*, where "grip" obviously implies the use of an "iron hand". The phrase "grim Oppression" is also found in *On the Death of Lord President Dundas*. More interesting is the Miltonic image of "bright-ey'd Hope" in stanza 5, which finds a strong echo in "white-rob'd Peace" from *The Brigs of Ayr* and "Thou young-ey'd Spring, gay in the verdant stole" in *Sonnet on the Death of Robert Riddell* - written by Burns a few months after the new *Elegy*. Also, the line "To strew his lonely path with fairy flowers" is similar to "And strew'd the lea wi' flowers" from *Now Spring Has Clad the Grove in Green*, written after *The Scotian Muse*. Thus far, the imprint of Burns is emphatic.

Throughout the *Elegy* there is a masterly use of Miltonic abstraction, a skill particularly marked in Burns's writing. In fact, there are similarities with poetry from The Della Cruscan *British Album*, which Burns borrowed from Syme in 1793. In *Ode for Mrs Siddons*, Della Crusca wrote "While Sympathy with melting eye / Hangs on thy bosom's fervid sigh" which is very similar to "Sympathies endearing band" in stanza 5 of *The Scotian Muse*. The description "endearing band" is used by Burns in *Epistle to Davie*. The Miltonic descriptions "Stern Oppression" and "bright ey'd Hope" are employed in a more subtle and less cumbersome manner than the parade of abstract Miltonic forces in *The Brigs of Ayr*, where the "Genius of the Stream", "Spring", "Beauty", "Rural Joy", "Summer", "Plenty", "Autumn", "Winter", "Courage", "Benevolence" and "white rob'd Peace" are presented in the final stanza. So, there are subtleties and poetic skills evident in this poem which are employed in a superior manner to several known poems of Burns.

A subtlety of almost relaxed pastoral language deceptively carries the reader through the poem, aided by the gentleness of the feminine Muse, until the final stanza which linguistically jumps a gear to a level of forceful anger which is unexpected, but extremely effective. The forceful radical lines are in quotation marks, as though the author is calling up the forces of "Truth" as part of an incantational chant. There are 12 lines of Burns which begin with the word "Say" and 6 which begin "Ye powers", such as "Ye Powers of Honour, Love and Truth", from *Young Peggy*, and "Ye powers of peace and peaceful song", Nature's Law. The description "The time will come" that despots will get their just deserts is more fustian drama than "it's comin' yet for a' that", from *A Man's A Man*, but the sentiment is similar. The entire tone of the final lines may seem unlike Burns, which is understandable given that such lines could never have been printed under his own name during his lifetime. They do, however, carry the political fortitude of the *Washington Ode* which is stubbornly anti-despot or anti-tyrant.

Conscious that the pool of adjectives and adverbs within the letters of the poet are far richer than those found in his poetry, there are too few words not found in the poetry of Burns to pose a problem to his authorship of *The Scotian Muse*. For example, the word "accordant" is not found, but "accord" is. The word "unfetter'd" is not found, but "fetters" occurs at least 8 times. Nor does the word "phantom" occur in the *Wordfinder*, but "spectre", "ghost", and "ghaist" do. Words such as "blood-stained", "attunes", "languid", "lov'st" and "cling" are all found in Burns. So, there is no language problem, nor discordant phrases or imagery which strike a note out of tune with the writings of the poet. Within the Elegiac genre of Burns's poetry, the new *Elegy* shuffles into place neatly as a sister poem. Its dramatic burst of high-flown radical fury to close, may also be a stepping stone towards the strident, forceful *Washington Ode*, which appears to exist in fresh air when considered among the few democratic works which survived.

In the pen-name "Lysander", there is little to be found to fix the poem to Burns, although the ring of the name is very similar to "Sylvander", his pen-name for correspondence with Mrs McElhose, Lysander was, of course, one of the lovers in Shakespeare's *A Midsummer Night's Dream*. Overall, the rich continuity of echoes from known Burns works throughout *The Scotian Muse* point seriously to the strong possibility of his authorship. The Elegies of Burns were not a dominant feature of his published works and consequently imitation can be ruled out.

If there is a chance the poem is by a mystery poet X, then the poet, in one burst of creativity managed to outdo many poems by Burns by writing in a style which in some stanzas, surpasses Burns in this type of poem. It seems more likely that Lysander was one of the changing guises of a poet who knew how to "jouk and let the jaw flee o'er" in public, and was a master of pseudonymous poetic form, keen to stay "independent" in his radical views. With one eye fixed on the reality that Burns penned the cage-rattling *Washington Ode* in mid-1794, this poem, especially with its fiery close, appears to be his work. In a detailed search of all the published poetry of the period, there is no sign of another poet, other than Burns, who published work of this quality and merit. Thus, the stylistic evidence points quite convincingly to Burns as the only possible author of the new *Elegy*.

A6. New Song, Or a Wet Day at Walmer Castle

O! Willy is a wanton wag,
The blythest lad that ere I saw
And has so well the gift of *gab*,
He makes John Bull his purse-strings draw.
He can armies raise and navies,
He can venture on a war;
Men and money how he levies -
His like is neither near nor far.

For *Catskins* when he went to fight,
Of insults offer'd loud did bawl,
And honest John, who thought him right,
At last agreed to pay for all.
But Willy then was in a passion,
Swore he'd give John, *Nootke Sound*;
Yet by his fam'd negotiation
John got ne'er an inch of ground.

With Russia then he would be fighting,
For Aczakow, to please the Turks;
But John not much in war delighting,
Fox soon exposed his humbug works.
For Willy's plans are always droll,
Nor saw he Poland in his map;
All Liberty from Pole to Pole,
He threw in Kate's voracious lap.

And now he's gone to war with France,
Where men and money he must send:
In short he leads John such a dance,
That God knows when his wars may end.
From East to West, from South to North,
O'er Europe all the sword he'll draw,
And not content, he'll still hold forth,
And quarrel with America.

As he can drink, and not be drunk,
As he can fight, and not be slain,
As he can speak and strike the trunk,
That never dar'd to strike again;
Then what cares he for thousands lost,
Or what cares he for thousands slain,
What cares he what wars may cost,
For Widows tears, or Mother's pain!

And so for Sport he's gone to Dover,
With D——, R———, and I.————,
Tho' bad at dashing into cover,
They say he can do nothing wrong.
And they're a set of wanton wags,
The blythest lads that e'er we saw;
While o'er their bottle Harry brags,
That honest John must pay for a'.

Duncan Davison *as an Anti-War Song.*

New Song or a *Wet Day at Walmer Castle* was published in the *Gazetteer* of
15th October 1703. It is a biting satirical attack on "Willy", William
Pitt and how he and "Harry", Henry Dundas, have conned the British people - symbolised as John Bull - to raise taxes in order that
Britain can fight the French. The comic-satire exaggerates the personal and boisterous cunning of senior politicians in their glory hunting campaign in the name of "John Bull". The theme of this witty
song is the expediency an unprincipled, corrupt government and
their exploits in conning the public. Such critical sentiments are not
difficult to find among the letters of Burns during this period. So,
the overall thrust of the song is certainly in the Burnsian mould.

The first two lines of the song are taken from the song, *Willie Was a
Wanton Wag*, song 137, in Johnson's Scots Musical Museum of 1788:
"Willie was a wanton wag, / The blythest lad that e'er I saw...". Composed by a Mr Walkinshaw, this quaint song is an innocuous, weak,
mediocre piece, clumsily out of meter, with no political nuances. It
contains several regional Scots dialect words never used by Burns.
Also, it does not possess the "sprinkling" of English words employed

in the *New Song* - a distinctive feature evident in many auld Scots songs improved by Burns. This process of "sprinkling" English words through old songs was mentioned by Burns to George Thomson, almost as though the poet was offering him a menu of stylistics to chose from. The *New Song*, possibly based on the same tune as Walkinshaw's old song, is a more mature, radical song. The mysterious Mr Walkinshaw, who either submitted, or composed the old song, cannot be traced as a writer of any work after 1788. He can, therefore, be ruled out as the author of the *New Song*. The original and oldest song of the name *Willie was A Wanton Wag* was composed by William Hamilton in the early 18th century which Burns was also familiar with. (CL 588).

In stanza 3, the mention of "Kate", is a reference to Catherine, Empress of Russia. Burns had mocked her notorious immorality in the bawdy song *Why Should Na Poor Folk Mowe*, verse 5: "Auld Kate laid her claws on poor Stanislaus, / And Poland has bent like a bow:" Only Burns, in the 1790's, can be found to mention Catherine, as "*Kate*", using the standard Scottish derivative of Catherine. There is little possibility any other writer could have copied or imitated Burns manner in *Why Should Na Poor Folk Mowe*, since it was not a known Burns song in 1793. Although it was written a few months prior to the *New Song*, it did not see publication until the start of the 19th century. So, if this textual overlap is not mere coincidence, then only Burns could have written the *New Song*.

Stanza 5 contains 2 lines which are almost identical to the Burns' song, *Duncan Davison*. In fact, the same 8 line stanza and 8 syllable lines indicate the *New Song*, may have been written to the same tune, the air *Duncan Davison* or the air *Willie Was a Wanton Wag*. Verse 3, lines 5-8 of the song *Duncan Davison*, reads -

> A man may drink, and no be drunk;
> A man may fight, and no be slain;
> A man may kiss a bonie lass,
> And ay be welcome back again!

The New Song reads -

> As he can drink, and not be drunk,
> As he can fight, and not be slain,
> As he can speak and strike the trunk,
> That never dar'd to strike again;.

This overlap reveals a strong similarity between the two songs. The probability both songs were composed by two different authors independent of each other would make the textual overlap pure fluke. Such a remarkable phenomenon is surely outwith the bounds of chance. The connection - if they are from different authors - could be explained by the possibility the lines in the *New Song* were copied from Burns' song *Duncan Davison*, written in 1788, (see no. 202, p.391, Vol. 1, Kinsley). Any imitation of Burns' song could not have been deliberate, if it occurred at all, given that the song was published without the poet's name and merely signed "Z" - the letter used by Burns for songs he partly modified.

During his border tour Burns had collected an old bawdy song and cleaned it up to make *Duncan Davison*. Of all the songs to mimic or adapt a phrase from, *Duncan Davison* must rank as one of the most unlikely pieces to mimic. It is not one of Burns' best songs. The person most likely to throw into a new song several lines so similar to one in a 1788 songbook, was Burns himself. It is widely known he was heavily engaged in re-working songs from the *Orpheus Caledonius* and Ramsay's *Tea-Table Miscellany* and knew every edition of Johnson's *Scots Musical Museum*. So, as the main Scots writer polishing up old songs during the 1790's, there can be little doubt Burns, having already re-vamped *Duncan Davison*, was the most likely person to adapt old, familiar lines he had already written. There was also the safety of knowing, during the time of sedition laws, the old song was composed by someone called Z. The chance the *New Song* would be traced back to him was extremely remote.

The final 4 lines in stanza 5 criticise the callousness of Willy Pitt and ring strongly of another Burns song, *Logan Braes*. The same strong language mourning the deaths caused by war and "window's tears" is used in both songs. While there is little overlap in exact word usage with *Logan Braes*, the subject, sentiment and tone are the same: verse 4 -

O wae upon you, Men o' State,
That brethern rouse in deadly hate!
As ye make mony a fond heart mourn,
Sae may it on your heads return!
How can your flinty hearts enjoy
The widow's tears, the orphan's cry:
But soon may Peace bring happy days
And Willie, hame to Logan Braes.

This is the final verse which Burns completely re-wrote. The original lyrics are those of a simple love song. What is striking about Burns' final version is its forceful anti-war posture, which is the theme of *New Song*. In the *New Song*, the same posture is adopted:

Then what cares he for thousands lost,
Or what cares he for thousands slain,
What cares he what wars may cost,
For Widows tears, or Mother's pain!

The significance of the manner in which Burns re-wrote *Logan Water* with its political overtones in the final verse indicate that even on his hobbyhorse of re-writing songs, his strongly felt political views could not be suppressed - they come bursting through. *Logan Braes* was composed and sent to George Thomson in June, 1793 and given the seditious tone of the final verse, it was unwise of Burns to trust Thomson with the song, unless he had planned to publish the song marked with a "B" or "R" to keep his name anonymous as he had done with several songs sent to Johnson. It was not published until after the *New Song* appeared in *The Edinburgh Gazetteer*. So, the overall sentiment, tone and forceful language of the *New Song* are in perfect harmony with the views of the poet at this period.

Quite strikingly, stanza 5, displays so many textual overlaps, nuances and echoes from Burns's writings, that from considering it alone, the case for his authorship is very strong. There is hardly a known Burns song which can stand such close comparison to his other songs, as the *New Song* does in stanza 5. Moreover, imitation of Burns can be ruled out on the basis that textual overlaps occur in two works which the poet had yet to see published. Imitators, of course, would have been restricted to viewing Burns as the "heaven taught ploughman" and had a very narrow, limited perspective on the songs he was writing and re-working.

The final verse mentions 3 names which were dashed out and difficult to guess from the original, who have gone to Dover with Willie Pitt to celebrate the naiveté of the public in handing over their money to the "*set of wanton wags*", (in Scots) or *parcel of rogues* (in English), ruling the nation. The final scene is of "Harry", Henry Dundas, boasting in his boisterous manner, that the public will pay for everything.

In sum, the song is certainly in the style of Burns although it does not display great flashes of genius so often expected from the bard, but it is more than comparable with many of his songs and contains too many consistent textual overlaps and actual lines from Burns' known songs for the case of his authorship not to be very strong indeed. It was an overtly seditious work in 1793, but is now, with hindsight, only mild satirical wit. Having already shown the bard was still writing radical effusions after early January 1793 and considered other poetic voices from the period - who composed nothing in this manner - the logical conclusion is that its author was Burns. His wit and satirical mockery are evident throughout the song.

A7. Lines on Ambition

As Caesar once period's the warlike page,
    Frought with the acts of Macedonia's Chief,
Discordant passions in his bosom rage,
    And sudden tears declare his inward grief.
And when his anxious friends, who round him stood,
    Ask'd, what disturb'd the quiet of his breast -
While yet his eyes distill'd a briny flood,
    The future tyrant thus his cares express'd -
"[unreadable] my years attain'd,
    His triumphs round the earth's wide orb were spread;
And [unreadable] seat the hero gain'd,
    And Conquest twin'd her laurels round his head.
While I remain unnotic'd and unknown,
    A novice yet among the sons of Fame;
Where are the trophies I can call my own?
    What spoils of victory can Caesar claim?"
Thus Julius, burning with Ambition's fire,
    At length; thro' Roman blood, to empire rose -
But henceforth may that wretch accurs'd expire,
    Whose glory on his country's ruin grows.
May fortune always their endeavours bless,
    Who struggle to defend their country's cause,
May victory crown their labours with success,
    Who fight for Freedom, and for Patriot Laws.
But those who dare a people's rights invade,
    Who millions, for dominion would enslave;
May all their toils with infamy be paid,
    Not tears - but *curses* visit them to the grave.
In deep oblivion may their acts be hid,
    That none their despot victories may lead;
As Greece her sons, to sound his name forbid,
    Who, to be known, perform'd a villain's deed.

A Briton.

The last two lines refer to Erestrates, who, to perpetuate his name, set fire to the temple of Diana - to Esphus.

A Briton Revisited

The first pointer to suggest *Lines on Ambition,* published in *The Edinburgh Gazetteer,* December 1793, may have been written by Burns is the pseudonym, A. Briton. In 1788, in a letter published in the *Edinburgh Evening Courant,* Robert Burns first used the pseudonym A. Briton. When Burns enclosed a copy of the letter signed "A. Briton" to Mrs Dunlop, he told her it was *for her eyes only.* (CL 290) It was not widely known during Burns's lifetime that he had been the author of the letter in the *Courant* nor that he was "A. Briton". If no other writer employed such a pen-name - and there is no evidence to suggest any other author did - then it follows, Burns wrote *Lines On Ambition.* However, the poem itself must stand up to rigorous scrutiny in comparison to the bard's works before any certainty of provenance can be established.

Was the pen-name "A Briton" common during the 1790's? No evidence supports such a view. From extensive reading of British newspapers during the period 1788-1798, there are only three examples of the pen-name "A Briton". The first was by Burns in his 1788 letter, then it appears with *Lines on Ambition* 5 years later, in *The Edinburgh Gazetteer.* Then, 2 years after the publication of *Lines on Ambition,* the pen-name re-surfaces in *The Morning Chronicle,* during late 1795, a newspaper Burns promised to send occasional poems. The example from *The Morning Chronicle,* a song entitled *The Cob Web,* is also being attributed to Burns on contextual and stylistic evidence. A detailed scan of newspapers after the death of Burns reveals no further examples of A. Briton. It is surely a significant coincidence that a pen-name used by the poet can be found on only two further occasions during his lifetime, then disappears with his death. Beyond doubt, *Lines On Ambition,* based on the pen-name alone, merits serious consideration as a lost work of the bard. The discovery of the poems signed A. Briton is surely an indication that the newspapers of the period have not been researched in detail by modern Burns scholars. No serious scholar of Burns could by-pass such poetry without close scrutiny, knowing that the bard had employed this known pen-name. So, there can be little doubt that this poem is new to the 20th century.

The first impression of the poem is that it is set out in even ten syllable rhymes throughout. The control of language is indicative of a poet who has confidence in their skill. The poem, particularly near the end, is of considerable quality. Regrettably, several words near the start of the poem are illegible due to the age of the faded newspaper.

The poem is strikingly similar to four lines written by Burns during 1793. In *Lines on Ambition*, the lines which refer to "ruin" of the country by political ambition bear a striking resemblance in form, tone and sentiment to lines penned by Burns in June 1793 in *The British Album*, a collection of verse edited by Robert Merry (known under the pen-name of Della Crusca):

> Perish their names, however great or brave,
> Who in the DESPOT'S cursed errands bleed!
> Who but for FREEDOM fills a hero's grave,
> Fame with a seraph-pen, record the glorious deed!

A close comparison reveals the similarity of "Perish" and "expire" and "accurs'd" and "cursed". The praise to be heaped upon those who "fight for Freedom, and for Patriot laws" in *Lines on Ambition* is also echoed in "Who but for FREEDOM fills a hero's grave, / Fame with a seraph-pen, record the glorious deed!". These lines are accepted to the canon by Kinsley, (no 412C). These accepted lines reinforce the A. Briton pen-name evidence and make the bard's authorship almost undeniable.

However, MacKay comments that the four lines accepted by Kinsley to the canon, have not "so far been admitted to the canon" in his *Wordfinder* Appendix B, number 92. This is clearly a serious error since Kinsley accepted the lines as authentic. The lines are of course, political, so controversy is to be expected. MacKay provides no evidence or authority to support their rejection. A reading of various Burns journals from 1968 onward (the publication date of Kinsley) reveal no evidence to support MacKay's rejection or accidental omission. The very fact that he says that the lines have never been admitted to the canon is astonishing, given Kinsley's acceptance. They are accepted here on the authority of Kinsley, a Professor of literature. Moreover, there is no evidence to doubt their authenticity, merely a question mark over the sloppy omission of the biographer.

The lines by Burns in the Della Cruscan *The British Album* are not only stunningly similar to *Lines on Ambition*, they could easily be slotted in as part of the poem near its end. The only problem with doing so is that one line known to be by Burns exceeds the ten syllables found in the new poem. The four lines accepted to the canon by Kinsley are not so much a seamless dress to *Lines on Ambition*; they are, though, very similar and are effectively the same strong radical brew from the same vessel. It is highly probable that the origin of *Lines on Ambition* are the four lines by Burns in the Della Cruscan *The British Album*.

Lines on Ambition is a broadside attack on the opponents of the pro-democracy camp. The comparison of contemporary political figures to Caesar does not name specific individuals, but is loaded with general implication. The political upheaval in Caesar's Rome may have been superficially similar to the early 1790's and the contrast probably influenced "A. Briton" in December, 1793. For instance, in Shakespeare's *Julius Caesar*, in Scene 1, Act 3, after the death of Caesar, Cassius declares "...cry out 'Liberty, freedom, and enfranchisement'." These were the all important do-or-die words of the 1793-4 period. Brutus, contemplating the death of Caesar, pronounced "... ambition's debt is paid" and in Scene 2, recalled "... but as he was ambitious, I slew him ...death for his ambition. Who is here so base, that would be a bondsman?" (A Scottish translation of the last line might read - *Wha sae base as be a slave*..from *Scots Wha Hae*) Of course, many intellectuals and poets of the period would have read Shakespeare, so no exclusive link can be made to Burns from Shakespeare; although only radicals would have identified with the moral character of Brutus and viewed Caesar as a despot or tyrant. It is certain that the author of *Lines on Ambition* is a historically aware poet who was a fan of Shakespeare. So far, this profile includes Burns.

The meaning of "ambition" in *Lines on Ambition* is a narrow definition, focused mainly on politicians in public office. It is similarly found in the poet's *A Winter Night,* to describe the personal abuse of power by statesmen. The poet believed that many social inequalities were man-made, not accidental or the product of nature. The same point is made in *Man Was Made to Mourn*. In *A Winter Night*, stanza 8, the use of Miltonic abstraction is striking:

> See stern Oppression's iron grip,
>   Or mad Ambition's gory hand,
> Sending, like bloodhounds from the slip,
>   Woe, Want, and Murder o'er a land!

The ring of "mad Ambition's gory hand" reads as though it could easily have come from *Lines on Ambition* - Caesar's glory was gained "thro' Roman blood". The narrow meaning of the word "ambition" may have been common among the educated culture at this time, but the number of radical poets in December 1793 were few. The Burnsian image of "ambition" and its "gory hand" from *A Winter Night* finds strong echoes in *Lines on Ambition*.

When *Lines on Ambition* was published, many radicals had been imprisoned for sedition, or like Muir and Palmer, waited to sail to Botany bay, while their followers were largely neutralized. In such a culture of oppression, it took courage to stay true to the principles of the reform movement. Colonel Dalrymple was struck off the army list. Lord Daer gave up the Presidency of the Edinburgh Friends of the People. Many radicals were driven to underground activity. Dundas managed Britain's war effort and held almost absolute power in Scotland. It is well documented that Burns was not enamored by Dundas and would have been very likely to see him as an ambitious Scottish equivalent to Caesar. This point is valid if we consider the allusions of Burns to the Roman period which flowed naturally and extempore in his epigrams. In a local context, Burns lashed the feudal Lord Galloway as though his end was nigh -

> Bright ran thy line, O Galloway,
> Thro' many a far-fam'd sire:
> So ran the far-fam'd Roman way,
> So ended in a mire.

As an extempore flash of Burns's satirical wit, the epigram illustrates that the poet did compare what he considered to be the impending fate of the Pitt government with the fall of Rome. Rome fell through slavery, injustice and corruption; Britain, according to Burns, was on the slope of a sliding, venal age, to use the language of Thomson's classic poem *Winter*. The only reference in Burns to Caesar is his description of political in-fighting for ambition and glory in his extraordinary Miltonic *Election Ballad Addressed to Graham of Fintry*, stanza 10, "Heroes in Caeserian fight". So, contrasting his own time with Imperial Rome and mentioning Caesar are not entirely alien to the poet's writings.

Even when under the inquisitorial eye of the Excise the poet dared to describe the yawning gap between the principles of the British Constitution and the corrupt practice of politicians. Political corruption or the abuse of power in public office for self interest was viewed by the indignant Burns as an outrage to virtue, reason and law, which he believed every person of intellect should wish to see amended, as he indicated to Fintry and developed in his letter to Erskine of Mar in April 1793. In conversation with Chambers, Syme reminisced that the bard's indignant outbursts on the subject of the abuse of power by political leaders were extraordinary, that his eyes "glowed like burning coals". Even taken as a wild exaggeration, this personal testimony reveals the kindled passions of the poet on the subject of politics. The poet, therefore, clearly possessed the radical personality and motive to write the new poem.

It is known that the poet read Robert De Lohme's *The British Constitution* during 1793. De Lohme's work argues that the Constitution of 1688 had stripped away monarchical power to prevent tyrannical behaviour by Kings. It further states that there was an almost perfect equilibrium between the powers of the state, the King and the "Executive Power" in Britain which guaranteed freedom and prevented tyranny by parliament. If the "Protector", or political leader, is to abuse the trust of his office through ambition, says De Lohme, the "Protector becomes a tyrant".(p.198-199) The British Constitution, according to De Lohme, did not permit the possibility of one person's "accumulation" of power. He concluded that it was not possible for tyranny to exist in Britain. Moreover, De Lohme praises "the admirable institution" of "the Trial by Jury" (p.182). Contrasted against the realities of 1793, where Martial Law existed and draconian laws were implemented with force, the text reads more like a novel than a book on the Constitution. Burns must have wondered what relevance the theory of De Lohme's work had to the world of 1793. It was the "liberty" of the "subject" which was under attack from the government. This was not meant to be possible. By handing his copy of De Lohme's Constitution to the Dumfries library in September 1793 Burns may have calculated his act would be publicly seen as that of a loyal subject. In reality, he probably felt like throwing it into the river Nith in despair at the gap between the principles of the Constitution and the practice dished out by Dundas and Pitt.

During 1793 the poet also read the poetry of the Della Cruscan's *The British Album* and annotated the 2 volume work with comments. The poets of this radical volume are largely forgotten, but may have given the bard ideas which he developed into poetry. A few lines can be found on the theme of *Lines on Ambition*. For instance, from stanza 6, *Elegy written On The Plain of Fontenoy*, there is, "For thousands ev'ry age in fight to fall.../ And that is Fate, which we Ambition call". More akin to *Lines on Ambition* is Della Crusca's *Ode to Folly*: "Let others court Ambition's smile, / Or pant for Glory's laurel wreath". It cannot be argued that these writers did not influence Burns merely because Henderson and Henley blasted them as a "dreaded shoal" of radicals. Henderson and Henley were high Tories who detested radical poetry as their slight on *The Tree of Liberty* reveals. Thus, it is known Burns was reading poetic work on the theme of *Lines on Ambition* only months before the new poem was published.

The message of the poem is forthright. It argues that statesmen who abuse political power for self-aggrandisement are tyrants or despots. Caesar is cited as the classic historical case. The poem suggests that Caesar's greatness and glory were based on the blood and suffering of those he enslaved. The democratic thrust of the poem is that modern ambitious statesmen of Caesar's ilk should be condemned and their desire for fame turned to infamy. After damning Caesar in the specific, the poem turns to the general context of contemporary "tyrants", by implication Pitt and Dundas, and looks to a future when dictatorial leaders are spurned: "But henceforth may that wretch accurs'd expire, / Whose glory on his country's ruin grows." The context of "ruin" at a national level is found in *Strathallan's Lament*, "Ruin's wheel has driven o'er us". It is also found in *Prologue for Mrs Sutherland*, "Wrenched his dear country from the jaws of ruin". Burns believed Pitt and Dundas were taking Britain down the road to ruin by mid-1793.

Interestingly, the desire to see leaders brought to justice and exposed as tyrants who would ruin their country for fame is expressed in the second *Ghost of Bruce* poem in similar words - "curse", "blast the men", "Who owe their greatness to their Country's ruin!" The strong echoes in language and sentiment from the second *Bruce* poem, published three months before *Lines on Ambition,* suggest they were written by one author. It also makes sense that the bard would have penned and published a few other radical poems before being confident enough to use his old pen-name, A Briton. It is highly probable the pen-name was employed as a signal to a few close friends of the bard that he was back on the scene, despite the fact we only have a record of him telling Mrs Dunlop he was A Briton.

From what is known about Burns' political sentiments at this period, notably his opposition to the war, *Lines On Ambition* fits his sentiments like a glove. There can be little doubt the bard viewed Pitt's government as one led by *tyrants,* as the *Washington Ode* vividly suggests. It therefore would have been entirely in keeping with Burns' views for him to write:

> But those who dare a people's rights invade,
> Who millions, for dominion would enslave;
> May all their toils with infamy be paid,
> Not *tears* - but *curses* visit them to the grave.

Moreover, there are echoes from many Burns' letters in the use of the word "curse". To Peter Hill, Burns wrote "may the wrath and curse of all mankind, haunt and harass" those "who have involved a People in this ruinous business", in reference to the war with France (CL 553). In the same letter, he goes on "...CURSED be he that curseth thee", quoting from Deuteronomy, chapter 28, verse 29. The words quoted from Burns are of the same strong, passionate and indignant language found in *Lines on Ambition.*

Implicit in the radical sentiment of *Lines On Ambition* is the view that statesmen are morally obliged to be honourable and noble, that their actions should be beyond reproach, above corruption; and a bulwark to tyranny. The poem is, therefore, essentially idealist. It's *raison d'etre* is the frustrated desire of idealists down the ages, to see public leaders reflect the public will, without self-interest, for the public good. This ideal is contrasted with the expedient British leadership of 1793 - a sentiment expressed by Burns a few years previous in his pseudonymous letter addressed to William Pitt:

..our Country... (was) sacrificed, without remorse, to the infernal deity of Political Expediency! Not that sound policy, the good of the whole; we fell victims to the wishes of dark Envy and *unprincipled Ambition.* (CL unnumbered: p.510-511).

If these were the views of Burns in 1789, would his sentiments not have been more strident during the political tumult of the 1790's? The letter is an attack on "unprincipled Ambition" in the vein of *Lines on Ambition.*

The new poem is certainly not the work of an uneducated rhyming ploughman who wrote mainly Standard Habbie poetry in Scots vernacular. So, few contemporary readers would have guessed Burns as the author, given their narrow, parochial view of the bard. This, of course, was the objective of employing the style and language used. Modern readers, though, are far more aware that the range of the poet's stylistics are extraordinary and his poetic voices are diverse. This style is one Burns could have easily adopted. It is certain that *Lines on Ambition* cannot be an impersonation of Burns. He was not famed or known for this style of poetry. So, with impersonators out of the way, the evidence for the poet's authorship is enhanced and accumulating.

The description "Macedonia's Chief", referring to Alexander the Great, is echoed in Burns', "Then sat down, in grief, like the Macedon chief", from *Bonie Mary*, verse 3. In the frivolous bawdy song, *Bonie Mary*, the mention of "Macedon chief" is surprising and unexpected. It is interesting that the song was sent to Cleghorn at the end of October, 1793, only two months before the publication of *Lines on Ambition.* Moreover, an uncommon word in poetry of the 1790's, "Discordant", in the line "Discordant passions in his bosom rage" is also found in Burns' work, written less than a month after *Lines on Ambition* saw print. In *To Miss Graham of Fintry*, stanza 2, the poet wrote "Discordant, jar thy bosom-chords among", where "Discordant" and "bosom" form part of one sentence as in *Lines on Ambition.* While "perus'd" was not used by Burns in poetry, "peruse" can be found in *Epistle to James Tennant* and *Sketch - Inscribed to the Right Hon. C.J. Fox.* However, "perus'd" is found in several letters, including a letter to Mrs McElhose. (CL 462) The adjective "warlike" is seen in *When First I Saw*, verse 2, "Did warlike laurels crown my brow" and *Parcel o Rogues*, "Thru many warlike ages". There are over 90 examples where Burns used "tears", many similar to *Lines on Ambition*. The phrase "disturb'd the quiet of his breast" is echoed in *Man Was Made to Mourn*, stanza 10, "Disturb thy youthful breast". There are more than 80 examples of "breast" among the poet's works. The word "briny", uncommon to poetry of the 1790's, is found in *Poor Mailie's Elegy*, stanza 5, "An down the briny pearls rowe", where "pearls" are tears which "flood" in *Lines on Ambition*. The poem does, therefore, reveal distinctive language echoed in Burns's writings around the same period. The first four couplets, thus, clearly bear the imprint of Burns.

The word "henceforth" may seem unlike Burns. However, he used this word in *Epistle to James Smith, The Ordination* and in an epigram *On Mr. James Gracie*, "May he be damned to Hell henceforth". The description of Caesar, pining "unnotic'd and unknown" is echoed in Burns's "obscure, unknown" from *My Father Was A Farmer* and "unnoticed, obscure" in *The Ronalds of the Bennals*. The word "wretch" is found in Burns in more than 30 occasions. In *The Cottar's Saturday Night* the poet describes the glitter of titled pomp as "Disguising oft the wretch of human kind". In *Passion's Cry*, completed just prior to *Lines on Ambition*, the word "expire" also ends a line of poetry in the same way it does in the new poem, "Love grasps his scorpions, stifled they expire". In *The Brigs of Ayr*, the phrase "their country's glory" echoes line 20 of *Lines on Ambition* which refers to "his country's ruin". In line 22, "country's cause" is echoed in *On Glenriddel's Fox Breaking its Chain*, "Quite frantic in his country's cause". The notion of a tyrant's wrongdoing being the foundation of their glory is also found in *On Glenriddel's Fox* "Thought cutting throats was reaping glory". In stanza 5 of the same poem we find classic Rome "her fiat hurl'd / Resistless o'er a bowing world" contrasted with the contemporary "Billy Pitt" bleeding the country with taxation. "Rome" and "Greece" are mentioned in *Scots Prologue for Mrs Sutherland*. Thus, the comparison between ancient Rome and the political leaders of the 1790's is a familiar theme in Burns's poetry. So, the main body of the poem bears the imprint of Burns.

There is also a distinctive use of the word "May" which begins three lines of the new poem in lines 21, 23, and 27; "May fortune always their endeavours bless .../ May victory crown their labours with success /...May all their toils with infamy be paid". There are five such lines which begin "May..." in *Here's A Health Tae Them That's Awa*, one which strongly echoes *Lines on Ambition*, "May liberty meet with success". Also, in the Burns' poem *Lament for the Absence of Creech*, and in *Epistle to John Maxwell*, the word "May" is followed by "fortune", exactly as in line 21 of *Lines on Ambition*. Accordingly, the use of "may", prior to praise or condemnation, is a feature of Burns's poetry.

In the call for "Patriot Laws" and "rights" in the new poem, there is an echo *of The Tree of Liberty*, which calls for "And equal rights and equal laws, / Wad gladden ev'ry isle, man". The words "labours" and "toils" are found throughout the poetry of Burns, particularly in *The Cottar's Saturday Night* and *Epistle to Davie*. The rhyme of "cause" and "laws" is found in Burns's *Birthday Ode for the 31st December 1787*. The word "dominion" is used in *Westlin Winds*, "tyrannic man's dominion". Moreover, the ring and sentiment of the final line "perform'd a villain's deed" is similar to the line from the *Washington Ode* "damned deeds of everlasting shame". Both poems share the same condemnation of tyrants' "deeds" and "everlasting shame" is echoed in the notion that "curses" should "visit them to the grave. / In deep oblivion may their acts be hid". In fact, the entire tone and sentiment of *Lines on Ambition* can be read as a literary stepping stone in the evolution towards the *Washington Ode* which was written six months later.

Simple inductive logic suggests that if Burns could write a powerful democratic Ode in June 1794, he was certainly capable of writing other works of a similar nature after early January 1793. A work like the *Washington Ode* does not just "explode" into existence out of a cultural void: it is a representative snap-shot picture of the poet's radical thoughts in mid-1794 and conveys his view of the British government, the war being fought against France and the grinding of "ruin's wheel" over the virgin-green shoots of democratic hope and the suffocation of the voice of humanity. Of course, the government line was that the radicals were all "evil Jacobins", that the reform movement was insurrectionary, that the National Convention of the Friends of the People which met again in January 1794 was a revolutionary government-in-waiting and that the last thing Britain needed was the pernicious creed of "democracy" and "equality". *Lines on Ambition*, therefore, is almost certainly another lost "democratic" work of Burns.

From a detailed analysis of the words employed in *Lines on Ambition*, there is no cluster of four or five adjectives or adverbs which pose a problem to its authenticity. Most radical works of the time display at least four or more adjectives or adverbs alien to Burns. Works he did not write are relatively easy to spot. Indeed, the striking similarity between the poem and the four lines by Burns written in the Della Cruscan *British Album* during 1793, point to him as author of *Lines on Ambition*. The similarity is astonishing. Given the extent of detailed cross-reference in the poem to the known works of Burns, the lexical similarity in the four known lines by Burns, it is the known pen-name, A Briton, that clinches the argument. In the late 18th century in Scotland the evidence confirms that only one poet used such a pseudonym - Burns. On its own, the pen-name of Burns is not definitive; but, with the mass of stylistic evidence to corroborate the provenance of *Lines on Ambition*, there can be no doubt that the poem is the voice of the bard.

A8. To Messrs Muir, Palmer, Skirving and Margarot

"Among innumerable false - unmov'd,
Unshaken, unseduced, unterrify'd" - Milton

Friends of the Slighted people - ye whose wrongs
From wounded FREEDOM many a tear shall draw
As once she mourn'd when mock'd by venal tongues
Her Sydney fell beneath the form of law.

O had this bosom known poetic fire
Your names, your deeds, should grace my votive songs
For Virtue tought the bard's far-sounding lyre
To lift the PATRIOT from the servile throng.

High o'er the wrecks of time his fame shall live
While proud Oppression wastes her idle rage.
His name on history's column shall revive
And wake the genius of a distant age.

It shines - the dawn of that long promised day
For eager fancy bursts the midnight gloom
The patriot's praise, the grateful nations pay
And tears the trophy from the oppressor's tomb.

Yet what the praise far distant times shall sing
To that calm solace Virtue now bestows.
Round the dire bark She waves her gaurdian wing;
She guides her exiles o'er the trackless snows:
With Joy's gay flowers She decks the sultry wild
And sheds the beam of Hope where Nature never smil'd.

The Wings of Virtue and the Patriot Lyre

To Messrs Muir, Palmer, Skirving and Margarot was printed in the final
issue of the Edinburgh Gazetteer in January 1794. It is a historically
significant poem due to its subject matter, the sedition trials of Scottish radicals in 1793 and early 1794. Thomas Muir was tried in late
August and the Reverend Thomas Fyshe Palmer on September 12th
1793. William Skirving and Maurice Margarot were tried in early January, 1794. Muir and Palmer were sentenced to 14 years and 7 years
transportation respectively, and waited as prisoners on board a ship
ready to sail to Botany Bay in January, 1794. Skirving and Margarot
sailed with them. The trials of these democracy activists caused a
great outcry across Britain due to the severity of the sentences. The
"Sydney" mentioned in line 4, stanza 1, is a reference to the young
advocate Thomas Muir who was compared by his contemporaries to
the great 16th century English writer and statesman, Sir Phillip Sydney. Muir's crime was that he loaned a book to someone, Paine's *The
Rights of Man*.

It is documented that the trial of Muir was one of the key factors
which stirred Burns to write *Scots Wha Hae*. It is certain that Burns
would have watched the events of the sedition trials in January, 1794,
like a hawk. Aware that the judgment on Muir was essentially a farce
of rigged "justice", the bard would have been stunned by the rich
irony of Scotland's most promising young advocate being the first
main casualty of the sedition laws - "Her Sydney fell beneath the
form of law".

This poem may be a work of Burns for many different reasons. The
notion that Burns had stopped writing radical material on 5th January, 1793 has already been examined and shown to be false. Not only
has it been proven he was still in the radical vanguard, albeit covertly, but the poem *Lines on Ambition*, signed A Briton - a poem cer-

tainly by Burns - was published in December 1793 in the same newspaper. These two factors alone, prior to a textual analysis of the poem, open up the realistic possibility Burns wrote *To Messrs Muir, Palmer, Skirving and Margaret.*

The quote from Milton "Among innumerable false - unmov'd, / Unshaken, unseduced, unterrify'd" is significant. It can be read as a tribute to the unbending courage of radicals who stood charged with sedition and argued the justice of their case. It also indicates that the author of the poem believed in the cause of the radicals and was an unflinging supporter of the same ideals. It is interesting that a few months after the trials Burns wrote his most powerful radical poem, the *Irregular Ode for General Washington's Birthday.* It has been described as a Pindaric Ode but it is couched in the same strident language quoted from Milton in the new poem, and encourages radicals to bravery, to "dare the tyrant to his very beard". The noble, radical-minded, independent person idealised in the *Ode* is also a person who was "*unmov'd*" and "unterrify'd" by tyrants:

> Where is Man's godlike form!
> Where is that brow erect and *bold,*
> That eye that can, *unmoved,* behold,
> The wildest rage, the loudest storm,
> That e'er created Fury dared to raise!..
> ...Ye know, and dare maintain, The Royalty of Man.

The *Washington Ode* laments an England which can no longer boast a radical poet like Milton to strike the "patriot lyre" and rouse the "freeborn Briton's soul of fire". In stanza 2 of *To Messrs Muir, Palmer, Skirving and Margaret* the same rhyme of "lyre" and "fire" are employed also to describe the "lyre" of the "Patriot". Of course any poet could have quoted Milton, but of the handful of radical poets still vocal in Scotland in 1794, Burns was most likely to identify with these specific lines as the courageous *Washington Ode* shows.

Overall, the poem displays a strong belief in historical progress. It suggests that future generations will look back and see the wrongs committed on the pro-democracy radicals and will condemn the actions of "proud Oppression". So, even as the transportation sentences were being handed down, the author of the poem is pictured as sitting alone amid "midnight gloom" with almost a prescience of a future day which will "dawn" and historically correct the injustice of the period. The poem does not contain the over-optimistic Millennium spirit of Painite radicals which caused them to believe they were on the threshold of seeing a democracy being created in their lifetime and the end to all monarchy. It docs, however, show an unswerving optimism in the midst of melancholy, that "come it will, for a' that" the radical patriots of humanity would be lauded for their deeds. The penetrating historical awareness of Burns has been documented by Carswell and Crawford, notably in *The Vision* and *When Guilford Good*, but his hopeful sense of progress is best expressed in the last stanza of *A Man's A Man*. The belated historical victory in the poem is salvaged from a contemporary despair by a poet who appears to have almost a sense of their own immortality as a writer. Can it be accepted that all Burns had to write about Muir and Palmer was a comment in *From Aesopus to Maria* about his own fear of sharing the radical's fate? Did the "bard of Caledonia" really have no views on the January 1794 show-trials which transfixed the Scottish nation?

The poem is written in high rhetorical style, one which Burns could have easily employed given his ability to mimic any poetic form or style. The first line refers to the pro-democratic group, the Friends of the People, who have been "slighted". Burns' classic criticism of courtly acolytes, "venal contagion" or "venal bards" is distinctive in the first stanza, with the description "venal tongues". The "wrongs" are described as a national tragedy in the same way Burns wrote of "Stuart's wrongs", in *The Birthday Ode for 31st December 1787*, or "Wrongs injurious to redress" from *Strathallan's Lament*. In the combination of words such as "slighted", "wrongs", "wounded", "mourn'd", "fell" and "Oppression", there is a ring of *On the Death of Lord President Dundas* -

> Pale Scotia's recent wound I may deplore!
> ...Hearing the tidings of the fatal blow,
> She sank, abandon'd to the wildest woe....
> .....Wrongs, injurious, from many a darksome den,
> Now gay in hope, explore the paths of men.
> See from his cavern grim Oppression rise....
> ...To mourn the woes my country must endure:
> That wound degenerate ages cannot cure.

In the elegy to the Lord President, it is an abstract "Justice" which "sank, abandon'd". In the new poem, it is the spokesman of a similar abstract "Freedom", "Sydney" who "fell beneath the form of law". The phrase "From wounded Freedom many a tear shall draw" rings of another Miltonic description written by Burns, "Truth, weeping, tells the mournful tale" from *A Winter Night*. It is an interesting contrast that the battle-ready sense of moral indignation in *Scots Wha Hae*, "Freedom's sword will strongly draw" is turned to a stoical lament in "From wounded Freedom many a tear shall draw". Thus, the first stanza oozes words common to Burns's poetry.

The second stanza appears at first to pose a problem to Burns' authorship. There is an apparently self-deprecating line, uncharacteristic of the bard - "O had this bosom known poetic fire". Superficially, this might suggest a self-effacing poet. Yet, while this language seems unlike Burns, who had great confidence in his poetical skills, there are other examples where he feigned ignorance or implied he had little skill in the art of poetry - in fact his entire role-play as a "Heaven-taught ploughman poet" while in Edinburgh was a self-deprecating mask! In *Epistle to J Lapraik* he wrote "I am nae poet, in a sense/ But just a rhymer, like by chance". In *Epistle to John Goldie* he pretended "For me, my skill's but very sma'". He told Thomson, in the understatement of the century, *A Man's A Man* was "no song". Self-deprecation does, therefore, form part of Burns's characteristic style, whenever he wished to use it.

A reading of the second stanza within its proper cultural and political context in January 1794 makes it clear that the phrase "O had this bosom known poetic fire" refers to censorship and the sedition laws. If the line is read on its own as a sentence, it would appear to be merely self-deprecating. However, there is a moral intonation in the second line in the word *should* "Your names, your deeds, *should* grace my votive songs". The entire stanza suggests that the poet is a writer of songs - "my votive songs" - who would gladly dedicate songs to Muir, Palmer and so on, *if free* to compose and publish such songs. Moreover, the notion the author has little confidence in their poetic skill is dashed by the bold and confident lines "For Virtue taught the bard's far-sounding lyre / To lift the Patriot from the servile throng". This is no minor poet who writes songs; it is a major poet who is a "bard" confident of writing "far-sounding" songs and poetry, who has been taught by "Virtue" - a description almost synonymous with "heaven-taught". There is also a ring of the final stanza of *Verses Writ-*

ten With a Pencil, "Here Poesy might wake her heav'n taught lyre, / And look through Nature with creative fire". In fact, there are strong echoes of *A Vision* where Coila mapped out the role of Burns:

> Some rouse the patriot up to bare
> Corruption's heart;
> Some teach the bard - a darling care -
> The tuneful art.

In addition, Burns used the phrase "poetic fire" in stanza 5, *Nature's Law*, and *in To Robert Graham of Fintry*, he wrote "Till, fled each hope that once his bosom fir'd". Also, the word "bosom" is used in conjunction with "fir'd" in the first line of *Monody: On a Lady Famed for Her Caprice*, "How cold is that bosom which Folly once fir'd!" The word "servile" is prominent in Burns radical works such as *Scots Wha Hae*, "By your sons in servile chains"; and in the *Washington Ode*, "Avaunt! thou caitiff, servile, base". The final rhyme of "song" and "throng" is employed by *Burns in Prologue: Spoken by Mr Woods*, "Poor is the task to please a barb'rous throng; / It needs no Siddon's powers in Southern's song". So, stanza 2 displays a thorough Burnsian imprint.

Stanza 3, 4 and 5 develop the theme of the "patriot" being rescued by the "bard", confident that the wrongs of the age will be made right by the march of progress. Stanza 3 picks up the image from the word "lift" in the last line of stanza 2, and goes on

> High o'er the wrecks of Time his fame shall live,
> While proud Oppression wastes her idle rage.
> His name on history's column shall revive
> And wake the genius of a distant age.

If the line "Her Sydney fell beneath the form of law" from stanza 1 is recalled, stanza 3 displays a similar lexical structure to *Elegy on the Death of Sir James Hunter Blair*.

> My patriot falls, but shall he die unsung,
> While empty greatness saves a worthless name?
> No: every Muse shall join her tuneful tongue,
> And future ages hear his glowing fame.

The intonation and language ring like the *Muir, Palmer* poem. The phrase "While empty greatness" may be different from, but it describes the same type of people as "While proud Oppression". The words "proud Oppression" are echoed, with tone modification in the more robust, *A Winter Night*, "*stern* Oppression" and in *On the Death of Lord President Dundas*, "*grim* Oppression". The softer word "proud" is more appropriate in the elegy to *Muir, Palmer*, et al. The notion of Oppression's "rage", or the rage of tyrants and despots, is found in *Ode to the Departed Regency Bill*, "Deafening din and warring rage" and in the *Washington Ode*, which asks who is brave enough to stand up to "the wildest rage" of tyrants. Moreover, the final line of stanza 3, "And wake the genius of a distant age" strongly echoes *A Vision* "And when the bard, or hoary sage, / Charm or instruct the future age". So, by the end of stanza 3, the similarities between the new poem and known works of the bard hold the possibility of his authorship firm. Thus far, there are no lines, phrases, or specific words which cannot be found echoed in Burns.

The fourth stanza looks forward from the contemporary "gloom" to "the dawn of that long promised day" when the "patriot's praise" is sung by future, more enlightened generations. The words "eager fancy" are found in alternate lines of *To Robert Graham of Fintry* (*A-Z The Complete Wordfinder*, Appendix A, p689). Also, the words "grateful nations" are used exactly in *Prologue: Spoken by Mr Woods* The verb "bursts" is used in a more imaginative, unexpected and creative manner than in *On the Death of Lord President Dundas*, "The gathering floods burst o'er the distant plains". In fact, "bursts" in the context of "eager fancy bursts the midnight gloom" indicates a sudden flash, or picture in the imagination as though the poet has seen into the future and that future makes the present easier to come to terms with. It may have been Burns's whim and fancy, but he did boast on a few occasions that nature's bards like himself were second-sighted. This of course, may have nothing to do with the sudden mental insight into the future indicated by the use of "bursts", but it does partly describe the traits of a poet with a powerful and dramatic imagination akin to Burns's description of how *Scots Wha Hae* came to him in "sudden recollection" and "roused" his "rhyming mania". The alternate rhyme of "gloom" and "tomb" is also found in the political *Ode for the Departed Regency Bill*, "Then next pourtray a dark'ning twilight gloom ../ While proud Ambition to th' untimely tomb". Again, stanza 4 stands up to close comparison with the bard's writing.

The final stanza is astounding. In sixteen words there is one of the most stunning Miltonic images ever painted by a poetic imagination. The Miltonic force of Virtue, the collective embodiment of honour, justice, truth and all that is best in man as a species, is symbolised in Virtue as a giant godly-bird which "waves her guardian wing" around the transportation ship, "the dire bark" as it sails for Australia and Botany bay. She, Virtue, "guides her exiles o'er the trackless snow" and "decks the sultry wild" with "Joys gay flowers" and heaven-like, "sheds the beam of Hope" for Muir, Palmer, Skirving and Margarot. The pictorial image of Virtue flying with the ship partially embraced underneath her giant wing across the sea is breathtaking and worthy of the greatest paintings of Michelangelo or Blake. The poem does not have the action-packed cinematic drama of a *Tam O'Shanter*, but as an elegy this final cinematic stanza makes the poem superior *to On the Death of Lord President Dundas* and better than the best stanzas of *Elegy on the Death of Sir James Hunter-Blair*, which are both in the same style and language. The quality of this last stanza surely lifts the authorship of the poem away from a Kennedy, a Wilson, a Callander, a Dyer or any other known radical poet of the period. If literary critics have assumed political poetry is generally always hidebound doggerel, this poem proves the exception. The last image is worthy of a Burns in his "best manner".

The language of the final stanza is also in the Burnsian mould. In *Elegy on the Death of Sir James Hunter-Blair*, the line "Thro future times to make his virtues last" is akin to the description of the "praise far distant times shall sing". The phrase "far distant times" is echoed in a letter to Mrs Dunlop, 12th January 1795 when Burns wrote that he imagined the time would not be "far distant" when a person could criticise Pitt without being called an enemy of his country. The word "deck" is used in conjuction with "gay" in the song *The Gard'ner Wi His Paidle* and *Dainty Davie*. The description "gay flowers" is found in *Adown Winding Nith*. Eleven poems by Burns have a line which end with the word "bestow" or "bestows". The description that Virtue "sheds the beam of Hope" is similar to "And Virtue's light, that beams beyond the spheres" from *Elegy on The Late Miss Burnet of Monboddo*. In *Verses Written With a Pencil* there is a passage which is echoed in the "wrongs" suffered by the radicals and is composed in the same cadence of lament and "solace":

> Here, to the wrongs of Fate half reconcil'd,
> Misfortune's lighten'd steps might wander wild;
> And Disappointment, in these lonely bounds,
> Fine balm to soothe her bitter rankling wounds;
> Here heart-struck Grief might heav'nward stretch her scan,
> And injur'd Worth forget and pardon man.

The word "sultry" is found in Burns on four occasions. The description "beam of Hope" is echoes the "star of hope" in *Ae Fond Kiss* and "E'en ev'ry ray of Hope destroy'd" from *The Lament*. The final simile describing how "*Nature* never *smil'd*" upon the exiles finds its echo in "For *Nature smiles* as sweet, I wean" in *Behold, How Green The Groves*, also composed in 1794. In fact, if the variegated uses of the word "Nature" are looked at closely in Burns, the importance of "Nature" as a Miltonic force is central to his poetry. He considered himself a bard of "Nature's making" and wrote of nature's "wildest grace", "closed e'e", of nature "list'ning", that Nature "swears, the lovely dears", "honest Nature", "Nature's Law", "laughing Nature", "kind Nature" and so on. Clearly, the final stanza ends in perfect harmony with the ring of the Burnsian tuning fork.

There are no words alien to the bard throughout the poem, which would be expected in a poem he did not write. Research has shown that while many poems possess couplets or larger sections which ring of Burnsian language, there are normally several words or even two or three phrases which stick out as extremely unlike Burns. The consistent and clear comparison between the new poem and the language of Burns is continuous throughout the poem.

So, from a detailed statistical and textual analysis, there are no obvious words or phrases unlike Burns. The poet fits perfectly with Burns's strong calling as a poet and his radical idealism. The poem falls into place as part of his elegiac genre with *On the Death of Lord President Dundas* and *Elegy on the Death of Sir James Hunter Blair*. It reveals strong echoes from *A Vision*. The highly skilled use of language and the astonishing high Miltonic allusion found in the poem, coupled with the introductory quote from Milton all coalesce to suggest Burns as the most likely author. We know he continued to write radical material after January 1793. Thus, the attribution of *To Mssrs Muir, Palmer, Skirving and Margarot* is made with confidence that it was written by Burns. It is somewhat ironic that during the trial of Margarot, an architect called Robert Burns (no relation) was on the jury. In fact, aware of the poet's great sense of historical progress and his national role as the bard of Caledonia, it would be surprising if he had nothing to say in the poet's coin on the subject of the trials of early 1794.

Chapter 7

Poetry from The Morning Chronicle 1794-6

This section contains only five poems being attributed to Burns from *The Morning Chronicle* from the period 1794-1796. The contextual evidence outlined in *The Promise* illustrates the poet's offer to send writings to the newspaper after mid-March 1794. Conscious of intrusion by spies and informers, Burns was not going to put his name to any controversial work published by Mr. Perry. During these years there are many epigrams published in the newspaper, some signed "J.R." and "Thomas Fool". It is quite possible that many of the other epigrams are by Burns, but they have not been collected. Also, it is probable that there are works of the poet still to be found in the newspaper which were missed during this research and may yet be spotted and retrieved by other scholars. It would be unlikely that over a period of two years, Burns would only send five poems. If the argument of *The Lost Poems* is confirmed in the case of *The Edinburgh Gazetteer*, that around ten works were published by Burns, in a period of just over one year, then it would be likely that he would have seen a similar number of poems printed in the *Chronicle*.

Additional poems from the *Chronicle* of this period are printed under category B, as possible works of Burns. There is insufficient evidence to include them in category A . Computer-driven stylometrics may help to prove that a few of the poems from the *Chronicle*, listed in the B category, are authentic. The fact that the editor of the *Chronicle* wanted Burns to send him poetry is indisputable. The fact that the poet asked for a safe channel and address to send material is also indisputable. It is known that the poet published at least two songs and one poem in the *Chronicle* during 1794 and then an epigram in 1795. Moreover, the fact that the *Chronicle* was the first place to publish *Scots Wha Hae* and *A Man's A Man* with Burns named as the author, is also indisputable. The most important factor is that Burns was still writing radical works during the 1794-1796 period. Everything points to the likelihood that the *Chonicle* received and published material from Burns which has been unrecorded for two centuries because the poetry was published anonymously and the archives have never been scanned for potential "lost" poems.

A9. The Ewe Bughts

"Will you go to the Ewe-bughts, Marian,
      "And wear in the sheep wi' me?
"The mavis sings sweetly, my Marian,
      "But not sae sweetly as thee".
These aft were the words of my Sandy,
      As we met in the how of the glen,
But nae mair shall I meet wi' my Sandy,
      For Sandy to Flanders is gane.

How can the trumpets loud clarion
      Thus take a' the shepherds afar?
Oh could na' the ewe-bughts and Marian
      Please mair than the horrors of war?
But, oh, tis the fault o' them aw, Sirs,
      In search of gowd and of fame,
The lads daily wander awa, Sirs,
      And leave their poor lassies at hame.

Not a plough in the land has been ganging,
      The owsen hae stood in the sta',
Nae flails in our barns hae been banging,
      For mair than this towmond or twa.
Ilka Laird in the Highlands is rueing,
      That he drove his poor tenants away,
For naething is seen here but ruin,
      As the haughs are aw laying in lay.

There's gowd in the garters of Sandy,
      And silk in his blue-bonnet lug,
And I'm not a kaerd nor a randy,
      Nor a lass without blanket or rug;
Then why should he fight sae for riches,

Or seek for a sodger's degree,
Or fling by his kilt for the breeches,
And leave the dear Ewe-Bughts and me?

New Lyrics for An Old Tune

Ewe Bughts Marian was published in the London *Morning Chronicle* in July 1794, around two months after the appearance of *Scots Wha Hae*. It was unsigned. It is in the Burnsian mould of anti-war songs which include *Logan Braes, The Soldier's Return* and *On the Seas and Far Away* composed in 1793 and 1794. (The first publication of *The Soldier's Return* was September 26th 1793, in *The Glasgow Courier*, a fact not included in either Kinsley or MacKay. Kinsley's view that Thomson anglicized "sodger" to "soldier" is probably incorrect, since the *Courier* version reads "soldier" and would have been sent by Burns). *The Soldier's Return* was published under the poet's name and although it is not overtly anti-war, such as *Logan Braes*, it does imply an end to the hostilities with France, as in the first lines - "When wild war's deadly blast is blawn, / And gentle Peace returning". So, knowing the anti-war posture of the poet, his promise to send material to the *Chronicle* and the distinctive Scots ring to the song, the bard is a very likely author for this excellent song. In 1794 and 1795 there is no evidence of another Scottish songwriter/poet sending material to the London newspaper.

The story of *Ewe Bughts Marian* is the lament of a country girl, whose shepherd lover has wooed her with devotion "The mavis sings sweetly, my Marian, / But not sae sweetly as thee", but still he goes off to war "In search of gowd and of fame". She is perplexed that love's ties can seem to be so strong in the promises he has made, but the "trumpets loud clarion" and "the horrors of war" have tempted him to search for "fame". She moans that he has riches and still he goes off to fight in Flanders. In fact, the anti-war message of the song is that the war has taken so many shepherds and labourers from country farms that the countryside is suffering:

Not a plough in the land has been ganging,
The owsen hae stood in the sta',
Nae flails in our barns hae been banging,
For mair than this towmond or twa.

A "towmond" means a year's duration. So, the song refers to the time the war against France has been going on, almost one and a half years by July 1794. The line "For mair than this towmond or twa" is almost straight from the early Burns song *The Ronnals of the Bennals*, which reads, "For mair than a towmond or twa, man". Thus, in the romance of loss there is a strong echo of a known Burns song.

The poet first composed lines to an old tune called *Ewe Bughts Marion* with his song *Will Ye Go To the Indies, My Mary*, which was published in 1792; (Vol. II, number 387, Kinsley). He sent a song of the name *Ewe Bughts Marion* (Marion, not Marian) to James Johnson in 1795, commenting that it was "quite different" from the version previously published by Johnson (CL 684). Whether the poet meant new music or new lyrics is uncertain. No song of the name *Ewe-Bughts Marion* has ever been credited to Burns. It would seem strange for Burns to send the music to Johnson for *Will Ye Go To the Indies, My Mary* in 1792, then forward him a new set of music with the same title, *Ewe Bughts Marion*, without furnishing him with new lyrics. Is it possible that Johnson did receive these lyrics and simply never published them due to the anti-war theme? One thing is certain, *Will Ye Go to The Indies, My Mary* is proof that Burns was familiar with the tune called *Ewe-Bughts Marion*.

Burns knew of two old songs based on the melody, *Ewe Bughts Marion*. He was aware of the version collected by Allan Ramsay and an older version from the North of Scotland, " am not sure if this old and charming air be of the South, as it is commonly said, or of the North of Scotland. There is a song apparently as ancient as "Ewe - bughts, Marion," which sings to the same time, and is evidently of the North." The old North of Scotland lyrics bear no comparison to the new words found in the *Chronicle* -

The Lord o' Gordon had three dochters,
        Mary, Marget, and Jean,
They wad na stay at bonie Castle Gordon,
        But awa tae Aberdeen.

The second version known to Burns is the version found by Ramsay and is set in four stanzas of eight-lines:

> Will ye go to the ewe-bughts, Marion,
>   And wear in the sheep wi' me?
> The sun shines sweet, my Marion,
>   But nae half sae sweet as thee.
> O Marion's a bonnie lass,
>   And the blyth blinks in her e'e;
> And fain wad I marry Marion,
>   Gin Marion wad marry me.
>
> There's gowd in your garters, Marion,
>   And silk on your white hause-bane;
> Fu' fain wad I kiss my Marion,
>   At e'en when I come hame...
>
> /... I'm young and stout, my Marion;
>   Nane dances like me on the green:
> And gin ye forsake me, Marion,
>   I'll e'en gae draw up wi' Jean...

This original song is one of simple courtship where the hero proposes marriage and flatters Marion's vanity by his promises, but cautions, that if she will not have him, he will then go to his Jean. (Is it possible the Marian is meant to be Maria Riddell in the new version?) Clearly, the model for *The Ewe-Bughts, Marian* found in the *Chronicle* is the version from the "south" found by Ramsay. So, it can be safely established that the author of the newly found song was steeped in the *ouvre* of Scots songs.

The Ramsay version of *The Ewe-Bughts* possesses the same sweet, rural romance and naiveté found in John Mayne's *Logan Braes*. The anti-war brush-up and treatment of *Logan Braes* is surely repeated in the new version of *The Ewe-Bughts,* when compared to the original version found in *The Orpheus Caledonius,* published early in the 18th century. So, we need to ask ourselves how many Scottish poets were involved in song writing during this period? How many were familiar with Ramsay's *Tea Table Miscellany* and *The Orpheus Caledonius?* How many Scottish songwriters can be found with a track record of reforging old rural romances into contemporary anti-war heartbreak? The evidence strongly suggests the hand of Burns, although the song is not in his best manner nor is it too mediocre to be his.

In fact, the song is more clever than it first seems. There is a cleverly adjusted storyline which takes the "south" of Scotland version of the old song and places it in the Highlands. Surely only a poet familiar with both versions would lift the Ramsay version and place it in the Highlands? There are shades of *The Address of Beelzebub* in the new song, not in language, but in sentiment. The drive to get Highlanders into the British army proved a success because many viewed it as a temporary escape from poverty, akin to the message in the well known *The Twa Recruiting Sergeants* made famous by *The Corries*. Due to the number of people who left the Highlands to fight against France, the labourers on the land were sparse:

> Ilka Laird in the Highlands is rueing,
> That he drove his poor tenants away,
> For naething is seen here but ruin,
> As the haughs are aw laying in lay.

Burns was aware of the social problems in the Highlands, first mentioned in *The Address of Beelzebub*. In 1795 there was a shortage of labour on the land throughout Scotland. So it is possible the bard set out to unite the two old lyrics by using the version from Ramsay as the model but included references to the Highlands to add a flavour of the song from the North. It would have been characteristic of Burns to turn a regional song into a national song, in the way he wove together lowland lyrics with a Highland tune in *The Lea Rig*.

The new version of the song contains a "sprinkling" of English words, although it is predominantly written in Scots. Burns mentioned on a few occasions to Thomson that wherever it seemed appropriate he would throw a "sprinkling" of English words into an old Scots song to make it more intelligible to English readers. This feature is clearly employed in *Ewe-Bught Marian*, probably to suit its place of publication, the London *Chronicle*. This is not proof of the bard's authorship, but the "sprinkling" of English; the "critic's brush", is a distinctive feature of the bard's songwriting habits.

There is now a combination of factors which suggest Burns as the author. The poet was familiar with two sets of lyrics for the tune *Ewe-*

Bughts Marion. He had composed a song on the tune in 1792. He had turned a similar song of rural romance into an anti-war song with *Logan Braes.* There is a line in the new song lifted from the poet's own *The Ronnals of the Bennals.* There is a sprinkling of English words in the new song. He promised to send writings to the *Chronicle* in early 1794, prior to the song's publication. Moreover, Burns may have sent lyrics to Johnson in 1795 to the tune *Ewe-Bughts Marion,* but no song of that name ever appeared under the poet's name. Thus, in the absence of evidence to indicate any other Scottish songwriter, the most likely author is surely Burns.

A10. Exhoratory Ode to The Prince of Wales on Entering his 34th Year

"O, Prince! since you have reach'd that year,
When man-like wisdom should appear,
     And man-like virtues too,
For God's sake shew them - let us see
Some samples rare, of both, in Thee:
     O, Prince! we pray thee, do.

Thy Youth's Wild Oats have long been sown,
And too luxuriantly have grown:-
     'Tis time to pull them up.
Plant, in their stead, a better grain,
Some genuine Wheat, that may remain -
     'Till it produce a Crop.

Consider, you're a Married Man;
And be a father (if you can) -
     Of pretty *legal* Babbies:
Your follies and your freaks give o'er
At length - and caterwaul no more
     With meritricious Tabbies.

Consider, you were born to be
Th' Apparent Heir of Majesty,
　　　One day to fill a Throne:
To fill it - not with bulk of size,
But bulk of Brains; and, if you're wise,
　　　With Virtues, all your own.

For, if some Royal folks you ape,
You will not readily escape
　　　The fangs of Peter Pindar;
Whose caustic Muse, if in a rage
Will roast you, in her frying page -
　　　And roast you to a cinder.

Yet, Prince! avoid extremes - nor fall
Into the path of Prodigal,
　　　To shun the Miser's track:
Be gen'rous - but be also just;
The Nation's Gold is but a trust,
　　　That must be render'd back:-

That is, each Guinea which we give
Is only giv'n to make you live -
　　　And not to make you revel.
To meanly hoard - to basely lavish;
That would be sordid - *this* be knavish;
　　　But both transgress the level.

For Virtue, Science and the Arts
Reserve their well-proportion'd parts
　　　Of all that you can spare:
You only treasure up to Fame,
And to an everlasting name,
　　　Whate'er with *them* you share.

But, let not Luxury or Vice,
In any shape your hand entice
    To throw away your wealth:
Whate'er to those your hand may throw,
You on Ingratitude bestow -
    Besides, 'tis public stealth!

One council more:- If e'er you reign
O'er Britain's much-curtail'd domain,
    Ah, reign not like your Sire!
Be it your care to cherish Peace,
From Wars, and Contests vain to cease -
    Or dread a nation's ire.

Your former faults you may redeem,
And yet re-purchase that esteem
    Which, once, was thought your due:
'Tis ne'er too late, our Sages say,
To leave the perverse, crooked way,
    And honour's path pursue.

O, Prince! the Muse who thus exhorts
Is not a foe to Kings or Courts,
    Or Kingly, Courtly things:
She only wishes, hopes to see
A second Alfred rise in Thee -
    The best of earthly Kings.

Alfred, on Thy Starry-Throne!

The *Exhoratory Ode* was published in the *Morning Chronicle* on August 17th 1795, five days before *The Cob Web*, signed A Briton, a known pseudonym of Burns. The poet forwarded two other works with *Scots Wha Hae* when it was published in 1794, so it may be possible that he again sent more than one work to the newspaper - assuming, of course, that *The Cob Web* is his. After making the request for a safe channel and address to send material to the newspaper, during March 1794, he clearly intended to take advantage of the arrangement and compose radical works for Perry. However, there is little evidence that the bard delivered any significant amount of material during 1794, although the song *The Ewe-Bughts, Marion* and *To Certain Jurymen*, may also be from him.

The significant date from which Burns appears to have re-ignited his verve for radical poetry is early 1795, with composition of *The Heron Ballads*. It is plain that it would have been safer for the poet to write radical works for the *Chronicle* in English verse, than to pillory supporters of the Pitt government around the Dumfrieshire area, so close to home in a style and language recognisably his. That Burns wrote *The Heron Ballads* is sufficient evidence to consider the possibility that he was dabbling in radical works on a local, and therefore, on a national scale. The theme, style and language of the new *Exhoratory Ode-* written in Scots verse format, make it seem very likely that bard was at his old tricks.

The *Ode* brims over with the familiar irreverence found in *A Dream* written by Burns in 1786. In *A Dream*, the bard imagined himself transported to the King's Birthday levee in London. In stanza 10, after satirical remarks on various characters including "Willie Pitt", the Prime Minister, and the general pomp of courtly life, he turned to the Prince of Wales with a moralistic, wagging-finger:

> For you, young Potentate o Wales,
>   I tell your Highness fairly,
> Down Pleasure's stream, wi swelling sails,
>   I'm tauld ye're driving rarely;
> But some day ye may gnaw yer nails,
>   An curse yer folly sairly,
> That e'er ye brak Diana's pales,
>   Or rattl'd dice wi Charlie
>   By night or day.

This daring poem which described *God Save the King* as a "cuckoo sang" was iconoclastic from a poet from "peasant" stock. It is written in a tone and sentiment few poets would have been brave enough to put their name to. In fact, it is no surprise that Mrs Dunlop informed Burns that her London friends enjoyed most of his Scottish poetry and were learning "Scotticisms" to appreciate him fully, but they did not like *A Dream*. *A Dream* unequivocally warns the Prince of Wales about his behaviour and cheekily questions his manhood, precisely in the same boisterous and didactic language of the *Exhoratory Ode*. The first point of significance, therefore, is that this was familiar ground to Burns. He had already composed a poem and published it under his own name, which pointed the finger at the Prince of Wales in accusative, personal and irreverent language. Moreover, the find of a poem like the *Ode* with such a similar tone and posture as *A Dream* which is also in Scots verse form, makes Burns a likely contender as the author.

In *A Dream*, the bard looked forward to when the Prince might become King and dismissed the "clish-ma-claver" (gossip) about his inability to reign, coyly remarking that the Prince's "folly" might be mended. The line "So, ye may doucely fill a throne, / For a their clish-ma-claver" is strongly echoed in the *Exhoratory Ode to the Prince of Wales*:

> Consider, you were born to be
> Th' Apparent Heir of Majesty,
> One day to *fill a Throne*.
> To fill it - not with bulk of size,
> But bulk of Brains; and, if you're wise,
> With Virtues, all your own.

In 1795 there is no other work which offers such bold advice to the Prince, wishing to see the best from him, precisely in the manner of *A Dream*. The advice of Burns in the 1780's is given in Scots while the advice in the *Exhoratory Ode* is focused, emphatic English. For Burns, royalty was not a sacred, sacrosanct institution - like any other institution it could be abused and used in ignoble ways which bode ill for the general good. So, here again we have what appears to be the bard beating a familiar tune on an old drum, pointing his finger at "you, young Potentate o Wales" wishing to see "Virtues" all his own.

Also in *A Dream*, Burns gently raps the knuckles of the Prince for his effeminate reputation and lack of sexual conquests, as hinted in the description that the Prince was "driving rarely" "Down Pleasure's stream". It is a theme he hit on again in a poem written in 1789. The poem is rightly accepted to the canon by MacKay and rings strongly of *On Glenriddell's Fox Breaking its Chain* and several other works, including parts of *The Address of Beelzebub*. It is titled *To A Gentleman:*

Who had Sent a Newspaper and Offered to Continue it Free of Charge. Lines 30-36 mention

> The news o princes, dukes and earls,
> Pimps, sharpers, bawds, and opera-girls;
> If that daft buckie, Geordie Wales,
> Was threshing still at hizzies tails;
> Or if he was grown oughtlins douser,
> And no a perfect kintra cooser:

Here we are almost into the rich Braid Scots of Ferguson and need to decipher the old words for consumption in our modern anglicised Scotland. "Geordie Wales" of course, is a reference to the Prince of Wales. The word "hizzies", means hussies or girls. The poet wonders if the Prince has grown lazy or sedate - "oughtlins douser" - towards women, or turned out to be a "kintra cooser", or country stallion. Although this work would have utterly confused the Prince if he had read it, the theme of the future King's sexuality is returned to and developed in the new Ode:

> Thy Youth's Wild Oats have long been sown,
> And too luxuriantly have grown:-
>   'Tis time to pull them up.
> Plant, in their stead, a better grain,
> Some genuine Wheat, that may remain -
>   'Till it produce a Crop.
>
> Consider, you're a Married Man;
> And be a father (if you can) -
>   Of pretty *legal* Babbies:
> Your follies and your freaks give o'er
> At length - and caterwaul no more
>   With meritricious Tabbies.

Under the guise of anonymity, the Ode is more boisterous and mocking than the two previous works of Burns, with the cheeky slight "(if you can)" casually placed in brackets. Not only is this language couched in farmer's imagery - "Wild Oats" - it is on the same Burnsian theme, the sexual prowess of the Prince. So, the Ode is on the distinctive theme we find in at least two works of the bard with the same irreverent wit.

The thrust of the poem is to demand the Prince show manly virtues, brains and a two-way system of trust in the honour of his position, which is deemed to be propped up by public esteem and public taxes. This type of commentary might be expected from a poet who had closely studied De Lohme's *The British Constitution* and whose close friend Robert Riddell, was a radical specialist in constitutional reform. The responsibilities of the Prince's future Kingship are marked out in black and white terms:

> Yet, Prince! avoid extremes - nor fall
> Into the path of Prodigal,
> To shun the Miser's track:
> Be gen'rous - but be also just;
> The Nation's Gold is but a trust,
> That must be render'd back:-
>
> That is, each Guinea which we give
> Is only giv'n to make you live -
> And not to make you revel.
> To meanly hoard - to basely lavish;
> That would be sordid - *this* be knavish;
> But both transgress the level.

The wit and advice is clever, incisive and poignant. It embodies the same anti-corruption values displayed in the recently discovered work, *New Song*, from the *Gazetteer*, which pillories Pitt and Dundas who are blamed for conning the public by ever-increasing taxation, while swigging their celebratory, "bragging" bottle. Irreverence aside, the Ode is even-handed in its seemingly impertinent advice. If we employ the practice of Burns and translate into prose the language, tone and sentiment of the stanzas in *A Dream* which relate to the Prince of Wales, and place it alongside the new Ode, they are identical.

The daringly irreverent wit of the Ode is certainly in the mould of the bard's direct style. The kernel thrust of the Ode is to warn the Prince to wake up to the oppression and troubles across Britain. If he does not learn to lead honourably by example, it is suggested that an anti-Monarchist rebellion, such as happened in France, might occur:

> One council more:- If e'er you reign
> O'er Britain's much-curtail'd domain,
>   Ah, reign not like your Sire!
> Be it your care to cherish Peace,
> From Wars, and Contests vain to cease -
>   Or dread a nation's ire.

This stanza is seditious and a highly treasonable warning, or caution. The advice, though, comes from the voice of democratic reason. Regional famine occurred throughout Britain in 1795. The war against France was deemed unnecessary and unreasonable by reformers. How close Britain did come to a domestic rebellion is not known, but many thinkers of the period saw the trouble coming to a head in 1794-6, not merely Burns. The anti-war posture of Burns, witnessed in the dramatic close of *Logan Braes*; cleverly woven into *The Soldier's Return* of mid-1793, and expressed with indignant force in the *Washington Ode* - and evident in the final stanzas of *The Dagger* - is found here again. The advice of the Ode is that a future King must display honour and justice in the role as monarch.

Although the Ode conveys the view that the Prince is a weedy, feeble character, it is not wholly anti-royal. In fact, it closes with the desire to see the Prince become a stronger and more virtuous man, fit to rule trouble-torn Britain. The final stanza insists the Prince turn out to be another King Alfred:

> O, Prince! the Muse who thus exhorts
> Is not a foe to Kings or Courts,
>   Or Kingly, Courtly things:
> She only wishes, hopes to see
> A second Alfred rise in Thee -
>   The best of earthly Kings.

The use of "She" is merely a feminine reference to the poet's Muse. Burns hoped his eldest son would turn out to have the character of a Wallace or an Alfred, as commented to Mrs Dunlop. There can be little doubt Alfred was one of the poet's great icons, probably more because he set up the Jury system in Britain and beheaded 44 corrupt judges, than for his monarchical position. The poet identified with Alfred's independence of mind, his integrity and honesty, which made him act out of a sense of conscious public virtue towards the nation. It is in the *Washington Ode* that Burns wrote "Alfred, on thy starry throne / Surrounded by the tuneful choir" in eulogy to Alfred the Great. So, the final stanza of the *Exhoratory Ode* turns out to be a positive salutation to the Prince of Wales, hoping he would take over from George III and become a King who would nurture and "maintain The Royalty of Man". The key message, therefore, is that the Prince should be an innovative and radical King in the honourable mould of Alfred the Great.

It might seem that the most likely English poet to have written the Exhoratory Ode was Peter Pindar, the pen-name employed by Dr Walcot. It was not until the early 1800's that he gained a reputation for satirizing the Royal family. There are several reasons why we can exclude Pindar as author. First, he always signed his material with his pen-name, Peter Pindar. Second, he never put his pen name in a poem - he is mentioned in stanza 5. Most importantly, he made one poor attempt in Scots verse form which is inferior to the new Ode. It is not in his collected works and it would sit uncomfortably next to any of his effusions. Pindar's poetry was generally written in ballad or song format and it is widely accepted that, although his version of *Lord Gregory* is of reasonable quality, most of his writing is distinctively poorer than the Ode. Moreover, the Ode displays a mocking, satirical, boisterous tone galvanized with a seriousness which Pindar did not, and could not, write. In fact, it displays a daring irreverent wit beyond his talents. Pindar is the only other possible contender for authorship of the Ode and he does not even come close.

It would have been quite characteristic of Burns to out-do Pindar in wit and style and mention his name in such a witty manner in the body of the poem. Despite the volume of radical work in the *Chronicle*, which sometimes reveal a tone and language similar to Burns, it is effectively impossible that any other active poet could have written the Ode other than Burns. Had it been written in Scots, the case for provenance would have been almost unquestionable and obvious from the first read. As it is, the stunning similarities with *A Dream*, its Scots verse form, its boisterous wit and its distinctive eulogy to King Alfred - mentioned only by Burns in works of the mid-1790's - make the case for attribution persuasive. If the bard was to have re-written in English, the stanzas from *A Dream* which mention the Prince of Wales and put them in Scots verse form in a contemporary context for 1795, adding and updating the poem with the political flavour of the time, the final product would surely have been the *Exhoratory Ode.*

A11. Address to Justice

Best friend of Human Race - best friend assign'd
By Heavan's high will! O, Justice, how divine.
Thy look, when meekly aweful, at thy shrine
Thou sitt'st, with upright, uncorrupted mind,

Sustaining the dread Scales of Life and Death!
No gloomy Vengeance lowers on thy Brow,
No Passion rankles at thy heart, but thou
Art Righteous as thine Author! Like the breath,

Of vernal Eve, when hush'd is the still air,
Gentle thy voice is heard: while 'neath thy Throne,
Kneels Mercy, list'ning to the Captive's moan,
And breathes for Penitence her plaintive pray'r -

Then may my feet approach thine awful state,
And, if some brother of my kind to die
Thou doom'st in guilt, in shame, in infamy,
O may thy voice pronounce his dreadful fate!

But when Ambition - when dark Interest -
When foul Corruption, cringing on her knee
At Guilt's command - when low Hypocricy
Blasts the fair Virtues blooming at thy breast -

When, basely prostitute to Tyrant's Pow'r
Thine arm, the tool of a detested Crew
Thy Vengeance hurls at the Illustrious Few
Who, Freedom, in her last expiring hour

Cherish and love - still to their Country, just,
'Mid dangers, tortures, and stern Death's alarm!
When these bless'd Patriots, by thy ruthless arm,
Fall murder'd, foully murder'd, to the dust,

I weep, that Man should so his nature stain,
Insult his God, and his best gift profane.

"Justice, The High Vicegerent of Her God" – Burns

The language in the first few stanzas of this new poem does not immediately strike a chord as being in the bard's "style". However, such an immediate response belies a crude assumption, that there is such a thing as a single, fixed style in Burns. As any literary scholar knows, he had more than one "voice". It is undeniable that the poet's chameleon skill of poetic synthesis and range of style is remarkable. Burns had many different "voices" because of his extraordinary command of both the Scots and English language and his versatility in verse form. So, his poetic "dress" or "mask" could be selected from a range of mostly dead, great poets.

For instance, would the bard have used old English spelling, such as "sitt'st" and "doom'st"? A superficial response might be, no. A con sidered answer is, yes. The song *Sleep'st Thou* reveals such spelling and "Wauk'st Thou" in the title. In the *Washington Ode* the examples of such spelling are "tremblest", "erst", "accurst" and "link't". In fact, the poet mixed such old spelling with Scots and more general English words, often in the one song. In *Elegy On the Late Miss Burnet of Monboddo* Burns wrote "Thou left'st us, darkling in a world of tears" but adapted the line to "And left us, darkling in a world of tears in the *Epistle to Robert Graham of Fintry*. So, words such as "sitt'st", "doom'st" and many others - thou'st, can'st, dost, didst, mind'st, strik'st - were regularly employed by Burns for the best effect whenever it suited him. So, in terms of style and language, *Address to Justice* is a poem he could easily have written.

In fact, a count of key Burnsian words in the first 12 lines of the poem, those used at least 20 times among the poet's writings, reveal a total of 23 such words. In a 12 line block of poetry, a count of 23 common Burnsian words is higher than the total found in most of the known radical works of the poet. While this is not particularly significant as a pointer to authorship, it indicates that *Address to Justice* contains a density of words used regularly by Burns.

The *Address* paints a Miltonic scenario of a humble poet approaching the throne of Justice to plead that the powers given to the abstract personage of Justice by God, have been taken over and abused by a "detested crew" in Britain, meaning by implication, the Pitt government. To appreciate this work, it is helpful to imagine Justice on her throne as though the image is an art gallery sized painting. In this mental picture, almost cinematic, given the approaching poet before the throne, there are various other characters beneath and around Justice. They are Ambition, Corruption and Hypocrisy, who, together, have thwarted Mercy and debased the honour of Justice. This high level Miltonic caricature is a forceful portrayal of the political forces at work in Britain during the 1790's. It is far more akin to the extraordinary paintings of Blake than to the cartoon-like caricatures of *Punch* magazine during the 19th century. The *Address* is, therefore, a radical pro-democratic work forged into high poetic art form.

The poem falls into two basic parts, if we consider the use of language. Up until stanza 5, the flowery veil of high English poetry is maintained with great poetic skill, almost like a mask over the face of the poet who addresses Justice. From stanza 5 onwards, the mask falls away to be followed by a fiery burst of controlled indignation where, the anger and frustration of the author cannot be kept silent. There is a reverence for the great symbol of Justice in the first half of the poem which pivots from fixed respect and awe towards the forces of God on earth, to a furious outburst that the very powers given to man by God could be usurped and used by the factions of Corruption, Ambition and Hypocrisy. It is clear in the writings of Burns that he saw human hypocricy, excess personal ambition, and particularly corruption, as the enemies of a decent society. As Burns commented "Whatever mitigates the woes, or increases the happiness of others, this is my criterion of goodness; and whatever injures society at large, or an individual in it, this is my measure of iniquity". (CL 350) Burns's letter to Patrick Heron in the Spring of 1795, accords with the anti-Pitt government sentiments of the poem: it mentions their "dereliction of all principle ... profligate junto ...outraged virtue...violated common decency.. hypocrisy ... iniquity". Burns goes on to say that radical poetry which would "unmask their flatigiousness" and "deliver such over to their merited fate" is ".. innocent... laudable ...virtue". So, the burst of indignation from stanza 5 onwards is vintage Burnsian bombast.

The final stanza displays a religious despair, an anger of frustrated disbelief that men in political power could abuse their power without being troubled by their despotic acts. The poem brims over with idealistic angst at the contemporary world. It suggests a poet who holds faith in God, who sees the religious umbrella of God spanning over the natural world of man and Nature, within a holistic worldview - a religiously based nature-philosophy. Burns interpretation of the Bible and religion is distinctive within his poetry, where, on several occasions he directs requests openly to his Maker in semi-prayer form. In his letters he tells us religion and God are the only sensible way to make meaning out of life. He is no zealot and tolerates atheism in others. In the self-critical, rationalised Christian humanism of Burns, the peculiar and distinctive aspect to his belief, is that God *ought to be a pro-active force* in the world. Enlightenment driven reason combined with compassionate feelings leads him to this conclusion. It is clear that the views of the poet were rationally based and not merely an intuitive indignation against human wrongs. *Address to Justice* displays the same conceptual religo-political worldview found in Burns. Of course, this is not definitive evidence of authorship, as many other intellectual radicals would have expressed a similar holistic "mindset". It is the stylistic expression of these sentiments that is distinctive.

In *On the Death of Lord President Dundas*, stanza 3, the bard employs a Miltonic allusion of Justice, "Justice, the high vicegerent of her God, / Her doubtful balance eyed, and sway'd her rod". In the elegy on the Lord President the poet did not fully develop the Miltonic imagery of Justice to the level seen in the Address. There are seven examples in Burns of "Justice" as a Miltonic feminine being, "she". In *Address to Edinburgh*, Burns' employs the description "Here Justice, from her native skies, / High wields her balance and her rod". The image of Justice sitting on her throne is echoed in *Sonnet On Hearing a Thrush Sing on His Early Walk*, written in January 1793, "..in Poverty's dominion drear", where "Sits meek Content with light, unanxious heart". It is noteworthy that "meek" is found in the sonnet to describe the Mitonic personage, "Content", while in the Address "meekly" describes Justice as she "sits" on her throne. The same precise language in a Miltonic image is a striking lexical similarity. Also, the use of the word "aweful", seen in the *Address*, to describe the power of Heaven invested in the personage of Justice, is used by Burns in lines *Written at Friar Carse Hermitage*, "The smile or frown of aweful Heav'n". In *Stanzas, On The Same Occasion* the language "O, aid me with Thy help, Omnipotence Divine!" rings of *Address to Justice*, "O, Justice, how divine!" The same use of "how" is found in Burns' line "Sensibility how charming" from *On Sensibility*. A more striking textual overlap is found in the bard's *The Ninetieth Psalm Versified*, "O Thou, the first, the greatest friend / Of all the human race!" which is very similar to the first line of the *Address*, "Best friend of human Race - best friend assign'd". Moreover, four of these words overlap, "best" with "greatest", while "friend", and "human race" match exactly. So, what might have seemed superficially unlike Burns at first read, is indeed, packed with the phraseology of Burns.

In the second stanza there is a further similarity between the sonnet *On Hearing a Thrush Sing* where God is referred to as "Author of this opening day", while *Address to Justice* describes God, the father of Justice, as "thine Author!". The same description of God as "Author" is also found in *Stanzas, On The Same Occasion*. The use of "dread" as an adjective in the *Address* to describe the power of life and death, is found in *On The Death of John McLeod*, "Dread Omnipotence", and "O thou dread Power, who reign'st above", from *Prayer - O Thou Dread Power*. A similar echo, "O Thou dread Power, whose empire-giving hand" is seen in *Prologue: Spoken by Mr Woods*. The words "gloomy" and "Vengeance" are found in Burns. The description "gloomy Vengeance" is very distinctive, although a synonymous description is used by Burns in stanza 4, *A Tale* "In *sullen* vengeance, I, disdain'd reply". The adjectives used to describe the mood of vengeance, "sullen" or "gloomy", are almost interchangeable. While the word "Righteous" is only listed in *Burns: A-Z Wordfinder* once, the synonyms "Godly" and "holy" are common. The narrator in the *Address* observes that "No passion rankles at thy heart" when observing Justice. The word "rankles" is found in Burns as "rankling" in *Verses Written with A Pencil*, or "a-ranklin" in *The Address of Beelzebub*. So, unlike most newspapers poems of the period, the lexical structure of the second stanza rings true to the Burnsian mould.

Stanza 3 continues to paint the scenery around the grand personage of Justice, whose "Gentle" voice is heard, "Like the breath, / Of vernal Eve, when hush'd is the still air". The language sounds akin to Burns's "Her air like Nature's vernal smile" from *The Lass o Ballochmyle*, or "Her looks are like the vernal May" in *The Lass of Cessnock Banks* and "Here haply, too, at vernal dawn" from *The Humble Petition of Bruar Water*. The biblical figure Eve is mentioned by Burns in *On the Late Captain Grose's Peregrinations, The Mauchline Wedding, Epistle to Major Logan* and in alternate lines for *Address to the Deil* "An' Eve was like my bonie Jean", (no. 25 in Appendix A, Burns A-Z *Wordfinder*). The religious cadence of the *Address* and the similar sonnet styled rythmn and rhyme is found in *Sonnet on The Death of Robert Riddell* composed in April 1794 and also published in the *Morning Chronicle*.

> No more, ye warblers of the wood, no more,
>> Nor pour your descant grating on my soul!
>> Thou young-eyed Spring, gay in thy verdant stole,
> More welcome were to me grim Winter's wildest roar!

> ...Yes, pour, ye warblers, pour the notes of woe,
>> And sooth the Virtues weeping o'er his bier!
>> The man of worth - and "hath not left his peer"! -
> Is in his "narrow house", for ever darkly low.

By the end of stanza 3, it is clear the Address stands up to a close comparison with the writings of Burns. The case is turning out to be substantial but it is still questionable at this point.

In stanza 4 the line "Then may my feet approach thine aweful state" sounds similar to *Stanzas, On the Same Occassion*, where Burns wrote "I tremble to approach an angry God". In the same poem Burns asks how he can ammend for his own sins and writes of "mercy's plan", begging that he can "dare a lifted eye to Thee -". The language shows the same tone of humility employed in *Address to Justice*. The direct and personal "approach" to the throne of Justice is reflective of the bard's individualistic form of religious worship: the relationship between man's conscience and God. It is due to the strength of his religious views, the "noble anchor", that he could criticise "...Religion's pride, / In all the pomp of method, and of art; ...Devotion's ev'ry grace, except the heart*" in *The Cottar's Saturday Night*. The *Address* may not display criticism of formal religion, but it does reveal a strongly individual, thinking-person's interpretation of the relationship between man, religion, Justice and God. Such a perspective is found in Burns.

In stanza 5, the humility of the poet in the *Address* cannot be contained. The language and tone of the poem changes from the word "But". It is as though the narrator has stepped forward to the throne of Justice and has chosen to look Justice eye-to-eye and speak without restraint or fear. The pace of the language begins to rush in anger and frustration that Justice has been abused by "Ambition", "dark Interest", "foul Corruption" and "low Hypocricy". Together, these Miltonic forces "Blast the fair Virtues blooming at thy breast" and effectively take over the power, "thine arm", of Justice. The cinematic picture painted in the reader's imagination by this description is like an imagined *coup de tat* by the forces of Hell who now control Justice. We find "Ambition" blasted by Burns in *A Winter Night* as "mad" and a host of other Miltonic beasts such as "stern Oppression" and "Woe, Want and Murder". In a similar collage of Miltonic allusion there are flashes of the moral outrage found in the *Address* within the earlier *A Winter Night* -

> Not all your rage, as now united shows
> More hard unkindness, unrelenting,
> Vengeful malice, unrepenting
> Than Heav'n-illumin'd man on brother Man bestows!

> .....Ev'n in the peaceful rural vale,
> Truth, weeping, tells the mournful tale,
> How pamper'd Luxury, Flatt'ry by her side...

Miltonic influence is marbled throughout the poetry of Burns. In alternate lines to *Ode* to *the Departed Regency Bill* sent to Mrs. Dunlop (Appendix A, MacKay's *Wordfinder*), Burns also employs "Interest" in a strongly worded political context "And, Principal and Interest! all the cry!" In *The Vision*, Colia, the rural Muse of Ayrshire, tells the young Burns that poetic passions "...rouse the patriot up to bear / Corruption's heart". Is this not what *Address to Justice* sets out to do? The description "fair virtues" is found in Burns with "Again I might desert fair virtue's way" from *Stanzas, On the Same Occasion*, and "And certes, in fair Virtues heavenly road", from *The Cottar's Saturday Night*, or "Fair Virtue water'd it wi' care" in *The Tree of Liberty*. So, stanza 5 develops the Miltonic picture of the poem in a manner which is more refined than the cluttered pastiche of *A Winter Night*. Its language bears a strong Burnsian imprint.

The pictorial imagery of the Address is crafted with more care than *Inscription for an Alter to Independence*, also written in 1795. The radical tone of the inscription is akin to the language of the Address:

> Thou of an independent mind,
> With soul resolv'd, with soul resign'd,
> Prepar'd Power's proudest frown to brave,
> Who wilt not be, nor have a slave,
> Virtue alone who dost revere,
> Thy own reproach alone dost fear:
> Approach this shrine, and worship here.

The same biblical English - "wilt" and "dost" - is employed. The *Address* is a superior work because it is not merely anecdotal and develops its kernel Miltonic allusion with considerable skill into a grand pictorial image. Around the seat of Justice "Tyrant's Pow'r" has taken control of the "arm" of Justice and the "fair virtues blooming at thy breast" are blasted by the other Miltonic forces, Corruption, Interest, Hypocrisy and Ambition. There is a distinctive echo of "Tyrant Pow'r" in the *Washington Ode* where Burns wrote "England in thunder calls "The tyrant's cause is mine!" Thus, the language, imagery and radical politics of the bard converge and are focused with great skill in the *Address*.

The close of the poem rings true to the bard's radical sentiments turned from anger to art in the *Washington Ode* of 1794. The use of the "arm" either striking or falling is distinctive in Burns, as shown in the analysis of the second *Ghost of Bruce*. In the *Address* it is the "arm" of Justice which "hurls" "Vengeance" at "the illustrious Few". This rings strongly of the *Birthday Ode for 31st December*, "So Vengeance' arm" where the phrase "the base, usurping crew / The tool of faction" echoes "the tool of a detested Crew" in the *Address*. The mention of the "bless'd Patriots" who are cherished by "Freedom", which is "expiring" itself, is indicative of a poet observing the political feuds of the 1794-5 period and tells us the author feels the ideological battle is being lost. This feeling is portrayed in a letter by Burns of January 1795, when he wrote of the respite gained by London radicals who were found not guilty of Treason, "Thank God these London trials have given us a little more breath".

It may not be a mere coincidence that the rhyme of "Pow'r" and "hour" are found in the *Address* as they are in *Scots Wha Hae*. By early 1795 it was natural for him to focus his democratic hopes on the Whig Opposition led by Fox. In 1795 he saw how far Britain and Scotland were from the messianic democratic vision of the reform movement and in melancholic despair he could still envisage the democratic future, "comin' yet, for a' that". In his most serious frame of mind, Burns would certainly have written the closing couplet "I weep, that Man should so his nature stain, / Insult his God, and his best gift profane". The poem, therefore, ends in perfect harmony with the ideals and stylistics of the bard.

Thus, throughout *Address to Justice*, there is no language problem to the bard's authorship. It does not contain an array of words easily spotted in most newspaper poems of the time which are alien to Burns. The cross-relation to known works is consistent, strong and continuous throughout the *Address*. The cinematic Miltonic imagery is strikingly similar to Burns. The gentle start to the poem is in similar language to several poems by Burns, particularly his touching sonnet on Glenriddell. Moreover, the jump to a more strident, radical, religo-political indignation in the final stanzas is a qualitative change in language which displays considerable skill. So, aware the poet planned to send radical works to the Chronicle via a covert, safe channel, it is clear he had the ability, motive and opportunity to pen *Address to Justice*. In fact, if the Address is contrasted with the first two stanzas of the *Washington Ode*, the stylistic evidence for the Address is stronger and more "Burnsian" than the Ode. Therefore, the evidence for attribution is substantial.

A12. The Cob Web – A Song

The sweets of a blessing
Are had by possessing,
Hail! Britons! the cause is your own;
You are wonderful great,
You have Princes and State,
And the wisest and best on a Throne!

What a contrast is France,
Where is now the gay dance,
They are no way so happy as we;
We have flourishing Trade,
Plenty, beer, meat, and bread!
While madly they starve to be free!

It was once so for us,
Indeed it was thus,
Like them we once swore to maintain,
The blessing that God,
Sent to cheer man's abode,
And preserve free from blemish or stain.

Thus, they might suppose,
To be led by the nose,
Was not for a People, like them;
That we being free,
Should with freemen agree,
Nor those who sought freedom condemn.

But there they was wrong,
We have alter'd our song,
Resolv'd to have nothing to do -
With a good, full of evil,
Devis'd by the Devil,
That freedom for which the French rue.

Yet, lest it be thought,
We lov'd self to a fault,
We offer'd Court blessings to treat them;
Ah! could you expect
This they would reject,
And force us, unwilling, to beat them.

First a King, good as may be,
We made of a Baby,
Then demanded they'd fawn on the Child!
But, so wicked were they,
That they would not obey,
But beat us! for being so wild.

We brib'd to divide them,
Tried all arts to chide 'em,
To starve them, made a great fuss;
When, some Demon of Hell,
Inverting the spell,
Turn'd the picture of Famine on us!

So great is the blessing
We got by redressing
Each nation's faults but our own;
To destroy them, their Trade,
We, their country invade,
While our own is cut up to the bone.

But courage my Friends
We may yet gain our ends,
Perhaps in a circle they'll meet:
When, nine out of ten
They've kill'd of our men,
And the rest are left something to eat.

Signed A. Briton.

A Briton Fills "an Idle Column", 1795

This poem comes to notice in the pages of the *Chronicle* firstly, because of the pen-name, "A Briton", known to have been used by Burns.
The pen-name was first used by Burns in 1788 and is found only
twice thereafter in all British newspapers and does not appear again
after the death of the bard. If the pen-name "A. Briton" had been in
common usage it would be seen in the *Chronicle* prior to 1794 and

after July 1796. Outwith these years it is not to be found. The poem *Lines on Ambition*, also signed A Briton, has already been presented as a lost work of the bard with very strong evidence. Two years after *Lines on Ambition*, it is no surprise to find the pen-name A Briton employed in a newspaper Burns promised to send material to.

As mentioned in the case of *Lines on Ambition*, the geonym A. Briton had been around since long before Burns. There is, though, no evidence that it was a commonly used pen-name, as might first be assumed. Obviously, if it was a regular pseudonym from the era, it would diminish the prospects of *The Cob Web*'s authenticity. Intuition suggests that in the Britain of the 1790's everyone is potentially "A Briton". Yet, it is generally the case that most people who are born in England see themselves not merely as English first, British second; but they tend to equate the word "English" with "British" and often use the word "English" when they mean British - to the chagrin of some Scots. This is the case now and was the case during the poet's lifetime. This would indicate that an English poet was less likely to use the geonym "A. Briton" than a Scottish poet. Scots tend to see themselves as Scots first and British second. But it is a distinctive *second* with many Scots, not the blurred interchangeable English-meaning-British confusion characteristic of England. No Scot has ever used the word "British" to mean purely "Scottish". It therefore makes sense that the pen-name A Briton would be used by a Scottish poet, caught in the dual nationality culture of Unionist Scotland. A detailed search of every column of many national newspapers up until 1800 failed to find another occurrence of the pen-name, other than the poet's letter, *Lines on Ambition* and *The Cob Web*. It is therefore of considerable significance that the pen-name died with Burns, the only recorded poet known to employ it. Of course, this is not definitive, but it is strong contextual evidence.

Once again, the poetic form of *The Cob Web* seems unlike the poet's popular works. It does not immediately appear to have a familiar "Burnsian ring" to it. However, nothing written by Burns in English, other than one famous passage from *Tam O' Shanter* and *A Red, Red Rose*, gives a distinctive "Burnsian ring" - precisely because this silly, claustrophobic, reductionist phrase is an intuitive "gut feeling" which only means a "guid Scottish ring". There is more than a shot of mysticism in the notion that there is only one "ring" to the bard, and only the expert lug can hear it. When intuition and assumption meet with our subconscious impression of the poet's writing, they combine to give a subjective judgment which we often describe as the "Burnsian ring" or the "voice of the bard". Intuition is not enough and accordingly first impressions are not to be trusted.

The first problem with this song is the defective grammar in stanza 5. No-one would expect Burns to write "But there they was wrong." Yet, he did so in *John Barleycorn - A Ballad*, "There was three Kings into the east" (See Scott Douglas edition). Scott Douglas remarks that "Burns liked the antique euphony of *was*, in this line" (p.183). Subsequent editors changed the poet's grammar. An extensive search of other poetry from the period finds no other poet who used *was* instead of *were*. So, remarkably, the antiquated *was* points immediately to Burns.

Another apparent problem with *The Cob Web* is that it is not written in exact meter. If we assume everything from Burns' pen was written in meter, this work does not seem like a possible work of Burns. However, if known works of Burns which are written in a similar style are considered, we find they too are out of meter. For instance, in Kinsley, song 602, *There Was a Bonie Lass*, has an irregular meter. The first verse displays lines of 6, 7, then 9 syllables, followed by 5, 7 and 8.

> There was a bonie lass,
> And a bonie, bonie lass,
> And she lo'ed her bonie laddie dear;
> Till war's loud alarms
> Tore her laddie frae her arms,
> Wi' monie a sigh and tear.

Verse two shows a similar pattern of 6, 7, then 8 syllables, followed with 5, 6 and 9.

> Over sea, over shore,
> Where the cannons loudly roar;
> He still was a stranger to fear:
> And nocht could him quail,
> Or his bosom assail,
> But the bonie lass he lo'd sae dear.

The first verse of *The Cob Web* has 6, 6 then 8 syllables, followed by

6, 6 and 9 syllables. Verse 2 shows a meter of 6, 6 and 9, then 6, 6, and 8 syllables, which is uneven, but not as erratic as *There Was a Bonie Lass*. So, the fact that the new song is out of meter just as the poet's known song indicates that he did not seriously trouble himself with perfecting work in this style. *The Cob Web* is more verse propaganda, a political broadside, than it is literary art. This would explain why it did not have to be written in perfect meter.

The song *There Was a Bonie Lass* is surprisingly brief on lyrics. It was not published until 1803 in Johnson's S.M.M. and was written some-time in 1795, in the same year as *The Cob Web*. So, Burns had in fact employed the same style of *The Cob Wed* in his last years and com-posed an accepted song, probably to the same tune. None of his material in this style was publicly known during his lifetime, which means few would have suspected him of writing a work like *The Cob Web*, especially in English, and no-one would have attempted imita-tion of the poet in this form. So, although politics was "dangerous ground" for the bard to tred on, he was certainly on a safer plateau of Parnassus with *The Cob Web* than he was with the raggedly Scottish *Heron Ballads*,

Another work published by Kinsley (no. 607) and MacKay in the same style as *The Cob Web* is, titled *Ballad*. Kinsley comments it is "al-most certainly by Burns" and was written as a "companion-piece" to *Why Should na Poor Folk Mowe*. Despite Kinsley's apparent certainty of the songs' provenance he placed it in the chapter *Dubia*, with a ques-tion over its authenticity. MacKay, though, rightly accepts it to the canon. The song was first published in 1959 by Barke in *The Merry Muses*. The first stanza refers to the Excise investigation into the bard's political views while the second stanza mixes sex and politics, using the same style as *The Cob Web*:

> While Prose-work and rhymes
> Are hunted for crimes,
> And things are - the devil knows how;
> Aware o' my rhymes,
> In these kittle times,
> The subject I chuse is a mowe.

> Some cry, Constitution!
> Some cry, Revolution!
> And Politicks kick up a rowe;
> But Prince and Republic,
> Agree on the Subject,
> No treason is in a good mowe.

The song is clearly by Burns. The two stanzas are in balanced meter of 5, 5, and 8, then 5, 5 and 8 syllables, followed by an increase to 6, 6, and 8, then 6, 6, and 8 syllables, although the remainder of the song is more erratic. In *Why Should na Poor Folk Mowe*, the irreverent mixture of politics and the leveling power of sex is thrown into irregular meter of 5, 5, 8, then 6, 6, and 8 syllables, if the song is set out in the same manner as *The Cob Web* - it is normally published in four lines of two couplets with alternating twin-rhymes, followed by a chorus.

> Auld Kate laid her claws
> On poor Stalinlaus,
> And Poland has bent like a bow:
> May the deil in her ass
> Ram a huge prick o' brass!
> And damn her in hell with a mowe!

Moreover, the style of *The Cob Web* is very similar to the better known *The Kirk's Alarm*, a controversial satirical work Burns did not formally print in his lifetime, although he did send a few copies among friends: it is often printed in the same manner as *The Cob Web*, but with the final line of each verse repeated as a chorus (shown in italics):

> Orthodox! Orthodox!
> Wha believe in John Knox -
> Let me sound an alarm to your conscience:
> A heretic blast
> Has been blown i' the Wast,
> That what is not sense must be nonesense
> *Orthodox!*
> *That what is not sense must be nonesense.*

Dr. Mac! Dr. Mac!
You should stretch on the rack,
To strike wicked Writers wi' terror:
To join faith and sense,
Upon onie pretense,
Twas heretic, damnable error -
Dr. Mac!
'Twas heretic damnable error.

The first two verses of *The Kirk's Alarm* show an irregular meter, and run 6, 6, 10, then 5, 6, 9 syllables, ignoring the chorus; then 6, 6, 9, and 5, 6 and 9 syllables. So, with songs such as *There Was a Bonie Lass, Ballad* and *The Kirk's Alarm*, it is clear Burns had employed the style of *The Cob Web* on a few occasions. It thus turns out that by being obviously out of meter, *The Cob Web* is characteristic of compositions by the bard in the same style. It seems somewhat ironic that if *The Cob Web* had been written in perfect meter, then it would have been unlike the other songs of Burns and would have been suspect.

Moreover, if Henderson and Henley are correct that Burns modeled the style of *The Kirk's Alarm* on a political song published in *The Glasgow Mercury* on December 1788, it adds to our case. The old song is perfectly in the style of *The Cob Web*, without a chorus. (Kinsley's note on page 1308, volume III, copies the error of Henderson and Henley who printed in line 3 of stanza 1, "argumentation" when it should be "argumentum"). The song begins with erratic meter, but settles to a slightly uneven meter in the remaining verses:

Mr. Fox, Mr. Fox,
Thou'rt knock'd down like an ox,
By honest Will Pitt's argumentum;
'Twas a cursed mistake,
Such assertions to make,
Were they your's, or had LOUGHBRO' lent 'em?

'Twas madness, or folly,
Thus a nation to bully,
And thy tools will have cause to repent it;
From bad men to free us,
'Tis said that, "Quem Deus,
Vult perdere prius dementat"

If this song was the model for *The Kirk's Alarm* composed in 1789, then the poet had been familiar with the style for several years. So, in the years of political tumult which followed, this simple song format is one the poet could have employed standing on his head. The spark for a radical pro-reform poet to write such a poem as *The Cob Web* was probably reading the royalist and jingoist songs written in the same style and published in English newspapers of the 1794-6 period.

Thomas Crawford has documented several royalist songs written in the same format as *The Cob Web*. One example *The Life and Character of Mr Thomas Paine*, describes the radical pamphleteer as "Wicked Tom Paine" and counters the agitation of reformers by glorifying the "torch" of sedition and the great fight for "Freedom" against France - the exact opposite of the poet's views:

> Britons be brave,
> Let us such knave,
> Sedition's torch supply!
> For Freedom's cause,
> In equal laws,
> Resolve to live - or die!

Crawford then goes on to compare this to another radical broadside, *Whitehall Alarmed!*. In the same style as *The Cob Web*, it shows strong similarities with Burns's *Here's A Health Tae Them That's Awa*: "Here's Freedom to him that wad read, / Here's freedom tae him that wad write!" -

> To darken the mind,
> Let the press be confin'd,
> A LAW against Reading and Speaking
> Such bondage might pass,
> Among the low class,
> And let it be called their own seeking.

A further stanza depicts parliament "besieged by Reason" -

Nor can we by force,
Now alter the course
ENQUIRY and REASON are taking;
By Land and by Sea,
They cry to be free!
The powers of the world they are shaking.

It is clear from Crawford's research that the style employed in *The Cob Web* was adopted by right wing loyalists and radicals alike in a feud of verse propaganda during the mid-1790's, a microcosm of the wider ideological clashes. Aware that Burns had declared himself the poet laureate of the Whig Opposition in early 1795, prior to the publication of *The Cob Web*, it is difficult to believe the poet would not have been tempted to reply to the attacks on the reform movement, given his sentiments and habit of responding to issues in the press which outraged his sense of justice. If the manuscript for the broadside *Whitehall Alarmed* is still extant, it may be worth close examination to determine if it is in the handwriting of Burns.

The word "sweets" in the first stanza is distinctive and uncommon in 18th century poetry. Burns employed the word in *The Primrose*, "The sweets of love are wash'd with tears"; and in "While thro your sweets she holds hers way", from *Behold the Hour, The Boat, Arrive*, and in the final version of the same song, where the changes are slight, "While thro thy sweets she loves to stray". The greeting "Hail" in line 3 is found in Burns on sixteen occasions. In all, if we scan the adjectives and adverbs employed throughout poem there is not a cluster of four or more key words alien to Burns which would be grounds to reject the poem, as set out in the chapter on methodology. So, it passes our lexical test. Indeed, the poem is full of monosyllables, a distinctive trait of the bard's writing if we consider songs such as *A Man's A Man*. So, in style and language there is no barrier to attributing *The Cob-Web* to Burns.

The first two stanza of *The Cob Web* contains the same heavy irony of *Whitehall Alarmed!* and grab the reader's attention in the pretense that it is another right wing royalist song, praising British institutions which are in appearance, superior to France. The comparison goes on to argue that Britons "... have flourishing Trade, / Plenty, beer, meat, and bread! / While madly they starve to be free!" This is acute irony because during 1795 a poor harvest and the cessation of grain imported from America caused regional famine in Britain. Also, there is a distinctive Scottish rhyme with "Trade" and "bread", where "bread" is pronounced as the word "braid", and not with the emphasis on the "e" in an English pronunciation. The Scots pronunciation is a west of Scotland one, familiar to Burns. It is in this rhyme that the author of *The Cob Web* is lifted clear of the many English poetasters of the period who sent their work to the *Chronicle*. Moreover, the field is narrowed dramatically, since the number of poets of Scottish origin were few who published radical broadsides with Mr. Perry. The song, therefore, was composed by a Scottish poet - who employed the pen-name A Briton.

The origin of the title of *The Cob Web* may well be the song by William Roscoe which Burns quoted to Mrs. Dunlop on 12th January, 1795, *For the Anniversary of the French Revolution*. It is known Roscoe and Burns were friends and that Roscoe had sent him a copy of the song. The third stanza refers to the propaganda of Edmund Burke as though his views were "cobwebs" which might entangle the unwary:

> Let Burke like a bat from his splendour retire,
>   A splendour too strong for his eyes;
> Let pedants and fools his effusions admire,
>   Entrapped in his cobwebs like flies.
> Shall insolent sophistry hope to prevail
>   Where Reason opposes her weight,
> When the welfare of millions is hung in the scale,
>   And the balance yet trembles with fate.

Readers of the bard's letters will be familiar with the last two lines, used by Burns to stoically accept the value of the greater good in his reference to the execution of the King and Queen of France. The title *The Cob Web*, though, is merely a sarcastic simile for the predicament which British citizens were caught in during 1795, when Brunswick's plan of bringing France to its knees through starvation appeared to be happening in Britain.

The grinding irony of *The Cob Web* turns the "good" of loyalty to the Hanoverian government into a good "full of evil, Devis'd by the Devil" and goes on to comment that "some Demon of Hell, /Inverting the spell, / Turn'd the picture of Famine on us!" The anti-war tenor of the song is powerful in its simplicity. The indignant anger of Burns at Britain's involvement in the war with France comes through strongly. His anti-war view is recorded in the complex and more abstract Pindaric *Washington Ode*, "That hour accurst how did the fiends rejoice, /And Hell thro all her confines raise the exulting voice / ... the generous English name / Link't with such damned deeds of everlasting shame". The ironic wit of the final stanza concludes that the policy of Pitt to eradicate food shortages may still be achieved, after "nine out of ten" Britons are killed in the war "And the rest are left something to eat". This mocking irony is classic Burnsian bombast often found in his epigrammatic works.

Overall, the case for attributing *The Cob-Web* is strong. He was more than familiar with the style of song and was not particular about balanced meter in this radical broadside format. The wit and irony of the song are found in his writings. He had promised to write and send material to the newspaper. The fact that there is a clear Scottish rhyme in the song, points convincingly to a Scottish poet. This means a Scottish poet who employed the pen-name A. Briton. Burns was the only Scottish poet to do so. There is no cluster of alien adjectives or adverbs to alert us to a major shift in language usage. Therefore, circumstantial and textual evidence point overwhelmingly to Burns as the only possible author.

A13. *John Anderson My Joe*

John Anderson my Joe, John,
I wonder what you mean,
Approving of the Bills, John
The Bills you ne'er had seen! -
'Twas surely very foolish, John,
And how could you do so?
Pray had your tongue and say nae mair,
John Anderson my Joe!

The story of the Phaeton, John,
Was but an auld wife's saw,
And like another Phaeton, John,
You'll surely have a fa':
This talking will undo you, John,
And lack of truth much mo' -
You've neither brains nor gift o' Gab;
John Anderson my Joe!

This song appears in the *Morning Chronicle* on December 5th 1795. It is clearly the work of a Scottish poet and songwriter. This clearly narrows the field down to a few authors. It is too brief to analyse on a stylistic basis, but there are a few giveaway signs as to its author. Due to its marked similarity with *New Song, A Wet Day at Walmer Castle*, already ascribed to Burns from the *Gazetteer*, it seems inconceivable that it might be by any other Scottish writer but Burns. Given the poet's contacts with the London broadsheet, his epigram on phaetons, or high carraiges, which we know of; given the re-appearance of A. Briton in the *Chronicle* a few months earlier, plus his distinctive satirical wit, this cheeky adaption of *John Anderson My Jo* is surely his.

Chapter 8

From The Glasgow Advertiser *or* The Herald

A14. Remember the Poor

FRAE Greenland's snawie mountain high,
(Whare sleaks o' ice tumult'ous lye,
    An dismal scenes appear)
Bauld Boreas, wi' his surly train,
Rides howling thro' the mirk domain,
    And leads and guides the weir:
Nae mair the gowany field leuks gay,
    Nor flow'r-bespangled green,
To tempt our waunrin' feet to stray,
    Or charm our rovin' een;
        Mair dowie they grow ay,
            An' wither in the blast,
      I'm vext now, perplex now,
           To think their beauty's past.

Happy are they, wha, without dread,
Can hear the storm blaw owre their head,
    Nor danger needs to fear: -
Blest are ye, highly favour'd Great,
Wha coshly rest on beds o' state,
    Crown'd wi' ilk dainty chear; -
Enrag'd ay whan I do compare
    Your blythsome lives wi' mine,
(For mine's a life opprest wi' care,
    An' drudgery an' pine)
        I snarl and quarrell
           Wi' Fortune, that blind wh-re,
      That leuks down, and does frown
           On me, and hauds me poor: -

Reflect sae wretched's they maun be
That's doom'd tae pinchin' poverty
    And stern misfortune's blows;
An' O! thy pittance do thou grant -
It will banish their ilk' care an' want,
    An' rid them o' their woes:
Wi' sauls quite liberal an' free
    Your charity extend;
Now is the time, - an' credit me
    Ye'll no' miss't in the end.
        Mak' haste then, nor waste then
          Your siller on ought ill;
        Ease their need wi' a' speed
          Lest hunger does them kill.

Hail ye wha ha'e wi' open heart
Come forth o' late, an' ta'en their part -
    A noble gen'rous deed!
Is there, whate blude rins in yer viens,
A wretch, wha's cash , an' yet refrains
    Tae join ye wi' a speed —
(Uwordy's he to see the light
    O' day, that e'er wad scan,
An', for the sake o' riches, slight
    His fellow-creature, Man) -
        May his gear thro' ilk year
          Ay mair an' mair decrease,
        Wha'll no join wi' his coin
          To help fowks in distress.

Lang may ye live, Sirs, to defend
An' stand the poor man's constant friend
    In ilka time o' need;
Syne, whan Death at your doors does ca',
An' lays ye lifeless, ane an' a',
    Amang the silent dead,
Fame on her trump your praise will soun',
    An' mark ye in her pages,
That your deeds may be handed down
    Unto the latest ages; -
        An' may't be your decree -
            "Throughout an' endless day,
        "T'inherit by merit
            "The ever-sproutin' bay".

Jan 27th 1794, by JOB.

Taking a Neebor's Part - the Bard and Job

Remember the Poor was published in *The Glasgow Advertiser* of 27 January 1794. The *Advertiser* was the forerunner to *The Glasgow Herald*, now *The Herald*. The poem was composed in response to a clergyman's sermon published in the December issue of Dr. James Anderson's *Literary Weekly Intelligencer*, commonly called *The Bee*. The sermon, *"Address by a Clergyman"*, had been taken down and published from an anonymous preacher and describes the unemployment and hunger suffered in and around Glasgow in the winter of 1793-4. To introduce the sermon, Burns's poem *The Cottar's Saturday Night* was published in its entirety. (This highlights an error in *The Complete Letters,* which states "the only thing from his pen" published in *The Bee* was a letter to the Earl of Buchan. Further, *Verses Written on A Window In Breadalbane by Robert Burns* was also published in *The Bee* in 1792). The *Cottar's* was used to illustrate the worthiness of "the poor" and launch the charity plea. This places Burns' name and poetry in the forefront of the charity call.

Why *Remember the Poor* was published in *The Glasgow Advertiser* and not *The Bee* is an obvious question. *The Bee* closed in mid-January 1794. By printing the poem in *The Glasgow Advertiser* it widened the call for charity to a larger readership than the exclusive *Bee*. Moreover, *The Glasgow Advertiser* was a radical newspaper supportive of the pro-democracy group, the Friends of the People and the Anti-Slavery campaign prominent in Scottish politics in the mid-1790's. The *Advertiser* was, therefore, a newspaper which would have kept the poet's name anonymous. After all, he had promised to his employers he would keep out of controversy and was acting on his policy to "jouk and let the jaw flee o'er" - not to be caught in public wrangling on political matters.

Remember the Poor is the only newspaper poem in the bob-wheel stanza of *Epistle to Davie* during the 1790's. Most imitators of Burns who wrote in Scots verse employed Standard Habbie format almost ad nausea. By January 1794 the spate of imitators had subsided. In fact, the bulk of poems found in newspapers and journals during the early 1790's are in Augustan English and bear no resemblance to *Remember the Poor*. In fact, the average number of poems per year within Scottish newspapers during the 1790's is around 9. So, the dearth of high quality poetry in the Scots language within Scots verse format makes *Remember the Poor* virtually unique. It is astounding that this poem has not come to light before 1996. The only poet during this period who was known to employ the bob-wheel stanza with any real success was Burns.

It is known Burns subscribed to *The Bee*. At its launch, he was invited to compose for *The Bee* by Dr. Thomas Blacklock in September, 1790, who wrote to him in verse. Moreover, Dr. Anderson, who edited *The Bee*, requested Burns write for the journal. In his subscription response the poet declined the opportunity, but included a list of additional subscribers for Anderson. (CL 426). Burns loaned copies of *The Bee* to James Johnson, song collector, insisting that they be returned "take care of the two Numbers, as the loss of them would break my set". (CL 452) So, there is ample evidence to show Burns subscribed to *The Bee* and would have read the clergyman's article and noticed his own poem in re-print. He would have been delighted, proud and honoured to see his poem used to spearhead a humanitarian cause. He was, after all, in Daiches' apt phrase, a "passionate egalitarian".

Is it feasible that a poet of passionate humanitarian values would sit on his hands and do nothing on hearing a public call for charity in *The Bee?* Would Burns have ignored a call to help the suffering poor? The poet was charitable by personality: folklore tells that in Dumfries, even when his own family struggled, the bard and Mrs. Burns often gave aid to the hungry and destitute. He had suffered poverty's "cold blast" firsthand. So, from what is known about the poet's personality and views on poverty, it is clear he was not the type of person to do nothing. Indeed, his sentiments are a *prima-facie* motive to action. So, we can deduce with confidence that it would have been characteristic of the bard to help the plea for charity. What form of assistance would he have given?

There is no extant letter to confirm money was forwarded to the Glasgow fund by the poet. It is known the war against France diminished his income by almost a quarter, relying as it did on a percentage share of Excise seizures. In fact, on 24 December 1793, around the time when he would have read the call for charity in *The Bee,* Burns wrote coyly of his own and Scotland's "epidemical complaint" - "WANT OF CASH". (CL 605) Thus, we can sure that he was unable to contribute financially. In *Epistle to A Young Friend,* stanza 4, the bard suggested charity may have many forms other than "cash":

> A man may hae an honest heart,
> Tho poorith hourly stare him;
> A man may take a neebor's part,
> Yet hae nae cash tae spare him.

In a letter to James Hoy, Burns' told him poets could only pay in one "coin", that of "Rhyme". (CL 149) Also, a similar remark was penned to John McMurdo, "Kings give Coronets; Alas, I can only bestow a Ballad."(CL 571) So, aware Burns would have been keen to assist the public call for aid, the evidence suggests he would have *at the very least,* composed a poem to "take a neebor's part" and boost the call for charity.

The pseudonym "Job" is of interest. There is no secret code in the letters J, O and B. It refers simply to the Biblical name "Job" from the oldest book in the Old Testament, to hide the author's name. Its use suggests the author of *Remember the Poor* strongly identified with the Biblical figure. Job was a farmer with great wealth and power. In a trial of his faith, Job was cast into poverty, lost fame and family and was wracked with illness. Through his hardship, Job held to his faith and was supported by three friends. For Job, faith was a hedge of protection. Are there echoes of Job's experience in the poet's life?

There are. The poet had been a farmer. He had gained fame and to some extent, wealth. He gave a large share of his wealth to his brother Gilbert. He lost Ellisland farm, a "ruinous bargain", due mainly to an excessive rent. His fame diminished sometime around 1794, as implied in *From Aesopus to Maria*-"The shrinking bard adown the alley skulks". He also wrote of "My enemies" and "those who wait for my haulting". He had three main friends in Dumfries, Syme, Maxwell and McMurdo. He had lost his own young twins and a daughter. He had suffered periodic illness and a broken arm at Ellisland. He had to ride up to two hundred miles a week on Excise duties, doing what he considered to be the devil's work. In the teeth of misfortune's "blast", he also held onto his faith in God, and told one correspondent that he kept on his desk at all times a reminder of the benefits of "Religion", an eight line quotation beginning "'Tis this my Friend, that streaks our morning bright".(CL 524) There can be little doubt that the hardship suffered by Burns provided him with many echoes which link his experience with the Biblical figure Job, especially on the theme of poverty.

However, only a poet with a distinct fascination for the *Book of Job* would employ the pen-name. The references to Job in Burns's letters are numerous. For instance, to Charles Sharpe, he described himself as a "misbegotten son of Poverty & Rhyme ...beggared" with barely "a shirt on my back" whose "pilgrimages" in singing ballads from town to town was something "not even the hide of Job's behemoth could bear". (CL 446) To Mrs. Dunlop he wrote "in the language of the Book of Job" he was waiting for "..the day of battle and of war" (CL 362). Also, to Robert Ainlsie, he complained of the difficult life of a tenant farmer but stoically remarked, in the language of "Job, or some one of his friends..."Why should a living man complain?""(CL 248) In a letter to Dr. Moore, in 1790, the bard remarked "..but I am fond of the spirit of young Elihu shews in the Book of Job - "And I said I will also declare my opinion" (Job 32: 10)". (CL 404) Indeed, there are more references to Job in Burns's letters than to any other book of the Bible, 11 in total. (CL Index, p819) No other Biblical figure features as often as Job in passages where the bard has written on poverty or life's trials of hardship - the specific context of *Remember the Poor*. Hence, the pen-name does, after all, become a hook Burns would have hung his hat on.

Of course there was a considerable degree of Biblical language within the mindset of educated people during the late 18th century. However, few aristocrats or nobles who penned poetry would have identified with a figure who suffered poverty - it was the lot of the peasantry. It is significant, that of all the sections of the Bible, the bard had an inordinate interest with the story of Job. The notion that every rhymer and poet of the period scribbled over *The Book of Job* is surely preposterous. So, prior to a textual analysis of the poem, contextual evidence strongly points to Burns' authorship.

Stylistically, the poem is in the distinctive form of the bob-wheel stanza employed by Burns in *Epistle to Davie, To Ruin, Love and Liberty* from *The Jolly Beggars; Despondency, An Ode*, and *The Farewell*. It is a poetic form Burns lifted successfully from Montgomerie's old ballad *The Cherry and the Slae*. The poem is a well crafted work with an evenly balanced syllable count. Clearly, it is not the work of an amateur. It is a flawless example of the poetic form.

The ring of the poem sounds as though it is from Burns's existing Scots vernacular genre. In sentiment and language it is echoed in *Man Was Made to Mourn, The Twa Dogs, Lines Written on a Banknote, A Winter Night, A Man's A Man* and particularly, *Epistle to Davie*. It does not read as an amateur attempt at mimicry. It displays the distinctive Burns' style of setting a scene by painting a cinematic, dramatic image of nature first. The first stanzas of *Epistle to Davie* are remarkably similar to *Remember the Poor:*

While winds frae aff Ben-Lomond blaw,
And bar the doors wi drivin snaw,
    And hing us owre the ingle,
I set me down to pass the time,
And spin a verse or twa in rhyme,
    In hamely, westlin jingle:
While frosty winds blaw in the drift,
    Ben to the chimla lug,
I grudge a wee the great folk's gift,
    That live sae bien an snug:
        I tent less, and want less
            Their roomy fire-side;
    But hanker, and canker,
        To see their cursed pride.

It's hardly in a body's pow'r,
To keep, at times, frae being sour,
    To see how things are shar'd;
How best o chiels are whyles in want,
While coofs on countless thousands rant,
    And ken na how to ware't;
But, Davie lad, ne'er fash your head
    Tho we hae little gear;
We're fit to win our daily bread,
    As lang's we're hale and fier:
    Mair spier na', nor fear na',
        Auld age ne'er mind a feg;
    The last o't, the warst o't,
        Is only but to beg.

A distinctive feature of *Epistle to Davie,* which is also found in *Remember the Poor,* is the criticism of the "great folks" or "highly favour'd Great" compared to the worthiness of the poor. Immediately, this tells us the author of *Remember the Poor* is not a wealthy landowner or member of the Edinburgh Literati, but someone who has known hardship. Distilled in the first two stanzas of *Epistle to Davie* is the style, language and theme of *Remember the Poor* in the same bob-wheel stanza, rich Braid Scots, with a distinctive Burnsian brushstroke - employing a description of nature's scenery to set a mood and scene

- and the familiar contrast between rich and poor from a radical perspective. The bob-wheel stanza is not a poetic form an amateur could easily adopt with its intricate meter. Both poems were written in the month of January and are separated by a period of 9 years.

The cinematic imagery which begins *Remember the Poor* is a dramatic Miltonic image. Winter is symbolised in the personage of Bauld Boreas, the God of the North wind. Boreas is described as "howling" a destructive war of elements from Greenland, through mountains of "tumult'ous" ice "wi' his surly train". The casual use of brackets for "(Whare sleaks o' ice tumult'ous lye,/And dismal scenes appear)" suggests a confident poet intent on conveying an image of other worldly forces at work in the destructive power of winter. It creates an atmosphere which could easily have been the start of a Scots-styled *Ancient Mariner*. The phrase "dismal scenes" is not found in Burns' poetry, but can be traced to another poetic icon of Burns, Edward Young, in *A Poem on The Last Day*, line 143. Bauld Boreas has brought decay and laid waste the "flower-bespangled green" - summer's blossom. The first stanza fully develops the underlying theme of nature and closes with a sense of loss, allowing the tone to change from winter to poverty and suffering. The first stanza is striking in its strong poetic voice, the tone and clarity of language employed, which set the scene and mood. It is distinctively in the Burnsian mould.

Stanza 1, line one, "Frae Greenlands snawie mountains high" is echoed in Burns' *Now Spring Has Clad the Grove in Green*, "O, had my fate been Greenland snows" and sounds more Burnsian than "Farewell to the mountains, high-cover'd with snow" from *My Heart's in The Highlands*. The adjective "tumult'ous" is used by Burns in *On A Bank of Flowers*. verse 3. The word "dismal" is employed in a similar fashion in *On Mrs Riddell's Birthday*, stanza 1. The adjective "surly" is found in *Young Peggy*, verse 3, to describe "..surly, savage Winter" or "...aged Winter, 'mid his surly reign", from *On Hearing a Thrush Sing During A Morning Walk* and employed in a similar context in stanza 1, *Man was Made to Mourn*, "When chill November's surly blast". The phrase "winter war" in stanza 3, *A Winter Night*, means the same as "weir" in *Remember the Poor* where Boreas "leads and guides the weir" - a war of winter elements. Also, the use of "dowie" - listless or worn out - occurs in Burns' *The Young Highland Rover, Highland Harry Back Again* and in *Poor Mailie's Elegy* and is only used by poets such as Ferguson and Ramsay, who were both dead in 1794. The spelling of "snawie" is the same found in *To A Mountain Daisy*. So, the language of the first stanza rings true to the Burnsian mould.

When the Miltonic description "Bauld Boreas, wi' his surly train" is compared to Burns' works, a strong echo is found in the radical song *The Fete Champetre*, written by Burns in 1788 - "Cauld Boreas, wi his boisterous crew". The similarity of language is striking: "Bauld Boreas" matches closely "Cauld Boreas", while "surly train" and "boisterous crew" are synonymous. The only other poet of the 18th century known to use the phrase "Bauld Boreas" is Allan Ramsay (1686-1758) in *The Nipping Frost and Driving Sna'* and his *The Vision*. There can be no mimicry of Burns in the lines found in *Remember the Poor* since *The Fete Champetre* was only published under his name posthumously. The Miltonic image of "Bauld Boreas" in *Remember the Poor* is bolder and more powerful than Burns' line in stanza 1, *The Mauchline Wedding*, "When rotting rain and Boreas bauld". In all, the first stanza stands up well to close comparison with Burns' writings and shows flashes of improved poetic quality to some works of the bard, particularly the striking Miltonic image of winter. If Burns is not the author of this poem, the precise lexical overlap with *The Fete Champetre* is astounding coincidence which tests the limits of probability.

It is significant that there is a strong echo in the first stanza of *Remember the Poor* from Robert Ferguson's *The Daft Days*. The Edinburgh poet wrote in stanza 3:

> ...Wi' frozen spear,
> Sends drift owre a' his bleak *domain*,
> *And guides the weir*
> Whan Winter, 'midst his nippin' *train*.

The rhyme and the final description in the new poem are strikingly similar -

> Bauld Boreas, wi' his surly *train*,
> Rides howling thro' the mirk *domain*,
> And leads and guides the *weir*.

In addition, the line "Or charm our rovin' een;" is taken partly from Ferguson's *Leith Races*, which reads "To charm our rovin' een". There is no dispute about the influence of Ferguson on Burns, with strong links between *The Farmer's Ingle* and *The Cottar's Saturday Night* and echoes from Ferguson's *Hallow Fair* in Burns's *The Holy Fair*. The two poetic eulogies dedicated to Ferguson and the headstone Burns erected to him are testament to the influence he had on the bard. Burns was more than capable of lifting these lines from Ferguson and being steeped in the Scottish literary *ouvre* he could have employed the phrases from Ferguson almost subconsciously. The Ferguson-like lines in *Remember the Poor* are not mimicry; they are part of a focused and developed image from a poet who had matured beyond Ferguson. In the 1790's the only known Scottish poet who was likely to lift phrases from Ferguson and apply them in a *superior* manner was Burns.

Superficially, stanza 1 appears to possess a few words alien to Burns. They are not the glaringly obvious parochial spellings or words employed by Alexander Wilson, for instance. There are no examples of the words "sleaks", "flower-bespangled" or "vext" and "perplext" in known Burns' writings. However, "flower-bespangled" is more or less the equivalent of "flower-enamour'd" in verse 3, of Burns' *Delia*. A few apparently "strange" words do not, linguistically, pose a problem to Burns' potential authorship. The entire *raison d'être* of the poetic imagination is to search for and use new, sharper defined images in more precise, descriptive words. The poetic fusion of intellect and imagination, like a welding rod, is a process which strives to constantly improve and add to an existing store of words and imagery. The poet's goal is, therefore, always to find a new description, the elusive chase after the unique and original. The notion a poet's stock of words never changes is nonsense - although the pattern of how adjectives, nouns and verbs are employed might not change. The first song must differ from the second, and so on. Since originality cannot always be achieved, its substitute is to lift a particular phrase or word from an admired poet. The word "coshly" in stanza 2 of *Remember the Poor* is only found in Robert Ferguson's *Elegy on John Hogg*, among all Scots vernacular poems of the 18th century. A phrase, "dismal scenes" from Young, has already been indicated. In fact, several of the new words which critics might seize upon to argue Burns never used this or that word, reinforce his likely authorship precisely because they are taken from Ramsay, Young and Ferguson; stock and trade sources which feature in Burns' poetry.

Stanza 2 compares the luxury of the wealthy and powerful in Scotland with the peasant's life of endless work. The worries of the poor contrast dramatically with the comfortable "beds o' state" with which the "highly favour'd Great" are "Blest". The rich and powerful are described as free from winter's storms or "danger" and "dread". In *To Ruin,* Burns uses the words "storm" and "dread", "The storm no more I'll dread". Also, the words "Blest", "Fortune" and "favour'd" used in *Remember the Poor* can be found in *A Dedication To Gavin Hamilton* - "Are blest with Fortune's smiles and favours". The word "Great", which refers to nobles and aristocrats, finds many comparisons: in *Bess and Her Spinning Wheel* "state" and "great" form the rhyme - "O, wha wad leave this humble state / For a' the pride of a' the great?" In the final stanza of *Elegy on Captain Matthew Henderson,* the same rhyme echoes "Go to your sculptur'd tombs, ye Great, / In a' the tinsel trash o state!". It is repeated in *On Dining with Lord Daer,* stanza 7, "I watch'd the symptoms o the Great - /The gentle pride, the lordly state". Then again, in *Second Epistle to J. Lapraik,* "Were this the charter of our state,/On pain o hell the rich and great". In the anti-war *Logan Braes,* the unfeeling stately "Great" are blasted for their callousness - "O, wae upon you, Men o State,/ That brethern rouse in deadly hate!" Even in judging the death of his fellow poet, Ferguson, "my elder brother in misfortune", Burns accuses the "great" of Edinburgh society of starving him, "Yet Luxury and Wealth lay by in State, / And, thankless, starv'd what they so much admir'd". Also, the idle luxury of the "Great", comfortable in their "beds o state" is echoed in *A Winter Night,* "Oh ye! who, sunk in beds of down, / Feel not a want but what yourselves create, / Think, for a moment, on his wretched fate, / Whom friends and fortune quite disown!" *A Winter Night* goes on to shame those who have no feelings for the fate of the destitute poor. This sentiment in *Remember the Poor* is turned in stanza 4 to curse those who would "scan" and "slight" "His fellow-creature, Man", hoping "...his gear" would "mair an' mair decrease". Here is a clear echo of *Address to the Unco Guid,* "Then gently scan your brother man". The moral ending to *A Winter Night* "The heart most benevolent and kind / The most resembles God" echoes the religo-humanitarian sentiment of *Remember the Poor.* Pricking the conscience of the "highly favour'd Great, / Wha coshly rest on beds o' state" or condemning their cotton-wooled luxury, their "post" and "pension", is a well known motif in Burns' social comment poetry.

The frustrated anger in *Remember the Poor* at the unequal distribution of wealth, an intrinsic feature of semi-feudal rural Scotland, is featured in many letters of Burns (see CL 244, 358, 335, 347, 510, 319, 605, 638, 411B) where the epithet "snarl an' quarrel" is often apt. A classic example of Burns' indignant fury in full flight can be found in the passage to Peter Hill beginning "Poverty! Thou half-sister of Death, thou cousin-germain of Hell .... (which ends) ...while shallow Greatness in his idiot attempts at wit shall meet with countenance & applause". (CL 430) Clearly, the poet of *Remember the Poor* has suffered poverty and hardship and displays passionate feelings. Moreover, in December 1793, the poet quarreled with the Riddell's after being set-up in an aristocratic prank, the now infamous "Rape of the Sabines incident", which may have been the psychological background for the lines "snarl and quarrel, / Wi' Fortune, that blind wh-re".

The semi-autobiographical impression in stanza 2 reflect the author's strongly held views. It is of interest to find similar expressions throughout Burns's poetry where he could be said to "snarl an' quarrel,/ Wi' Fortune..." They include *The Creed of Poverty*, with its warning, if "mean thy fortunes be,/ Bear this in mind, be deaf and blind,/ Let Great folks think and see". Also in *My Father Was A Farmer Upon The Carrick Border,* the poet mentions his own struggle against "Fortune" - "In many a way, and vain essay, I courted Fortune's favour; O/ Some cause unseen, still stept between, and frustrate each endeavour; O". The song goes on to mention "fortune's vain delusion; O" and "Tho' fortune's frown still hunts me down with all her wonted malice; O". The teeth of the bard's radical humanitarianism is also found in lyrical "snarl" in *Lines Written on A Banknote*, where he "... vainly wish'd, / To crush the villain in the dust...". Moreover, when *Remember the Poor* moves from "snarl an' quarrell" to "...that blind whore,/ That leuks down, and does frown/ On me, and hauds me poor", it provides a further autobiographical clue about the author. In 1794 Burns may have been the famed bard of Caledonia, but he continued to struggle against poverty.

The introductory note to his first *Commonplace Book* echoes the phrase "hauds me poor" which suggests an author who desired to be wealthier. The poet described himself as "a man who had little art in making money, and still less in keeping it". Given Burns's fame and the publication of the 1793 Edinburgh edition of his works, which did not earn the poet any money, it is clear he would be able to relate to the notion of "Fortune" holding him in poverty. His hope of promotion to Supervisor in the Excise was not professional ambition, it was a dream of getting greater time to devote to poetry, with extra income as a bonus. He was regularly anxious about poverty and commented to Mrs. Dunlop, that his "old companion, Poverty, is to be my attendant to the grave"(CL 638). As early as his *First Epistle to Robert Graham of Fintry*, the poet affirmed his dogged determination not to sell his soul for the King's shilling: "The pie-bald jacket let me patch once more, / On eighteen pence a week I've liv'd before." Also, in stanza 6 of *Epistle to Dr. Blacklock*, the poet made it clear he would do anything to keep his family from destitution "But I'll sned besoms, thraw saugh woodies, / Before they want". So, even in the vague and shadowy self-portrait of the author in stanza 2 of *Remember the Poor* itself, the image, like a photograph slowly developing in solution, paints a reasonably acceptable picture of Burns's experiences. In a sense the bard was obsessed with the paradox of his fame and his poverty. Thus, in stanza 2, the personal Burnsian imprint is striking.

In *Remember the Poor*, stanza 3, lines 1-3 read as though they are straight from *The Twa Dogs* where the language is synonymous with "wretched", "doom'd", "pinchin' poverty" and "misfortune's blows". One of *The Twa Dogs*, Luath, explains that if one disaster happens to the poor, "...they maun starve o cauld and hunger". The use of "stern Misfortune's blows" where "doom'd" is also employed is seen in *Address Spoken by Miss Fontenelle*, written by the bard around December 1793, one month before *Remember the Poor*:

> Thou man of crazy care and ceaseless sigh,
> Still under bleak Misfortune's blasting eye;
> Doom'd to that sorest task of man alive -
> To make three guineas do the work of five.

(Although Burns used the word "doom'd" only 6 times, he always dropped the "e", as found in *Remember the Poor*.) In *Epistle to James Smith*, stanza 25, the exact words "Misfortune's blows", used in *Remember the Poor*, are found "I jouk beneath Misfortune's blows". If a writer can be known by their use of adjectives, *those found in Remember the Poor* are in key with Burns' best poetry.

Stanzas 4 and 5 celebrate those who have already pledged aid to the poor and condemns those who would "...for the sake o' riches, slight" "Their fellow-creature, Man". These words are echoed in the quotation used at the start of *Address to the Unco Guid*, "So ne'er a fellow-creature slight", where "fellow", "creature" and "slight" are matched. An echo can be found with "sake" and "slight" in *Here's His Health in Water*, verse 1, "'Till for his sake I'm slighted sair". The spelling of "blude", meaning blood, occurs 6 times among the bard's work, but is more commonly "bluid" (27 times) or the English "blood"(28 examples). One year after the composition of *Remember the Poor*, Burns chose the same spelling "blude" in *The Dumfries Volunteers*, "Our father's blude the kettle bought". The word "gear", meaning possessions, is found in 35 examples of the poet's work. The sentiment expressed in "May his gear thro' ilk year /Ay mair an' mair decrease", condemns the "great" who would not help the plea for charity. It rings of *Man Was Made to Mourn*, where the callous "lordly fellowworm" could "The poor petition spurn" and the indictment in *A Winter Night* that man's suffering inflicted on fellow man often far surpassed nature's wildest destructive havoc. Even the word "Uwordy" in stanza 5, meaning "unworthy", is far from alien to Burns. We find him using "wordy" on a few occasions, listed in *The Complete Wordfinder*. It is merely the opposite meaning. The poem therefore, does not merely ring of Burns in language, sentiment and nuance, it is almost as though we have struck a literary artery and each word is a blood vessel soaked by usage among the poetry of Burns.

Stanza 5's ".. the poor man's constant friend / In ilka time o' need" is echoed in *A Dedication to Gavin Hamilton*, "... the poor man's friend in need" and stanza 6, *Epistle to the Rev. John McMath*, "See him, the poor man's friend in need". The description in *Remember the Poor*, "Death, at your door does ca'" is similar to "Till death did on him ca'" from stanza 6, *Ballad on the American War*. Also, the phrase "Fame on her trump ..." rings like "Will gar Fame blaw until her trumpet crack", from *Scots Prologue for Mrs Sutherland*, stanza 4. The end of the poem, with its immortal blessing on the benefactors of the poor, who will receive their laurels in the form of praise from future "ages", rings like the end to *The Whistle, On the Death of Sir James Hunter-Blair, Election Ballad Addressed to Fintry* and the song *When First I Saw*, where garlands, bays or laurels are mentioned. The final stanza praises the "Good Samaratan" Christian act of giving, and thus knits the poem to its religious pseudonym, Job.

There are other poetic works on the theme of helping the poor in Scottish newspapers of the period, but they are poor and patchy in comparison to *Remember the Poor*, the only newspaper poem in bob-wheel stanza for the entire 1790's. For instance, *The Humble Address of the Industrious and Indignant Poor* from *The Edinburgh Evening Courant*, March 23rd 1795, is on the same theme - the best stanzas are 1 and 5

> Full five long weeks the frost has pinch'd us sore,
> And cold, with poverty, is hard to bear;
> But thanks to heav'n! we anchor on the shore
> Where tales of woe are heard with gracious ear....

> This well-trimm'd charity and kind relief
> Shall in our greatful hearts be treasur'd up;
> We'll bless all those who dissipate our grief,
> And kindly sweeten our embitter'd cup.

If this is an attempt at poetry from someone who suffered hunger and cold, it is grossly artificial and incongruous by employing such flowery, "humble" language on the subject of hardship and suffering, without a hint of being "indignant". It is a weedy effort which contrasts starkly with the confidence, skill and natural flow of language in *Remember the Poor*.

In sum, there are simply too many lexical overlaps with Burns in *Remember the Poor* to be coincidence. Most Scots poems from the 1780-1790's period bear virtually no textual comparison to Burns and often illustrate regional word spelling absent from *Remember the Poor*. Stanza 1 is strikingly Burnsian in tone. The overlap of "Bauld Boreas, wi' his surly train" and "Cauld Boreas, wi' his boisterous crew" suggests more than simple mimicry of the bard. Indeed, there are flashes of poetic genius in *Remember the Poor* which surpass some of the bard's works - a feature which would be expected 9 years after *Epistle to Davie*. Moreover, there are a few lines which are so simple, such as "... to see the light o' day" and "...for the sake o' riches" which are simply too relaxed to have come from an imitators pen. The intricate meter of the bob-wheel stanza does not make it an easy Scots verse form to mimic. Contextually and textually, the evidence points firmly to Burns as the author, a poet who had a fascination with the *Book of Job*. It is inconceivable that Burns would have been unaware of the call for charity around Glasgow and would have callously ignored the plight of the hungry. Given that there was no-one in Scotland at this time who could write Scots verse poetry to this level, other than Burns, it is *beyond reasonable doubt* the bard's work.

A15: The Remonstrance and Petition of Rover, A Poor Dog

Hard-hearted, sour, unpitying Dent -
Will thy stern spirit ne'er relent?
    The curse of man and dog!
Tir'd, for a while, with Negro banging,
Thou'd'st take a turn at spaniel hanging,
    And flog, and hang, and flog.

O thou hast got a dainty heart!
Go to Jack Ketch, and learn his art;
    Halters are pretty trifles;
Learn how to pull a kicking leg,
Tuck up a puppy on a peg,
    Or give a hound the stifles.

And yet that heart, which, hard as stone,
Felt nothing for poor *Mungo's* moan,
    Is grown so mighty tender,
That an old wedder cannot bleed,
But Dent abhors the unrighteous deed;
    Of flocks the stout defender.

For lambs are such soft pastoral creatures,
And have such dear bewitching features;
    What mortals can withstand 'em?
'Tis their white coats this mercy brings,
Had Nature dy'd them *black*, sweet things,
    We might have killed at random.

Now, lambkins, ye may safely stray;
This pious shepherd guards your way:
    How jealous for his mutton.
Curse on the dog who picks a bone,
Scarecly three shillings can atone,
Or save thy weazand, glutton.

When Pitt to save these harmless dears,
Has pull'd *his House* about our ears
    Away we curs must scamper.
E'en Dash, the guard of Holywood geese,
Who like his master, loves to fleece,
    No more his guts must pamper.

Three shillings for your dog per ann!
Good Master, save me - if you can;
    The threat'ning noose throw by:
O think how many theivish curs,
Tho' clothed perhaps in richer furs
    Want hanging more than I.

Ah, let me live! - not great the cost; -
If dogs all die, the State is lost,
    For Pitt must have his taxes:
And shou'd we slip his fingers thro',
From cats he'll squeeze a shilling too,
    To save from cords and axes.

Not much of service can I boast; -
Humble, and faithful at my post;
    Kind Sir, then pray relent.
But if my kneck can not be spar'd,
I die, - ye cruel fates, how hard,
    I die by an ill-Dent.*

*A sudden stroke, vulgarly supposed, of witchcraft, and portentous of death.

From Luath to Rover

In *The Glasgow Courier*, 20 June 1796, the poem *The Remonstrance and Petition of Rover, a Poor Dog*, was published unsigned. It is written in Scots verse format. It is a satirical broadside on the Dog Tax which was about to be brought into law in July 1796. Obviously, the author was not a dog named Rover, but a poet who had their pulse on British legislation going through the House of Commons. The poem is a satire on the wider issue of William Pitt's tax raising power during the war against France. Burns was never enamoured by apparently unnecessary tax increases and sarcastically jibed at Pitt "I'm no mistrusting Willie Pitt, /When taxes he enlarges..." in *A Dream* and wagged his finger at Scottish M.P.'s in *The Author's Earnest Cry and Prayer* and *Scotch Drink* on the issue of legislation to increase liquor duty and apply it to the Forbes distillery at Ferintosh. Even as late as 1795 there is evidence of Burns' satirical pen being aimed at new taxation, the introduction of a hair powder tax: "Pray Billy Pitt explain thy rigs, /This new poll-tax of thine!" The wit of the poem is intense and in a few stanzas, verges on bawdy humour which might not appeal to genteel readers.

It is well known Burns owned a dog called Rover while he lived in Dumfries. In fact, a question put to the public on Radio Scotland in January, 1996, to be answered by telephone, was "What was the name of Robert Burns's dog when he lived in Dumfries?" "Rover" was the winning answer. So, of all the astonishing factors to tie a poem to Burns, his dog's name is probably the most unlikely imaginable. However improbable the connection might seem, it is a link to the poet which cannot be dismissed easily. Probability suggests every dog in Scotland in 1796 was not called Rover. Of the dogs who were called Rover, few would have been owned by a poet. Even if another poet did own a dog of the same name, would they too have been experts in humorous poetry? The balance of probabilities tips in favour of this poem being a composition of Burns.

The notion Burns could not have written this work because he was too ill to write does not stand up to scrutiny. He was still writing letters right up until a few days before his death. Moreover, he was re-writing old songs and composing his own, up until June and sent two letters to George Thomson in July, 1796. An article in *The Herald* in January, 1996 suggested Burns was an ailing man during his last three and a half years and implied he was not fit to have composed the "new" radical poems, despite contradictory evidence to confirm he had composed well over 100 songs in the last three years and penned over 50 letters to George Thomson alone, dispatching in excess of 150 known letters in the same period. Physical illness, therefore, did not seriously impede Burns mental enthusiasm for correspondence or composition. Thus, the poet was certainly capable of writing this poem during late May, or early June 1796, with time to see the poem dispatched to Glasgow for publication. Even if the poet had been confined to bed during this period - which he was not - it is very likely sheer boredom would have driven him to write poetry or songs. Moreover, there is proof he was still sending poetry to newspapers during 1796, in a letter dated 25th February, 1796. (CL 691)

In wit and satire there are several savage indictments of government policy written in flowery Augustan language which appear in London newspapers during the 1793-96 period, but no newspaper poetry compares to the daring wit employed in this work. Burns admired the humorous poems of Peter Pindar (Dr Wilcot) who assisted Thomson's song collection, but Pindar never wrote a poem on a par with Holy Willie's Prayer nor the Rover poem. The M.P. proposing the Bill to tax dog owners was Mr Dent. The poem may be *fustian doggerel*, exaggerating the nasty, wicked pastimes of a Tory M.P. who, to financially aid the war effort against France, was prepared to tax everything which moved. What dog ownership had to do with the war effort is surely the central question of the poem.

In stanza 1 Rover gets his teeth into Dent and does not let go. He is accused, by inference, of abusing coloured people - with great public abhorrence at the slave trade in the 1790's this slight is probably based on rumours of the time - and capable of hanging and flogging even poor spaniel dogs, endlessly. In fact, Dent is so nice a chap he is compared to the infamous hangman and axeman of the 17th century, Jack Ketch, who took 8 swings of a blunt axe to behead an English Lord. The poet knew of and mentioned "Jack Ketch" to Peter Stuart (CL 388) when he sent him, *Ode Sacred to the Memory of Mrs Oswald of Auchincruive* under the pen name, Tim Nettle. By the end of the second stanza Dent is a butcher, capable of hanging puppies on hooks. There are echoes from stanza 1, *On Mrs Riddell's Birthday*, composed in 1793 "My dismal months no joys are crowning, / But spleeny, English hanging, drowning". There are flashes of a macabre wit which Burns was renowned for amongst friends.

Stanza 3 mentions "poor Mungo's moan". In Scottish folklore this is a reference to the same Mungo in Tam O'Shanter: "Whare Mungo's mither hang'd hersel". According to Rover's sarcastic wit, Dent was such a callous person he would have offered to help those who would hang themselves. In terms of theme and imagery, the jump from Axe-weilding, gallow hanging Jack Ketch to "poor Mungo's moan" is natural and continues the macabre tone running through the poem. It is extremely unlikely another poet would have made reference to Mungo's hanging, even when Burns's epic tale was well known. So, by the end of stanza 3, there is pretty convincing evidence to argue Burns was the author.

Burns had already dedicated *The Twa Dogs* to the immortality of Luath, his first collie and put words into Luath's mouth. In the Rover poem, we again meet a dog who speaks his mind on serious issues of the day. Rover, though, displays a black and white satirical wit set on seditious mockery; while Luath was a clever, philosphizing collie with a shiny glossed coat, out to impress the Edinburgh Literati. Worried for his fate and horrified at maybe having to be put down, or hanged, ("..a meeting worse than Woolwich hulks") Rover expostulates in desperation:

> "Three shillings for your dog per ann!
> Good Master, save me - if you can;
>   The threat'ning noose throw by:
> O think how many theivish curs,
> Tho' clothed perhaps in richer furs
>   Want hanging more than I.

He then begs for his life, gasping in exclamatory terms that if dogs are so important to the state and are all killed, Britain will go, not to the *dogs* in ruin, but to the *cats* - and they will be taxed also. The absurd and iconoclastic image of Pitt actually squeezing a shilling out of cat come to mind as the rollicking, boisterous satire comes towards its close.

> "Ah, let me live! - not great the cost; -
> If dogs all die, the State is lost,
>   For Pitt must have his taxes:
> And shou'd we slip his fingers thro',
> From cats he'll squeeze a shilling too,
>   To save from cords and axes."

Frustrated and in a life or death dilemma, Rover pleads he is worthy to survive and puts his defense. He is humble and faithful at his post. Then, with his last gasp of pleading, he charms that if he is to die it will not be by his owner's hands, but by an "ill-Dent". Whatever this ailment might be, it sounds like a death worse than any imaginable.

> "Not much of service can I boast; -
> Humble, and faithful at my post;
>   Kind Sir, then pray relent.
> But if my kneck can not be spar'd,
> I die, - ye cruel fates, how hard,
>   I die by an ill-Dent."

The footnote, to explain the meaning of an "ill-Dent" is simply a play on Dent's name, with classic tongue-in-cheek humour, pretending such a death is real. An "ill-Dent" is supposedly, death brought on by a shock induced stroke: "a sudden stroke, vulgarly supposed, of witch-craft, and portentous of death". This is, of course, to be taken as seriously as the hilarious line that suggests had lambs been black, they might have been killed at random. Quite simply, from the wit and humour in Burns's satirical pieces, this poem - not a work of art; nor a bad poem either - is far too clever and satirical not to be by the king of satire in the 1790's, Burns. It takes mockery and ridicule to a ridiculous and absurd level. Had it been written in braid Scots, it is certain no-one could have questioned the authenticity of the poem. No doubt this hilarious epistle may well be a bone of contention for literary and linguistic experts to chew over.

Chapter 9

The Possibles: Category B

The eight poems printed in this section do not display the strong textual and contextual evidence of those in category A. It is for this reason that several of them may be the work of the Scottish bard and a few are probably not. They all show varying degrees of similarity with his work. In the absence of agreed academic rules to determine the provenance of anonymous or pseudonymous poetry from late 18th century newspapers, I have set out the basic reasons why a few of the poems are almost certainly by Burns. There are also included a few works I originally suspected as his work, which failed to pass the textual analysis set out in the methodology. So, the notes given in this section are essentially an outline sketch of ideas to explain why the poems have been collated to assist expert linguists and Burns scholars in making further, more definitive judgements.

A detailed scan using the Mitchell Library's CD Rom Poetry Database, which contains all known published poetry for the 18th century, with many obscure authors, failed to find patterns of language which could pin down a specific author for any of the category "B" poems. There is certainly a reasonable case that a few of the poems are by Burns, but the evidence is not strong enough to ascribe the works to Burns with any confidence.

B1. More Treason

To simple John Bull says imperious Pitt,
"Don't you hear my Alarm Bell? - Pray listen to it:
Thicves! thieves! Look about you: these Jacobin Dogs
Will steal your Roast Beef; - and they'll feed you with Frogs!
Of their Treasons and Plots should your faith have the staggers
Burke will show you, in proof, his invisible Daggers!"
John, apt to be frighten'd at rumours like those,
Star'd round, to discover his pilfering Foes:
But while he was dreaming of Peachums and Lockits
He found the fly Premier had rifled his pockets.

The Morning Chronicle of 18th March 1795 published this small witty piece signed "B". Burns signed many songs sent to Johnson for publication in the S.M.M. with the same initial, "B". There is no other known poet of the period who signed "B" as an initial, other than Burns. When compared to *Sketch - Inscribed to C.J. Fox*, there are striking similarities. The same style is employed. The same wit is evident. The metre, just like the *Sketch*, is somewhat erratic. The last line echoes quite strongly the final lines of the *Sketch* "Then feats like Squire Billy's you ne'er can atchieve 'em, / It is not, out-do him, the task is, out-thieve him)". The poem mocks the invasion scares of the period. The real problem with such a piece is that its brevity makes it difficult to determine Burns' authorship on purely stylistic grounds. However, the signature "B" for a poem so similar to the *Sketch* dedicated to Fox, found in a newspaper the poet promised to send material to, plus the fact that there is no evidence to show that the simple one-letter, initial "B" was used as a signature by anyone other than Burns, all point to this piece being his work.

B2. Sonnet On The Tree of Liberty Being Planted in Savoy

Rear'd with warm zeal, by Gallia's patriot bands,
Symbol of Liberty! Immortal tree!
Whose cherish'd plants shall bloom in distant lands,
Type that the wretch is blest, the slave is free!

Thy parent root, tho' fix'd in Gallia's plain,
Firm as the rock that mocks the angry flood;
Yet ah! that root which storms assail in vain,
Has been cemented to the soil with blood!

Then would my aching bosom seek repose,
To Savoy's vales my pensive fancy roves;
Where general bliss, exempt from partial foes,
Has realis'd those dreams the Poet loves,

Where war's chang'd form assumes a moral grace,
And comes the guardian friend of human race.

Dated as written on 10th August 1792.

Comments on this sonnet are given with the next poem *To A Great Nation*: both were signed under the same pen-name.

B3. To A Great Nation

Rise, mighty nation! in thy strength,
And deal thy dreadful vengeance round;
Let thy great spirit, rous'd at length,
Strike hordes of Despots to the ground.

Devoted Herd! thy mangled breast,
Eager the R——! Vultures tear:
By friends betray'd, by foes oppress'd
And Virtue struggles with despair.

A trumpet sounds! arise, arise,
Stern o'er each breast let country reign
Nor virgins plighted hand, nor sighs
Must now the ardent youth refrain.

Nor must the hind, who tills thy soil,
The ripen'd vintage stay to press,
'Till rapture crown the flowing bowl,
And Freedom boast of full success.

Briareus like, extend thy hands,
That every hand may crush a foe;
In millions pour thy generous bands,
And end a warfare by a blow.

Then wash with sad repentant tears,
Each deed that stains thy glory's page;
Each phrensied start impell'd by fears,
Each transient burst of headlong rage.

Then fold in thy relenting arms,
The wretched outcasts where they roam;
From pining want and war's alarms.
O call the child of Misery home.

Then build the tomb - O not alone,
On him who bled in Freedom's cause;
With equal eye the martyr own,
Of faith revered and ancient laws.

Then be thy tide of glory stay'd,
Then be thy conquering banners furl'd,
Obey thy laws thyself hast made,
And rise - the model of the world?

The Muse of Colia - a Lady?

Sonnett on the Tree of Liberty being planted in Savoy was published in the
Gazetteer on 16th November, 1792, its first issue. It was inscribed "Written by a Lady". On 12th November 1793, a year later, the same "Written by a Lady" appears with the poem *To A Great Nation*. It would
seem fair to judge that the same author wrote both poems. The second poem is therefore looked at here with the first, since it is clear

the author of the first merely took the opportunity one year later to employ the same pen-name again. This pen-name does not occur again anywhere in British newspapers other than in these two poems. There is no known female poet in Scotland in 1792 and 1793 who composed radical poems of this quality. There is no indication that they might have been penned by Janet Little or Maria Riddell. The crux of the problem is, who did write them?

Were Burns the author of both, such a pen-name would certainly throw any spy or informer off the trail of a radical poet-come-Exciseman. So, does this end the possibility of Burns's authorship? The simple answer is no. In fact there is evidence which might be relevant in a letter to Thomson, where Burns enclosed a song informing him it was a " "For a' that & a' that" which was never in print: it is a much superior song to mine. - I have been told that it was composed by a lady". (CL 676) In footnote number 6 to the letter MacKay comments that the "lady's verses" were rejected by Thomson and the "lady" was never identified. The "For a' that" sent to Thomson was probably by Burns; part of *The Jolly Beggars*. Is it possible the reference by Burns to a "lady" might give hint of a previous subterfuge in the *Gazetteer*?

The "Written by a Lady" does suggest a poet who wished to detract readers from their real identity and may refer to the feminine "Muse" so often mentioned in poetry of the period. This is conjecture which is far too insubstantial for any conclusion. However, the possibility of Burns as the author cannot be ruled out. If Burns was still active writing radical material for the newspaper, as seems apparent from *The Dagger* and so on, then he must be considered as a likely candidate. After all, the entire process of writing potentially seditious material during this period was fraught with the necessity of employing a hit-and-run procedure of changing one's pen-name on a regular basis.

Textually, both poems are strong contenders in depth of Burnsian language. *The Sonnet on the Tree of Liberty* contains 24 words used more than 20 times by Burns throughout his works, a count markedly higher than most of his known radical works. In stanza 2, the line "Firm as the rock that mocks the angry flood" is very similar to "Firm as the rock, resistless as her storm" from the *Washington Ode*. Several lines of Burns begin with the word "Firm", such as "Firm may she rise with generous disdain" from *Prologue Spoken by Mr Woods*, and "Firm as my creed, Sirs, 'tis my fix'd belief" in *Address Spoken by Miss Fontenelle*, composed around the end of 1793. The word "fix'd" is not common to period poetry, but is used many times by Burns - for instance, in *The Rights of Woman* written a month after the sonnet. Around 29 lines of Burns's poetry end with the rhyme of "plain". In fact, there are no words in the sonnet which pose a problem to Burns's authorship on a textual basis. One noun, "Savoy" is not found in his poetry, which, given the subject of the poem, would be expected. Also, the word "cemented" is not found in Burns, but the present tense "cement" is used in *Scotch Drink*, stanza 13. So, from a detailed scan of the language found in *Sonnet on the Tree of Liberty*, it passes the qualitive test of displaying no words, adjectives or adverbs, which immediately indicate that Burns would not be the author. Of course, this is not definitive proof of his authorship, but it certainly opens the door to the possibility.

There are many echoes in the sonnet which point to the possibility of Burns as author. The language of *The Vision*, "Scarce *rear'd* above the *parent earth*" is akin to "Thy parent root" in the new *Sonnet*, which also uses the word "Rear'd". The phrase "parent stem" is found in Burns's *On the Birth of A Posthumous Child*. The description of "fancy roves" is akin to "Fancy's flights" from *A Bard's Epitaph*. Moreover, in *The Gloomy Night is Gath'ring Fast* the same phrase "Fancy roves" is used and also finds its rhyme with "loves". In *Mary Morison*, "To thee my fancy took its wing" is akin to the notion of the poet's imaginative "fancy" travelling to Savoy. The description of "Gallia's patriot bands" is echoed in *Here's A Heath Tae Them That's Awa* where Burns refers to Fox's "band" of patriotic supporters. The word "Gallia's" is found in *The Tree of Liberty*, "Wha pitied Gallia's slaves, man". In the same poem by Burns, there is an echo of the "Symbol of Liberty" as a tree in "Sure plant that far-fam'd tree, man". The word "seek" is common to Burns and also found in *The Tree of Liberty*, "But seek the forest round and round". It may be that the *Sonnet on the Tree of Liberty* is the literary origin of Burns's *The Tree of Liberty*, which certainly employs many of the same words, although it is written chiefly in Scots.

Further echoes are found in Burns's *New Year's Day to Mrs Dunlop*, where the description "in vain assail" is turned round to "assail in vain", in stanza 2 of the sonnnet. The phrase "my aching bosom seek repose" is echoed in "There seek my lost repose" from Burns's *Had I a Cave* where the verb "seek" is also employed. The words "general bliss" are akin to "gen'ral mirth" in *The Vision*. The description "the guardian friend of human race" is strongly echoed in *The Ninetieth Psalm Versified*, "O Thou, the first, the greatest friend / Of all the human race". Thus, there are no language differences to highlight a problem in attributing the sonnet to the bard. There is every possibility it was the first poem sent by Burns to the *Edinburgh Gazetteer*. If this is the case, it is understandable that the poet would not have mentioned it to Graham of Fintry, given the poem's overt political nature.

Did Burns have the opportunity to send the poem to the newspaper and see it printed in the first issue? Burns' initial letter to the editor, Captain William Johnston, is dated as 13th November, when the poet read the *Prospectus* for the new paper. He did not hang about and write a week or so later. He wrote immediately to Johnston. There is no record to show that the letter of 13th November contained poetry. Conversely, there is no proof that it did not contain poetry. In fact, the only poem formally recorded as being sent by Burns to the *Gazetteer* is *The Rights of Woman*, in a letter dated 27th November. The poem duly appeared on 30th November, three days later. The delay of three days is important, as it suggests the time span required to get a poem from Dumfries and into print with the *Edinburgh Gazetteer*. *Extempore Stanzas on the poet Thomson* was published in the *Gazetteer* in the second issue, 23rd November. Surely if this had went to Johnston with the poet's first letter, it should have appeared in the first issue, next to the sonnet? If the known Burns poem was sent in the first letter, it would be a surprising editorial judgement for Johnson to print as his first poem, a work written by someone other than Burns, if he received the *Stanzas* in the poet's first letter. If the *Stanzas* on Thomson were not included in the first letter from Burns to Johnson, then there is a letter missing.

The facts indicate that the second and third issues of the Gazetteer contained poems by Burns and no other poet. (The fourth issue published no poetry). So, Burns was off his mark pretty fast. The appearance of the new radical newspaper, *The Edinburgh Gazetteer*, was an excellent platform for pro-democratic poetry and indeed, a God-send to any radical poet in Scotland. The poet's enthusiasm for the democratic editorial angle of the newspaper would suggest that if he had any radical poems laying in his desk he would have carefully chosen a poem for Johnson, to be dispatched immediately with the order for the newspaper. It does not fit the character of Burns to burst with enthusiasm for a newspaper about to be launched and not send a relevant poem. A headnote to *Sonnet on the Tree of Liberty* places its composition or completion, on August 10th 1792. So, the author held onto the poem for three months. There can be little doubt that if Burns was the author of the sonnet he would have put it in his first letter to Johnson, in time for publication in the first issue. This would mean that the bard saw his poetry published in the first three issues of the *Gazetteer*.

The sonnet is a worthy piece of poetry and is executed in better style than *The Rights of Woman*, which, although it is not one of the bard's best works, is carried more by its sentiment than by its quality. There is also a distinctive hole in the Burns canon in terms of sonnets. The very few sonnets in his Collected Works is a surprising gap. Major poets with an admiration for Shakespeare are bound to write several quality sonnets in their career. During the 1791-76 period there are a couple of sonnets from Burns, but there is not one on the pro-democrtic theme, which is surprising. Since so many of his radical works were suppressed until the middle of the 19th century, it would seem reasonable to expect there would be two or three sonnets among the lost, "democratic effusions". Naturally, it follows, that if the new sonnet is his, *To A Great Nation* is also his work.

Given the strength of evidence for the new poems, *Lines on Ambition*, *The Dagger* and both *The Ghost of Bruce* poems, it seems evident that Burns was back on the radical scene at the time the second poem was published, *To A Great Nation*. So, he is certainly in the frame as a possible author, especially given the evidence to suggest he wrote the first poem ascribed "Written by a Lady". The poems are both linguistically robust and were written by a poet who knew their craft with considerable skill.

To A Great Nation, without doubt, is by the same author as *Sonnet on the Tree of Liberty*. Like the sonnet, it is written in a language markedly different to the well known Scots poems of Burns. If he was the author, his contemporaries would not have suspected him, given their narrow and parochial view of the poet as a Scots rhymer only. There are 24 words in the first three stanzas which were used more than twenty times in the poetry of Burns. The average score for known radical poems of the bard is less than 20. This shows that the poem is in tune with the language of the bard. The word "Rise" at the start of the poem is found in Burns. The description "mighty nation" in line one, is similar to Burns's "To rule this mighty nation", from *A Dream*, "mighty England", in *Scots Prologue for Mrs Sutherland*, and "mighty Rome", *On Glenriddel's Fox Breaking its Chain*. The phrase "deal thy dreadful vengeance round" is similar to "Satire's vengeance hurls" in *From Aesopus to Maria*. The notion of the "great spirit" of "vengeance" being "rous'd at length" is echoed in Burns's *Address Spoken by Miss Fontenelle*, "Paint Vengeance as he takes his horrid stand, / Waving on high the desolating band, / Calling the storms to bear him o'er a guilty land?" The word "horrid" from the new poem and "dreadful" from the *Address* are synonymous. Also, the word "Rouse" preceeds "Vengeance" in the *Address* and is used in a similar context in *To A Great Nation*, "rous'd at length". It is interesting that the new poem was written just prior to the Address in late 1793. So, we would expect to see these lexical similarities. The word "despots" is found twice in the *Washington Ode*, alongside four occurences of "tyrant". So, the language of *To A Great Nation* is unequivocally in the Burnsian mould.

In the second stanza, the word "Herd" is uncharacteristic of most 18th century poems, but is found in Burns on twenty occassions - often in reference to religious factions, as in *Epistle to William Simpson* or *The Twa Herds*. The word "mangled" is also rare to period poetry but is found three times in Burns, one example being in *Tam O'Shanter*. The word "Vultures" is not in Burns's poetry but is found in at least one letter. The contrast between "friends" and "foes" is found in *The Whistle*, "his foe, or his friend". It also occurs in *The Gloomy Night is Gath'ring Fast*, "Farewell my friends! farewell my foes!" The use of "foes" is similar to the battle-ready posture of *Scots Wha Hae*, where "Oppression's" "chains" deserve vengeance, "Tyrants fall in every foe" - which rings of "Strike hordes of despots to the ground". Again, the Burnsian imprint is clear.

The third stanza lauches with a line that seems unlike Burns, "A trumpet sounds! arise, arise!" Yet, we find in *The Silver Tassie*, the poet wrote "The trumpets sound, the banners fly", which clearly echoes the new poem. Burns penned the song *The Silver Tassie* in September 1793, just prior to *To A Great Nation*. In the old song adapted by Burns, *Highland Laddie*, he wrote "Trumpets sound and cannons roar". The word "stern" is not common among period poetry, but is featured eight times in Burns to describe "stern Misfortune", "stern impulse", "stern Oppression's", "Stern Ruin's" and "Tyrant stern to all beside". The phrase "o'er each breast let country reign" is partly echoed with "And in her breast enthrone me", where "enthrone" and "reign" are almost synonymous. So, once again the language is consistently in tune with Burns.

By the third stanza it is clear the poet is perturbed at the political situation of Britain in the same manner of Agrestis in *The Ghost(s) of Bruce*. A rebellion of some sort is expected in Britain, but it is one which must be anti-vengeance, as clearly illustrated in stanzas, 6,7,8, and 9. The final view is that after the impending rebellion, the new society should "Obey the laws thyself hast made, / And rise - the model of the world?" This sounds very similar to Bruce's return, where he would "stay the hand of Vengeance, and bid Mercy take her place" *in The Ghost of Bruce*, version two. This may, of course, be imitation of the earlier poem also found in the *Gazetteer*. However, who would imitate an unknown poet called Agrestis?

At this juncture, there are no language problems which might suggest Burns could not be the author. The pivotal question of provenance, may depend on how *Scots Wha Hae* is interpreted. If it is seen to be loaded with strident political overtones - which it is, if we acknowledge the "Do or die" pledge of the Friends of the People and the origin of the phrase from the French Revolutionary Jacobin oath. The radical edge to *Scots Wha Hae* makes it quite probable, that, desiring a peaceful democratic society without tyrannic rulers, Burns continued the theme of the song with more specific reference to the political scene of late 1793. Such an interpretation would explain the continuity of his radical thought which links to the fiery, powerful *Ode for General Washington's Birthday*, composed several months after these poems.

In sum, these two poems fail to display a cluster of adjectives or adverbs alien to the writing of Burns. Surely, if he were *not the author*, there would be lines or passages which we could easily spot, that ring out of key with his known compositions? On purely textual grounds, they could be tentatively ascribed to Burns. The contextual evidence, though, is purely conjecture. It probably was Burns who was first off the blocks in November 1792 with the *Sonnet on the Tree of Liberty*, but firmer evidence is necessary before authenticity is certain. These works are certainly the kind of "democratic effusions" which were likely to be destroyed during the fiercely anti-radical period after the poet's death, if the manuscripts survived at all.

B4. Sonnet To The Earl Of Lauderdale

Maitland, accept the verse a muse would pay,
That looks on greatness with no envious eye,
Nor flatters vice tho' "impious men bear sway,"
And virtue droop while truth and honour fly.

Virtue that loves the quiet vale of life,
Yet haply deck'd with grandeur's ermin'd stole;
She ventures in the field of civil strife,
To prompt the ardours of some patriot soul.

Still in your bosom, rouse the generous zeal,
That rarely warms the hereditary great;
And by new efforts for the public weal,
Still merit censure from the tools of state.

Censure - the noblest praise a tongue can give,
That libell'd Franklin and defended Clive

Feb 1793 - One of the People

Comments on this sonnet are given with notes on the next poem, *To Lord Stanhope:* both were signed under the pen-name "One of the People".

B5. To Lord Stanhope

On Reading His Late Protest in the House of Lords.

Stanhope! I hail, with ardent Hymn, thy name!
    Thou shalt be bless'd and lov'd, when in the dust
    Thy corse shall moulder - Patriot pure and just!
And o'er thy tomb the grateful hand of Fame

Shall grave - "Here sleeps the Friend of Humankind!"
For thou, untainted by Corruption's bowl,
Or foul Ambition, with undaunted soul
Hast spoke the language of a Free-born mind,
Pleading the cause of Nature! Still pursue
Thy path of Honour! - To thy Country true,
Still watch th' expiring flame of LIBERTY!
O, Patriot! still pursue thy virtuous way,
As holds his course the splendid Orb of Day,
Or thro' the stormy or the tranquil sky!

Signed: One of the People

One of The People

Both *Sonnet to the Earl of Lauderdale* and *To Lord Stanhope* were composed by a poet who employed the pen-name "One of the People". The style and language of both works suggest the same author. Whether the pen-name sounds similar to "Ane o' the Swine" used with *The Dagger*, "One of the Multitude" found with the single Scots verse piece on Burke, or the letter defending Robert Riddell signed "One of the Rabble" published in 1791, is of interest but probably of no significance. It is important, however, that the sonnet on Lauderdale appears in the *Edinburgh Gazetteer* in February 1793, while the poem on Stanhope is found in the *Chronicle*, January 1795. Burns is known to have sent material to both newspapers.

The Earl of Lauderdale was the M.P. James Maitland. He was a friend of Burns, as confirmed by the poet's letter to John MacKenzie of January 1787(CL 73). In mentioning the breakfast meeting Burns had with Maitland in 1787 MacKay assumes wrongly that it was with the sons of the Earl, when it was with James Maitland himself and his brother. James Maitland was the same age as the poet, born in 1759. He was an active pro-democracy member of the Whig opposition. In early 1793, he petitioned the King and parliament on behalf of the people of Glasgow to complain of the economic, and therefore, social effects of the war.

It is certain the bard's esteem for Lauderdale was increased during the 1790's by the Earl's unstinting dedication to the cause of reform and his dedication to help the less fortunate. He is praised among the many radical Whigs mentioned in *Here's A Health Tae Them That's Awa*, composed by the bard a few months before the sonnet was published and also mentioned in *John Bushby's Lamentation*, "And my son Maitland, wise as brave". Undoubtably, Maitland was an enlightened aristocrat Burns held in respect.

Immediately, in the first stanza, the sonnet strikes a chord with the style of Burns. The poet often took pains to assert that he would flatter no living man, friend or foe. In *Verses on Dining with Lord Daer*, the bard mentions that he "watched the symptoms of the great" and so on, which is echoed in line 2, stanza 1 of the sonnet. Here we find a poet boldly stating that they do not look "on greatness" with an "envious eye", "Nor flatters vice tho' "impuious men bear sway"". Clearly, this quote lifted from John Gay's Fable III, is a sign the sonnet is by a writer steeped in the poetry of the early 18th century. Gay died in 1723. In fact, a detailed search through *The Complete Wordfinder* reveals echoes from the poet's writings in every line of the sonnet. In the first block of 12 lines, three stanzas, there are twenty three words which can be found used more than twenty times among the bard's poems. This is a higher count than most of the accepted radical works of Burns.

The sonnet, overall, does not possess the expected four or more adjectives or adverbs usually found among newspaper poems of the period which are alien to Burns. The questionable words are merely "prompt" and "hereditary". (It is quite likely that a scan of the *Complete Letters* would reveal both words, or that "prompt" is found in the poems of Burns, but like the word "haughty" is simply not listed in the *Wordfinder*). So, as we saw in a detailed consideration of the qualititive language differences between the poems of Burns, two or three new words are actually an expected creative transformation between poems. So, from the rules outlined in the methodology, the sonnet can, on textual grounds, be ascribed to Burns.

The work of Burns most similar to the new sonnet is *Sonnet on the Death of Robert Riddell*. There is maybe a subtle difference in tone, since the sonnet on Riddell is naturally more down-beat, as a lament for a close friend. In fact, the language of the sonnet on Riddell rings more of the elegiac verse in Burns, than any other group of his poems. It is interesting that "Yet haply deck'd with grandeur's ermin'd *stole*" rhymes with "soul" in the new sonnet, while in the Riddell sonnet, it is "gay in thy verdant *stole*" which rhymes with "soul". A mastery of English is evident in the high poetic skill of both works. Among living poets in all Britain during the 1790's there were probably only two or three who could write at this level.

There are many echoes from Burns throughout the sonnet. Without additional indicators, however, to reinforce the textual evidence, it is difficult to prove the the case. The fact that the Earl of Lauderdale was a friend of the poet's is supportive contextual evidence which is reinforced by three known references to the Earl in the poet's work. The fact that the poem passes our methodology test and does not have a cluster of words alien to Burns is significant. Together, these factors make the case for the poet's authorship attractive and appealing, but not definitive. This work certainly merits further detailed analyses by linguistic experts. The results of stylometric tests done in comparison to the works of Burns during 1793-4 would be interesting.

The subtitle for *To Lord Stanhope*, found in the *Chronicle* during January 1795, is "On Reading His Late Protest in The House of Lords". Stanhope was quoted in *The Glasgow Advertiser*, 27th January 1795, as saying in the House of Lords that he would "ever remain firm" in his opposition to the war against France, that it was destructive of British commerce and so on. His anti-war speech was very much on the theme of the protests by the Earl of Lauderdale. What is certain in both cases is that the author did not simply write two poems during the 1790's. Both are poems of high literary merit from a major democratic voice of the age, who had great poetic confidence and skill. So, the author of both works was clearly an active poet who simply used the pen-name twice and continued writing under a new pen-name. *Sonnet on the Earl of Lauderdale* is similiar to *The Scotian Muse: An Elegy*, found several months later in 1793 in *The Edinburgh Gazetteer* and ascribed here to Burns.

Like *Sonnet to the Earl of Lauderdale, To Lord Stanhope* owns echoes from Burns in every line that can be found by scanning *The Complete Wordfinder*. The words "Hymn", "bless'd", "corse", "moulder", "grave", "undaunted", "free-born", "virtuous", "stormy", "splendid" and "expiring" are all found in Burns. Only "untainted" and "tranquil" are not listed in the *Wordfinder*. This poses no problem to ascribing the poem to Burns since we know there is often at least two or three such new words found only once in many of the bard's works. So, there is no cluster of four or more adjectives or adverbs which would indicate the poem is not by Burns.

It is of interest that the pen-name "One of the People" is found on only one other occassion which pre-dates both poems. It is seen in *The Glasgow Mercury* for the 9th-16th August issue, 1791. This is around the time the bard's friend Robert Riddell was embroiled in a constitutional debate with Edmund Burke which occured in *The Glasgow Journal* and spilled over into *The Glasgow Advertiser*. Riddell himself can be excluded as a possible candidate to be "One of the People", due to his sudden death in 1794. This means he could not have written *To Lord Stanhope* which was composed and published in early 1795. Riddell only ever used one pen-name, "Cato". The brief article in *The Glasgow Mercury* is certainly on Riddell's hobby-horse theme, "Constitutional Facts 1791". And as mentioned earlier, Riddell found himself strongly supported by a correspondent who used the pen-name "One of the Rabble", which is quite likely to have been Burns. The influence on Burns by his constitution-specialist friend Riddell may have prompted him to be both "One of the Rabble" when defending Riddell, then "One of the People" when presenting facts on the constitution for readers of the newspaper. Of course, it is possible that the "One of the People" from the Mercury is a different person to the poet who wrote in the *Gazetteer* and *Chronicle*. However, since the pen-name is only witnessed on three occasions during the entire 1790's, it would be more probable that the Mercury pen-name is from the same person who later used the pseudonymn.

The only other realistic candidate for "One of the People", who was known to write on contitutional matters and wrote poetry, was James Thomson Callander, whose *The Political Progress of Britain* was serialised in *The Bee*. Although he was a leading radical commentator from 1792, Callander's poetry is not of the standard found in the new sonnet or *To Lord Stanhope*. So, the prime candidate for both poems is still Burns. Both poems may eventually be accepted to the canon if more rigorous "scientific" analyses supports the tentative conclusion here, that the poems are more likely to be by Burns than any other living poet.

B6. Ode - Inscribed to Certain Jurymen

Praise, bid the Angels, beside thy throne,
In shining order wait, and trumpet-tongued,
    Rehearse the deeds of those
    Whom future times shall bless,
Spread their far-sounding wings, and from the caves
Where Ocean steeps in lilv'ry shells his pearls
    Of purest, whitest ray,
    The chosen jewels cull! -
With thine own fingers, string the glittering gems,
And coil Twelve Crowns - and then another Twelve,
    And on their noble brows
    The eternal guerdon bind,
Who now, once more, the holy gates unbar
Of Freedom's long-forbidden, silent Fane -
    And to loud worship call
    Rejoicing Britain's Sons.

This little Ode is a stunning poem. It appears in *The Morning Chronicle,* December 11th 1794, just prior to the publication of Samuel Taylor Coleridge's *Sonnets on Eminent Characters.* At first reading the word "cull" seems to stick out as unfamiliar to Burns, but it is found in his poem on Maria Riddell, *On A Lady Famed for Her Caprice.* The overall impression of the poem is that is was written by a poet who adored Gray's *Elegy in a Country Churchyard,* which has "Full many a Gem of purest Ray serene, / The dark unfathom'd Caves of Ocean bear", which is clearly the language the poem strives to emulate. Gray's poem was one of Burns's favourite works in English. So, although the poem does not immediately strike the reader as in a known "Burnsian" style, he could have experimented with this type of Ode and produced this work with ease.

The Ode is briliant in its clever praise of the members of the jury who were selected to judge the trials of leading radicals, including Horn Tooke, in London during December 1794. Its primary purpose was to place on the jury a sense of their historical responsibility, prior to their actual judgement, which was not delivered until early January 1795. The message of the Ode is simple: history will judge the jurors if they fail to acquit the accused. If the jurors acquit the accused, the Ode suggests their praises will be sung and their names will be engraved in the pages of the democratic future. The author was watching the trials with anticipation and sought to sway the jury, if possible. Interestingly, we know Burns was aware of the trials and wrote "Thank God these London trials have given us a little more breath", to Mrs Dunop, 12th January 1795, when the accused were acquitted. So, aware that he had already published material in the newspaper earlier in 1794 and was a watcher of events in London, eager to see the freedom of the accused radicals (especially after the show-trials in Scotland in 1793 and January 1794), the possibility of Burns as author cannot be dismissed lightly.

The line "The eternal guerdon bind" seems unlike Burns. It appears to be more like some early work of Coleridge. The words "eternal geurdon" are found echoed in a poem dedicated to Burns by William Roscoe, where every verse of Roscoe's poem alludes to various lines of poetry by Burns. (See appendix B for the Roscoe poem). Coleridge altered his early radicalism in later years and many of his works were not published until the 1830's, so it may be his. If it turns out to be Burns or Coleridge, it is a worthy historical find.

B7. On William, Earl of Mansfield

Made to engage all hearts, attract all eyes,
Delight the witty, and instruct the wise;
With native sweetness to adorn his race,
Each manly sentiment, each polish'd grace;
Dear to the Nine, the Muse's better hope,
And Gloster's Patron and the Friend of Pope,
See Murray drop into the silent tomb,
Prov'd mortal only by the gen'ral doom!

Oh! greatly virtuous in a Land ingrate,
The polish'd Pillar of a sinking State!
With lips of fire to plead the injur'd cause,
Correct our judgements, and unravel laws;
Whose subtle Wit, and letter'd sense bespoke
The soul at once of Tully and of Coke!
A frame in Nature's happiest mould design'd,
Like a fair casket to the soul inshrin'd,
Which, spirit-like, ooz'd thro' its earthly bound,
Glow'd thro' each sense, and beam'd a sunshine round!
Whose courteous aspect was the counterpart
And lively image of a pregnant heart,
Where spoke at once the Statesman and the Sage,
And Youth's vivacity and the sense of age!

Such Murray was - his Country's honest pride,
Belov'd thro' Life, regretted when he died;
Enrich'd with all that length of days can give,
Or make the Great Man's memory to live,
Without a pang he gently breathes his last,
Like Golden Dreams, or Visions that are past:
So droops the AMARANTH without decay,
And in sweet scents exhales itself away!

"My Honoured Friend, Sir William Murray"

This worthy dedication to William Murray, the Earl of Mansfield, (born 2nd March, 1705 & died March 1793) was printed on 17th July 1795 in the *Morning Chronicle*. Murray was a Scot, born at Scone, in Perthshire. It appears from a note appended with this poem that it was written as an obituary dedication in 1793, but did not see print until July 1795. So, for whatever reason, the poem lay unpublished for around two years.

Around the time of his first Highland tour, Burns wrote an epigram which mentions "old Mansfield" who wrote like "the Bible". When at Ellisland, though, there is a greater sign of respect for Sir William Murray. In a letter to Graham of Fintry, written on 13th May 1789, Burns wrote,

... you talked of being this way with my honoured friend, Sir William Murray, in the course of this summer. You cannot imagine, Sir, how happy it would make me, should you two illuminate my humble domicile ... I expect your Honors with a kind enthusiasm. - I shall mark the year & mark the day, & hand it down to my children as one of the most distinguished honours of their Ancestor. (CL 341)

No biographer documents this visit. There is no evidence in any of the poet's letters to confirm that it did, or did not, take place. The elderly Murray was around at the time of the poet Pope, "Gloster's Patron and the Friend of Pope". Given the bard's immense respect for the English poet Pope, a visit from the Earl, already "my honoured friend" would have been taken as a great honour by Burns, who would certainly have lamented the passing of the great man. The excellent and clever dedication may indeed be a work of Burns. It is not an amateur performance.

B8. Ode for the Birthday of C J Fox

Let courtly bards, a fawning breed,
To Kings and Queens attune the reed,
    And dedicate their lays:
Be mine the province to rehearse,
In simple, but not venal verse ,
    An honest Patriot's praise.

O Fox ! the pride of Britain's isle;
May Heav'n propitious on thee smile,
    And guard thee from all harm.
This is the wish of ev'ry breast,
Which slavish dreams have not possess'd,
    And Freedom yet can charm.

What though a perverse, pension'd band,
Who swarm like locusts o'er the land,
    Calumniate thy name?
With all their malice, all their art,
They cannot wound thy noble heart,
    Nor stain thy spotless fame.

No; generous, candid, upright MAN!
The fellest of those fiends ne'er can
    Inflict a single wound:
Sputter they may, and threaten too,
But all their shafts, when aim'd at you,
    Fall guiltless to the ground.

How did thy fret, and fume, and rage,
When you explain'd the legal page;
    And dared our RIGHTS assert?
With impotency like to burst,
They raved, they roar'd, they rail'd, they curs,d,
    But could not controvert.

May ill betide the worthless crew,
Who would our liberties subdue,
    And forge for Freemen chains!
We trust the fate-spun morn is nigh,
When the stern Justice of the Sky
    Will pay them for their pains.

Then shall the TORIES of the day,
Be, like cobwebs, swept away,
    By CONSTITUTION'S brush:
Freedom be seated on her Throne,
And all her enemies laid prone,
    In one eternal crush.

Meanwhile, let Freedom's Sons prepare
To face her foes with skill and care;
⠀⠀⠀Be prudent, but be firm:
Those wily Greeks will try to steal
Tha PALLAS of the Common-weal;
⠀⠀⠀But will not dare to storm.

Full well they know what blood remains,
Yet uncorrupt in English viens;
⠀⠀⠀What love of Freedom grows
In English hearts - That native fire
Must kindle soon a nation's ire
⠀⠀⠀'Gainst all her trech'rous foes.

Led by the flambeau, that displays,
In Fox's hand, its vivid rays,
⠀⠀⠀Let us our course pursue;
While TEUCER leads, we need not fear
The issue of our joint career,
⠀⠀⠀The goal is full in view.

See Russells, Erskines, Maitlands, Greys,
Encrease the patriotic blaze,
⠀⠀⠀With genuine British oil!
See Sheridan, with attic wit,
Expose the sophistry of Pitt,
⠀⠀⠀And Windham's logic foil!

"O Grant! it grieves me much to see
So promising a youth as thee,
⠀⠀⠀Betray'd from virtue's plan:
We hope to see thee yet employ,
Thine eloquence, brave Highland boy!
⠀⠀⠀To venge the Rights of Man.

Enough, my muse! - with mirth and glee,
Let's solemnize the Jubillee:
   'Tis Fox's fiftieth year!
Freedom (no Papal Bull she wants)
A plenary indulgence grants,
   To all assembled here.

Freedom! before the sacred shrine,
We'll freely quaff the rosy wine,
   That cheers the human heart.
We'll quaff, 'till slumbers seal our eyes,
Then dream of Thee - and then, we'll rise
   We'll act, each man, his part.

The Poet Laureate of British Democracy

The *Ode for the Birthday of C. J. Fox* was published on the 37th birthday of Robert Burns, 25th January, 1796, in *The Morning Chronicle*. The 25th January was a Monday. The Sunday, 24th January, 1796, was the birthday of C. J. Fox, leader of the Whig Opposition. There was no Sunday edition of the newspaper, so the Ode could not have appeared on the day of Fox's birthday. One of the first distinctive features of the poem is that it is in Scots verse form, a rarity in English newspapers of the period. The date of publication is coincidental and cannot infer any link with Burns, although he may have smiled wryly to know one of his political icons had a birthday one day before his. An obvious error in the poem is that it mentions the 50th birthday of Fox which was still a few years away. So, the author either did not know the age of Fox or employed poetic licence to hype a semi-royal jubilee atmosphere that was somewhat premature. It is noteworthy that Burns erred with his inscription to Robert Ferguson by getting the year of his birth wrong and penned the Birthday ode to Washington months after the actual date.

   The poet had already shown favour towards his fellow Scot, Charles James Fox, in *Sketch - Inscribed to C. J. Fox*, composed in 1789. Political tensions across Europe had increased dramatically since 1789. During the early 1790's there are clear signs that Burns's political sentiments swung fully behind the reform movement and the Whig party.

This is clear in 1792 with the song *Here's a Health Tae Them That's Awa*, which celebreates the same pantheon of icons mentioned in the new Fox Ode. The known Burns song praises leading Whigs, but singles out Fox with the toast: "Here's a health tae Charlie, the chief o the clan, / Altho that his band be sma". By 1796, the political atmosphere was openly hostile against reform and reformers. Activists were slowly driven underground by the sedition laws which were sharpened by new legislation. Political paranoia was rampant, with widespread fear of an underground explosion by the peasantry and townsfolk. The Messianic optimism of 1789-1792 period among the followers of Liberty had faded and hope focused on the parliamentary Whigs, particularly C. J. Fox. In this crucible of ideological struggle, Burns views had clearly hardened against the war with France and his idealistic praise of Fox in 1789 had been galvanized to pragmatic reform by 1792. Were his ideals forged with enough fire to create a radical Ode, which, as Noble commented on radio Scotland in January 1996, would stand comparison with the very best radical works of Byron, Blake or Shelley?

Another clue which links Burns with this poem is his remark to Mr Oswald, in 1795, when he affirmed he had came forward as the "poet laureate" of the Whig Party. The "songs of triumph" sent to Oswald were probably fragments of *The Heron Ballads* written around that time. For Burns to call himself the "poet laureate" of a "respected political party" is of considerable interest. The word "party" means, the entire Whig party. The significance of this declaration from Burns himself, suggests he would take up the quill to dedicate poetry to the Whig Party and in particular, to Fox, for the second time.

The poem is in the style of *On Dining With Lord Daer* and the *Election Ballad to Graham of Fintry* which ends with the thumping line "...grind them in the mire!!!". There are strong echoes from known works of the bard throughout the Ode. The start of the poem reveals the same anti-venal bard tone employed in *A Dream*. Several words which initially seem unlike Burns - from a "gut feeling"- are found in *The Complete Wordfinder*. The words "attune", "province", "propitious", "spotless", "fiends", "prone", "prudent", "wily", "kindle", "Encrease","Expose", "grieves","employ","solemnize", "frecly", and so on, are all used by Burns. In the *Inscription to Miss Jessie Lewars* written by the poet in 1796, the words "...enrol thy name; / With native worth and spotless fame", are echoed in stanza 3 of the Ode. In all, there are around forty lexical correlations which point to Burns as a potential author. Given the forceful power of the *Washington Ode,* written in a style not instantly recognizable as from Burns, this Scots verse *Ode* cannot be simply rejected because we do not like its forceful message. Stylometrics may prove the work authentic.

New Epigrams

B9. Impromptu

When Gibbie the Dog of the Fox told A fib,
The House sat admiring his brass;
They all smok'd a Rat in the head of Sir Gib,
And some in his head smok'd the Ass.

This epigram appears in *The Edinburgh Gazetteer,* 19th February 1793, titled *Impromptu.* It is very similar to Burns's song, *Why Canna Poor Folks Mowe,* "May the deil in her ass, ram a huge prick o brass", a reference to the wife of the Emperor of Poland, Kate Stalinlaus. Its subject is the embarrassment of a Whig minister, of the name Gibson - "Gibbie" - who lied to the House of Commons. Since "Gibbie" is "the Dog of the Fox", it is clear he was a member of Fox's opposition. There are no other epigrams in the newspapers of the period which display the same wit as this little bawdy-political piece. It is almost certainly by Burns.

B10.

Burke, both passionate and rude,
Calls us a "Swinish Multitude",
⠀⠀⠀Which some think defamation;
But I his meaning thus define -
That, if the People are all swine,
⠀⠀⠀*Hog-drivers* rule the Nation.

Signed: One of the Multitude.

The second "epigram" is actually a single Scots verse stanza, found in the *Chronicle* of 1st January 1796. The pen-name One of the Multitude can only be found with this one verse of poetry, although it is akin to "Ane o' the Swine" employed with *The Dagger.* It is very likely to be from Burns.

Chapter 10
Conclusion: The Scottish Thistle

"To sin by silence when we should protest is to make cowards out of men."
Ella Willcox

The provenance of the fifteen poems now provisionally attributed to Robert Burns and the potential that poems in category B may be his work, is certain to re-ignite controversy in Burnsian circles. Old assumptions have been questioned and many have been found wanting. Accepted knowledge that goes unquestioned becomes fossilized. Fresh questions often lead to new answers. The new poems have been presented with supportive evidence, which is more than Barke allowed in his iconoclastic edition during the 1950's. The case for some is stronger than for others. Several of the new poems are undoubtably of a very high literary order, while a few are linguistically weak. In some instances I may be proven wrong, but it is better to present poems which may be the work of Burns and be proven wrong, than to leave potential works lay for another two centuries unknown in faded yellow newspapers. Under the lexical miscroscope, the evidence supports the view that this work is historical and contains genuine works of our national bard. In a few instances, the case is overwhelming.

No-one can deny the bard's promise to send radical, anonymous material to the London *Morning Chronicle*. No-one can deny that he declared himself the poet laureate of the Whig Party. No-one can *now* deny that he continued to write radical poetry from 5th January 1793. *The Washington Ode, The Heron Ballads, A Man's A Man, The Creed of Poverty, On Mr Pitt's Hair-Tax, Lines for An Alter To Independence, Logan Braes,* are all controversial, radical works. Most are seditious. A few are highly treasonable. *A Man's A Man* and *Scots Wha Hae* were printed anonymously after January 1793. He was still sending poetry to newspapers as late as February 1796. Moreover, the poet supported the democratic cause up until his last breath. Indeed, the force of the *Washington Ode* suggests that the Excise investigation galvanized his radical views and did not diminish them. In all, this throws the possibility of *The Lost Poems* as wide open as a barn door.

The notion that the new poems have been seen and rejected in the past is silly. If no one looked, then no one would find them. It is as simple as that. If no-one found them, they could never be ascribed to Burns. For them to be rejected they would first have to be found. Now that they are found and ascribed, they can be rejected. However, it would be false to reject the new works wholesale on an assumption that they must have been rejected in the past. MacKay made this error in January 1996.

The idea of missing poems is far from new. Chambers and Pinnington agreed that there were many lost democratic poems. The eye-witness account of "chiefly political" poems recited by Burns in late 1795 adds to our case. Manuscripts were burned, stolen and lost. A body of letters are unrecorded from the 1793 period onwards. Lost letters would have certainly contained additional poems and songs. Indeed, it was almost inevitable that democratic poems would have been a casualty to the fierce suppression of radicalism during the period. Kinsley is right. The Burns canon is unresolved

Does it not seem incredible that a poet of passionate democrat ideals would repeatedly assert his right to maintain an "Independence" in his own opinions and compose lines for an *Alter to Independence* in 1795, if he had become timidly silent, afraid of oppression? It does not add up. It makes more sense to see the few radical poems that survived as the chosen flotsam of an over-heated tumultuous period of fierce oppression. It is a startling fact that the first historical publication of both *Scots Wha Hae* and *A Man's A Man* under the bard's name, occured in *The Morning Chronicle*, and has went unnoticed for two centuries.

The relationship between Scotland and her national bard vis-à-vis his radical views has been a thorny issue since before his death. Hugh Blair remarked that "the ploughman bard's politics smell of the smithy".[1] During his last years, Burns was harangued in Dumfries for supporting the democratic cause and labeled a "Jacobin". From 1796 until the 1840's, his legacy was the subject of fierce debate. On one side were the loyalist Hanoverian Tories who poured scorn on his views and on the other side, radicals and Whigs, many, former friends of the poet. An archetypal opponent of Burns was Josiah Walker. In

1811 he blasted the bard as an uneducated poet whose views on the French Revolution were obnoxious:

> On subjects of this nature, Burns does not seem to have arranged with much deliberation or correctness. He surrendered his mind to one leading idea ...He was likewise disposed, from a constitutional temper, from education... to a jealousy of power, and a keen hostility against every system which enabled birth and opulence to intercept those rewards which he conceived to belong to genius and virtue. He had, therefore, I suspect... a secret wish for the mortification of those who were in the exercise of authority.[2]

Until the 1850's, this type of attack was the norm, spiced up with stories of booze and sex. No doubt, this personal abuse enhanced the appeal of Burns.

The friends of the poet give a less jaundiced impression. Alexander Wilson, a Paisley poet, came to the bard's defense in 1806 to condemn those who castigated Burns for his ideals during his lifetime, but who slowly became "Burnsians" when his fame was too high to be destroyed -

> Alas! I knew him when his country's pride,
> Yet left dark Poverty's cold winds to brave;
> And those who then the friendly hand deny'd,
> Now strew with flowers his green unconscious grave.[3]

A Dumfries poet, wrote *Verses Written for the Anniversary of Burns* in 1825, and stung the bard's critics:

> Yes! Campbell, well might'st thou bid discord and strife,
> Those foes to the living, - his memory save;
> For the *hatred,* alas! that oft scowled on his life,
> Has smiled sacrilegious, e'en over his grave....
>
> ... But his fame is secure with the lib'ral and good,
> Whose still voice alone can true genius reward;
> And perish the Scot, who malignant can brood
> On the faults of the man, when he thinks of the bard.[4]

In the comments of the poet's friends, Nicol, Gray and White, there is indication that a pent up dam of reactionary prejudice had burst after the death of Burns - from people who feared the biting satirical pen of the poet when living. It is a knock-out blow to the notion of Burns as a Hanoverian bard, that his supporters during the 1790's and the early 19th century were mainly radicals sympathetic to the Whig Party, while his critics, to a man, were loyalist Tory Hanoverians. Critics who bend *The Dumfries Volunteers* to suit the Hanoverian bard myth ignore the final seditious ring of the song "... we'll ne'er forget THE PEOPLE!". In the radical-loyalist divide, Burns was unequivocally on the side of democracy.

Henderson and Henley in 1896 had no illusions about the poet's radicalism. They detested the man and his views. They saw him as "too fearless and too proud to dissemble" his sympathies for the democratic cause in his last years.[5] He had a "rather noisy sympathy with the leading principles of the French Revolution". The poet, they assert, had no intellectual political principles, merely "jealousy of his betters". They continue, "to apologise for Burns is vain ... a peasant of genius perverted from his peasanthood, thrust into a place for which his peasanthood and genius alike unfitted him". They refer to the poet's "peculiar immortality", as though they did not consider Burns's fame justified. At the centenary of the poet's death, they smugly celebrated *that he did die so early* · "the best for him, certain necessary conditions being impossible, was to die". Burns, in their view, was not an honourable, loyal British Hanoverian. The new radical poems would have been a red rag to these bullish editors.

There is a strong case to argue that the radical views of Burns have been obscured into a protean blur since the 1850's. It was the literary high brow obfuscation of Christopher North who invented the Hanoverian bard notion. So, even MacKay's "Burns" is old wine in a new bottle. The broad Church of the Burns Movement, from the 1850's onward, allowed entry to people who were opponents of the poet's radical views. Scotland is probably the only nation in the world that could tolerate as leading commentators on a national poet, people who are wholly opposed to the radical message of the poet. Anti-Burns Burnsians are a uniquely Scottish phenomenon.

If we read or listen to Crawford, Noble, O'Hagan, Gaw, Bold, Hindley Fowler, Hendry, Paton, Simpson and Campsie, to mention only a few scholars, it turns out that they have quite a different view of Burns from the biographer, MacKay. Even McIntrye, the latest biographer, untainted by sympathy towards the poet's views, accepts that he did not change "his spots" in his last years. Burns cannot be a loyalist Hanoverian and the "poet of democracy" at the same time. The two impressions are mutually exclusive. He is either one, or the other. Loyalist Hanoverians detested reformers during the 1790's. The radical movement wished to see the loyalist Hanoverian government of Pitt booted from office. So, given that most scholars see Burns as a major radical poet, *The Lost Poems* fill the gaps, the missing jig-saw pieces of his final years.

Rather than wishing to suppress the radical ideals of Burns, McDiarmid wished to see the values of the poet's writings opened up and alive within the culture of Scotland. Despite his awkward relationship with the Scottish literary "establishment", Scotland's greatest poet of this century made a valuable contribution:

> the need to follow his lead at long last is today a thousand times greater than when he gave it... We can still affirm the fearless radical spirit of the true Scotland. We can even throw off the yoke of all the canting humbug in our midst. We can rise and quit ourselves like men and make Scotland worthy to have had a Burns ... and we can communicate that consciousness to the ends of the earth... if ... we won't, the Burns cult will remain a monstrous monument to Scotland's refusal to follow Burn's lead - a monument to the triumph of his enemies.[6]

If the view of McDiarmid is to be ignored and dismissed, then it would seem that Scotland is unworthy of ever having had a McDiarmid, let alone a Burns.

Hitherto, no work on Burns adequately explains the apparent quantum leap from the poet's so-called silence in 1793 to the powerful *Washington Ode* in the middle of 1794. If we are to believe biographers, it drops out of the sky. In the development of the poet's thought, it is clearly not the one-off composition that it appears to be. It seems almost certain that *On the Year 1793, The Dagger, The Ghost of Bruce* poems and *Lines on Ambition,* and several other new radical poems, represent the missing stepping stones in the evolution of the bard's thought and poetry towards the *Washington Ode,* and after it.

In the light of considerable evidence which suggests that there was no other Scottish poet capable of writing works like *The Dagger* and *Remember the Poor*, these two poems are surely more than worthy of entry to the canon. Moreover, the strong similarities between *On the Year 1793*, *The Ghost of Bruce* poems and *Lines on Ambition*, all point to Burns as the only possible author. No evidence can be found to show that any other poet employed the pen-name "A. Briton" during the 1790's. Furthermore, both *Lines on Ambition* and *On the Year 1793* reveal a stunning similarity to pieces of poetry we know are by the bard. Given that poems are missing from the canon, it seems clear that Burns continued to send and see published pro-democratic poetry in *The Edinburgh Gazetteer* and, ipso facto, published similar poetry in *The Morning Chronicle*.

Burns was driven on a wheel of compassion. It turned from Love to Liberty, his two favourite subjects. He was first a patriot to truth and God; second was he a Scottish patriot, by his passion for his wounded Scotia and its rich culture; only third was he a British "patriot", seeking the pragmatic solution of democracy and an end to the war with France. The extent of his "British patriotism" was no more than a specific geographical focus of his international humanitarianism, which ran head on against the anti-democracy "patriotism" of Pitt and Dundas. His loyalty to the constitution was loyalty to its principles, applied to all - not the corrupt abuse of it by the few. He was no loyalist Hanoverian bard. His passion for Scotland was always greater than his pragmatic acceptance of the Union. When he remarked that a Scottish prejudice would run in his *veins until the floodgates of life shut in eternal rest*, he meant it. His unflinging commitment to the cause of the reform movement during the mid-1790's, under the constant fear of persecution, certainly contributed to his early death. Burns was, effectively, a martyr to the cause of democracy. He was prepared to risk his life, to "Do or die!", in his covert, underground struggle against oppression, on the tightrope of controversiality. Burnsians should adore him more for his courage, bravery and his dream of the coming democratic world. *The Lost Poems* do not make him more radical. They are proof of his passionate humanitarianism, his love for freedom and justice for all. It is tragic that Scotland's national bard died an underground poet, shunned and persecuted for his views by many in the country he loved.

Footnotes

1. William Scott Douglas, *Poetical Works of Robert Burns*, p.185, Vol. 1, The Kilmarnock Edition, Thirteenth Edition, Glasgow, 1938.
2. Josiah Walker, *Poems By Robert Burns*, p.xcix-c, Edinburgh, 1811.
3. Alexander Wilson, see Appendix C.
4. *Verses Written for the Anniversary of Burns* in 1825, signed "M", published in *The Penny Magazine*, 1825.
5. T. F. Henderson & W. E. Henley, *The Poetry of Robert Burns*, Vol. IV, p.341, T.C. & E.C. Jack, Edinburgh, 1901.
6. Hugh McDiarmid, from Andrew Noble's "Burns and Scottish Nationalism", p. 180, *Burns Now*, ed.by Ken Simpson, Edinburgh: Canongate, 1993.

New Versions of Poetry by Burns

This poem was originally published in the *Edinburgh Evening Courant*, 6th Sept. 1787, after the poet's Highland Tour. It is listed in MacKay, as *Verses Written with a Pencil.* The new version has over 20 differences to the known version.

Verses Written on a Window in Breadalbane, By Mr Robert Burns, dated May 9th 1790

Admiring nature in its wildest grace,
These northern scenes with weary feet I trace,
O'er many a winding dell, and painful steep,
Th' abode of covey'd grouse and timid sheep,
My savage journey, curious, I pursue,
Till fam'd Breadalbane opens on my view!
A rifted hill each deep sunk glen divides,
The woods wild scatter'd clothe their ample sides,
Th' out-stretching lake embosom'd 'mong the hills,
The eye with pleasure and amazement fills,
The Tay meand'ring sweet, in infant pride,
The palace rising on its verdant side,
The striking arches o'er the new-born stream,
The village glitt'ring in the noon-tide beam,
The lawns wood-fring'd in nature's native taste,
Nor with one single goth conceit disgrac'd.

Poetic ardours in my bosom swell,
Lone wand'ring by the hermit's mossy cell,
The sweeping theatre of hanging woods,
Th' incessant roar of headlong tumbling floods.
Here poesy might wake her heaven taught lyre,
And look thro' nature with creative fire,
And to the wrongs of dust half reconcil'd,

Misfortunes lighten'd, steps might wander wild,
And disappointments in these lonely bounds,
Find balm to soothe her bitter-rankling wounds,
Here heart-struck grief might heaven-ward teach her scan
And injur'd worth forget and pardon man.

Published in *The Bee*, March 28th 1792.

O Wat Ye Wha's in Yon Town

"Song, By Robert Burns, (Never Before Published)", from *The Glasgow Magazine* Sept 1795. There are over 20 differences from the version published in MacKay.

O wat ye wha's in yon town,
    Ye see the e'ening sun upon.
The dearest maid's in yon town,
    That e'ening sun is shining on.

Now haply, down yon gay green shaw,
    She wanders by yon spreading tree.
How blest ye flow'rs that round her blaw!
    Ye catch the glances o' her ee.
How blest ye birds that round her sing,
    And wanton in the blooming year:
But doubly welcome be the Spring,
    The season to my Jeanie dear.
chorus
The sun blinks blyth on yon town,
    Amang the broomy braes sae green;
But my delight in yon town,
    And dearest pleasure, is my Jean.
Without my fair not a' the charms
    O paradise could yield me joy;
But gie me Jeanie in my arms,
    And welcome Lapland's dreary sky.
My cave would be a lover's bower,
    Tho' raging winter rent the air,

And she a lovely little flower
That I would tent and shelter there.
chorus
O sweet is she in yon town
The sinking sun's gaen down upon.
The dearest maid's in yon town
His setting beam e'er shone upon.
If angry fate be sworn my foe,
And suff'ring, I am doom'd to bear,
I'd careless quit ought else below:
But spare, oh! spare me Jeanie dear,
For while life's dearest blood runs warm,
My thoughts frae her shall ne'er depart;
For as most lovely is her form,
She has the truest, kindest heart.
Chorus

Stanzas to the Memory
of Robert Burns

Many poems were written in dedication to Burns after his death. Included here is an excellent poem by William Roscoe, the Liverpool friend of the poet's first biographer, Dr. James Currie. Roscoe is believed to have been heavily involved with the bard's biography and would have been privy to the bard's manuscripts which went to Liverpool.

> Portentous sigh'd the hollow blast,
> Which, sorrow-freighted, southward pass'd,
> I heard the sound, and stood aghast
>   In solemn dread:
> The mournful truth is told at last,
>   And Burns is dead!
>
> Ah! sweetest minstrel, nature's child,
> Could not thy "native wood-notes wild,"
> Thy manly sense, thy manners mild,
>   And sprightly glee,
> The ghastly tyrant have beguil'd
>   To set thee free?
>
> Unfriended, desolate and young,
> Misfortune o'er thy cradle hung;
> And penury had check'd thy song,
>   But check'd in vain;
> Till death, resistless in his wrong,
>   Has clos'd the strain!

Thus, 'midst the cold of winter's snows,
The unprotected snowdrop blows;
A while in native beauty glows,
        And charms the eyes;
Till past some ruthless spoiler goes,
        And crops the prize!

But not for thee, O bard, the lot,
In cold oblivion's shade to rot;
Like those unhonour'd and forgot
        Th' unfeeling great,
Who knew thy worth, but hasten'd not
        To soothe thy fate.

Whilst love to beauty pours the sigh,
Whilst genius shall with nature vie,
Whilst pity from the melting eye
        Shall claim regard;
Thy honour'd name shall never die,
        Immortal bard!

But, oft as winter o'er the plain
Shall pour at eve the beating rain,
The hind shall call his cattle train
        Around the fire,
To listen to some thrilling strain
        Of thy lov'd lyre.

Whether to heaven's eternal King
Thou strike the deep-resounding string,
Whilst, rising on devotion's wing,
        Hope soars above,
To happier realms of endless Spring,
        And boundless love;

Or whether lighter themes beguile
The moments of relaxing toil,
Bidding, on labour's front, the smile
        Of pleasure fit;
The roof re-echoes all the while
        To genuine wit;

Or if wild fancy seize the rein,
Whilst horror thrills thro' every vein,
And sprites and elves, an aweful train,
        Their orgies keep;
And warlocks o'er the frighted plain
        At midnight sweep:

As works the spell, the list'ning band,
Aghast in mute attention stand;
Again thou wav'st thy magic wand,
        Of pow'r so rare,
And all the scene, by Fancy plann'd,
        Dissolves in air.

Thine too the charms of social hearts,
Where wit its vivid light'ning darts,
And Converse keen to age imparts
        The fire of youth,
Whilst, from the fierce concussion, starts
        The spark of truth.

What tho' the wild untutor'd strain
The Critic's pedant laws disdain,
Not all the wire-cag'd minion train
        E're poured a note
So sweet, as echoed o'er the plain
        The woodlark's throat.

Old Coila, first whose brakes among,
Thy infant hands the wild harp strung,
Shall flourish in thy deathless song
　　　　With lasting fame;
And Ayr shall henceforth roll along,
　　　　A classic stream.

But thou, O Bard, in silence laid -
Ah! what shall sooth thy pensive shade,
For worth and genius ill repaid,
　　　　With bounty scant;
And hours of sorrow unally'd,
　　　　And toil and want?

See o'er thy song, as loud it swells,
The lordly Thane delighted dwells;
Or to his fair his rapture tells,
　　　　By thee inspir'd;
His bosom, as the strain impels,
　　　　Or thaw'd or fir'd.

Around him, see, to guard his state,
A train of pamper'd minions wait;
And see, to form his daily treat,
　　　　Each climate join;
While Iceland's frost, and Asia's heat,
　　　　Their gifts combine.

Yet, whilst he revels unconfin'd
Thro' all the treasures of thy mind,
No gen'rous boon, to thee consign'd,
　　　　Relieves thy care;
To Folly or to Vice assign'd
　　　　What Pomp can spare!

For rights with-held, or freedom sold,
Corruption asks he promis'd gold;
Or, in licentious splendour bold,
   Some titled Dame
Squanders, in riot uncontroll'd,
   What Worth should claim!

From hill to hill, from plain to plain,
Wide spreads the Chieftan's proud domain,
That, half a desert, asks in vain,
   For culture due;
Whilst cold inaction chills the vein,
   And rusts thy plough.

Meanwhile thy youthful vigour flies,
The storms of life unpitying rise,
And wounded Superstition tries
   To thwart thy way;
And loath'd Dependence ambush'd lies,
   To seize her prey.

Yet high above thy reptile foes
Thy tow'ring soul unconquer'd rose -
Love and the Muse their charms disclose -
   The hags retire;
And thy expanding bosom glows,
   With heav'nly fire.

Go, builder of a deathless name!
Thy Country's glory, and her shame!
Go, and th' immortal geurdon claim,
   To Genius due;
Whilst rolling centuries thy fame
   Shall still renew!

The Edinburgh Magazine, 1797.